Culture Contact in the Pacific

Culture Contact in the Pacific

Essays on
Contact, Encounter and Response

Edited by Max Quanchi and Ron Adams

Contributors

Ron Adams
John Anglim
Peter Bellwood
Marion Diamond
Bronwen Douglas
Clive Moore
Doug Munro
Vijay Naidu
Max Quanchi
Caroline Ralston
Andrew Thornley

CAMBRIDGE
UNIVERSITY PRESS

Published by the Press Syndicate of the University of Cambridge
The Pitt Building, Trumpington Street, Cambridge CB2 IRP, UK
40 West 20th Street, New York, NY 10011-4211, USA
10 Stamford Road, Oakleigh, Melbourne, Victoria 3166, Australia

National Library of Australia cataloguing-in-publication data
Culture contact in the Pacific.
Includes bibliographies and index.
ISBN 0 521 42284 1.
1. Acculturation—Pacific Area. 2. Colonies—Oceania—History. 3. Pacific Area—History.
I. Quanchi, Max. II. Adams, Ron.
303.4821823

Library of Congress cataloguing-in-publication data
Culture contact in the Pacific/edited by Max Quanchi and Ron Adams; contributors,
Ron Adams ... [et al.].
Includes bibliographical references and index.
ISBN 0 521 42284 1.
1. Oceanians—Cultural assimilation. 2. Oceanians—History. 3. Oceania—Discovery and exploration.
4. Europe—Colonies—Oceania. 5. Acculturation—Oceania—History. I. Quanchi, Max.
II. Adams, Ron (Ron W.).
GN663.C85 1992
303.48'295—dc20

A catalogue record for this book is available from the British Library
ISBN 0 521 42284 1 paperback

Transferred to digital printing 2004

Contents

Acknowledgements

The editors and publisher are grateful to the following for permission to reproduce copyright material:

Allen and Unwin, *Sea Routes to Polynesia*, London, 1968;

Angus & Robertson, for an extract from Noel Fatnowna, *Fragments of a Lost Heritage*, Sydney, 1989, pp. 101–2, 104;

Australian Journal of Politics and History, for an extract from J.W. Davidson, 'The transition to independence: The example of Western Samoa', 7:1 (1961), p. 15;

Australian National University Press, for an illustration from David Lewis, *We, the Navigators*, p. 204; extracts from Ron Adams, *In the Land of Strangers: A century of European contact with Tanna, 1774–1874*, 1984, pp. 10–12, 31–2; an extract from F.O. Kolo, 'Historiography the myth of indigenous authenticity', in P. Herda et al. (ed.), *Tongan Culture and History*, Department of Pacific and Southeast Asian History, 1990, p. 1;

Bellwood, Peter, for maps;

British Library, London, for an illustration;

Dixson Library, Sydney, for an illustration;

Doubleday / Transworld, for an illustration from David Lewis, *From Maui to Cook*, Sydney, 1977, p. 1;

Ethnohistory, for an extract from Roger M. Keesing, 'The *Young Dick* attack: Oral and documentary history on the colonial frontier', 33:3 (1986), pp. 278–9;

Hakluyt Society, Cambridge, for an extract from J.C. Beaglehole, *The Life of Captain James Cook*, 1974, p. 206;

Hilliard, David, for a table;

Ivy Thomas, for an edited extract from 'History of My Mother's Life', written in the 1960s (unpublished);

James Cook University of North Queensland, for tables from Doug Munro, 'The origins of labourers in the South Pacific', in C. Moore et al. (eds), *Labour in the South Pacific*, 1990, pp. xxxix–1i;

Mansell Collection, London, for illustrations;

Mana Publications, for extracts from *Rexford Orotaloa, Suremada: Faces from a Solomon Island Village*, Suva, pp. 5–6;

Melbourne University Press, for extracts from Jules S.-C. Dumont d'Urville, *An Account in Two Volumes of Two Voyages to the South Seas ... Vol. 1: Astrolabe 1826–1829*, 1987 (translated and edited by Helen Rosenman); an extract from Greg Dening, *Islands and Beaches: Discourse on a silent land: Marquesas 1774–1880*, 1980, p. 264; an extract from Stewart Firth, *New Guinea under the Germans*, 1982, p. 174;

Mitchell Library, Sydney, for illustrations; for documents from Jardine Matheson Papers collection;

National Library of Australia, for an illustration;

National Maritime Museum, London, for an illustration;

Oxford University Press, for extracts from J.W. Davidson, *Samoa mo Samoa: The emergence of the independent state of Western Samoa*, Melbourne, 1967, pp. 58, 400–1; an illustration from Peter Bellwood, *Man's Conquest of the Pacific*, 1979, p. 271;

Pitt Rivers Museum, Oxford, for an illustration;

Rigby, for an extract from Faith Bandler, *Wacvie*, Adelaide, 1977, pp. 14–15;

South Pacific Creative Arts Society, for five poems from S. Ngwele, *Bamboo Leaves: A collection of poems*, Suva, 1989, pp. 5, 15, 24, 28, 42;

Sydney Talk, for part of a speech by Patelisio P. Finau SM, at the Pacific Islander Migration and Settlement Conference, Sydney, September 1990;

Thames and Hudson, for illustrations;

The Journal of Pacific History, for an extract from Brij V. Lal, 'Girmitiyas: The origins of the Fiji Indians', Canberra, 1983, p. 129;

Turnbull Library, Wellington, for an illustration;

University of Queensland Press, for an extract from Paul M. Kennedy, 'Germany and the Samoan Tridominium, 1889–98: A Study in Germany in frustrated imperialism', in John A. Moses and Paul M. Kennedy (eds), *Germany in the Pacific and Far East, 1870–1914*, Brisbane, 1977, p. 100;

University of the South Pacific, for an extract from B. Narokobi, *Lo bilong yumi yet: Law and custom in Melanesia*, Suva, 1989, p. 23; an extract from P. Hempenstall and N. Rutherford, *Protest and Dissent in the Colonial Pacific*, Suva, 1984, pp. 147, 152; for an extract from *Pacific Constitutions, Vol. 1: Polynesia*, Suva, pp. 283–4, 289, 455;

V. N. Kneubuhl, for extracts from *The Conversion of Ka'Ahumanu* (unpublished script of a play), 1988, pp. 50, 73–4;

World Council of Churches, for an extract from John Garrett, *To Live Among the Stars*, 1982, pp. 184–5;

World Council of Indigenous People/National Aboriginal Conference, for an extract from Jacqui van Bastolaer, 'French Occupied Polynesia', in *Indigenous Struggle in the Pacific*, 1984, pp. 33–4.

A Note for Teachers

1 Teaching history

The book has been compiled to meet the requirements of current history teaching practice in school and college courses. The eleven themes were selected specifically to meet the syllabus of the Year 12 Victorian Certificate of Education Course, 'Culture Contact in the Pacific', though they also complement a wider range of senior school, college and university foundation studies on history in the Pacific.

2 Theme and structure

The overriding theme of the collection is culture contact. Each essay informs discussion on a specific element of the interaction between islanders and Europeans in the nineteenth century and early twentieth century. There are also two essays on pre-contact societies and two essays on political developments in the latter part of the twentieth century Pacific. We hope the book will:
- inform students of a variety of historical interpretations
- provide evidence and factual background for their own descriptive and theoretical explanations
- provide a general outline and understanding of history in the Pacific
- introduce elements of the historian's craft (e.g. interpretation, use of evidence).

The use of subheadings throughout the essays indicate the themes, interpretations and evidence presented.

Each part is preceded by a short editorial comment introducing several chapters grouped around a central theme.

3 Illustrations

Each chapter is supported by maps, diagrams, tables and black and white illustrations, nineteenth-century etchings or contemporary photographs.

4 Evidence, documents and sources

The essays are supported by documents, extracts and other sources which reflect changing historical representations over time. The opinions and evidence presented in the essay are extended by the illustrations, extracts and documents. These are designed to extend the author's commentary and to offer alternative interpretations.

5 Questions and activities

A set of questions and activities follow each chapter. They are based on the documents and on material from the essay. The questions and activities are analytical and involve students in critical processes and the formulation of interpretations. The questions involve some recall of material from the essay, but after being presented with the further extracts and sources which extend the opinions and evidence presented in the essay, they lead students to form their own opinions.

6 References

There are three chronologies (on missions, port towns and beach communities, and colonial annexations) and each chapter is supported by a list of sources from which the authors drew their ideas and evidence, or to which they wish to direct the reader's attention for further research.

Max Quanchi, Brisbane
Ron Adams, Melbourne

PART ONE
PRE-EUROPEAN PACIFIC SOCIETY

INTRODUCTION

Despite the work of archaeologists, ethnographers, demographers, geographers and linguists, there is still much that is unknown about the origins of Pacific peoples and the societies they created in the islands. For example, there is still a debate over the direction, timing and pace of arrival of the first to inhabit the widely dispersed atolls and islands of the eastern Pacific and the more closely settled islands of the western Pacific.

What was the impact of the introduction of large-scale agricultural drainage systems in Papua New Guinea? What clues can be found in the spread of Austronesian languages? When did the sweet potato arrive and where did it come from? What does the geographic range of the use of lapita pottery suggest? How important were gender and hereditary links in selecting chiefs in New Caledonia and Tahiti? What was the meaning of Roy Mata's mass burial site? Chapters 1 and 2 offer answers to these questions by introducing a range of evidence.

To what extent did the Pacific share a common history of adaptation and absorption of new ideas, institutions, foods, techniques and technologies? Bellwood and Douglas point to the impact of these changes and the European inability to recognise both the impact of pre-contact changes and the differences and similarities in language, social, economic and political organisation that existed across the Melanesian–Polynesian boundary. How did Europeans justify the use of the terms 'Melanesian' and 'Polynesian', as the people of the western and eastern Pacific became known?

Chapter 1
The Origins of Pacific Peoples

Peter Bellwood, Australian National University

The human colonisation of Australia and New Guinea was initially the achievement of stone-using hunters and gatherers who crossed the sea channels of eastern Indonesia, perhaps 60 000 years ago. Beyond the Solomon Islands the first settlements were considerably more recent, commencing about 3500–4000 years ago when agricultural populations with skilled techniques of canoe navigation began to enter the vast ocean expanses of remote Oceania.

Both of these episodes of colonisation are among the greatest achievements of human prehistory recorded anywhere in the world.

The geographical background to Pacific colonisation

The islands of the Pacific are customarily divided into the three geographical and cultural regions of Melanesia, Micronesia and Polynesia. They are scattered across an immense region which spans about 13 000 km from western New Guinea to Easter Island, and 8500 km from Hawaii to New Zealand. With the exception of New Zealand, all lie within or very close to the tropics. Temperatures are thus warm all year round except in the interior Highlands of New Guinea and most areas (except those close to the equator) have distinct wet and dry seasons in terms of rainfall. There are also seasonal patterns of winds and currents to the north and east of the Solomon Islands which were especially important for ancient voyagers.

In terms of size and geology, the major Melanesian islands are large (New Guinea is the second-largest island in the world) and contain a wide range of landforms and environments. They are also located close together in major archipelagoes: the Bismarcks, Solomons, Vanuatu, New Caledonia and Fiji. New Zealand, despite its isolation, is similarly large and varied in geological structure. The other islands of Micronesia and Polynesia, however, are for the most part formed only of volcanic rocks and/or coral. Atolls are formed entirely of low coral islets spaced around a central lagoon. These islands and atolls are small, often scattered far apart, and were generally lacking in natural resources (apart from fish) when humans first reached them.

For example, a large number of useful and edible plants which eventually became domesticated by humans, existed in the wild in Indonesia and the western part of Melanesia. These included species of yams and taro, bananas, breadfruit, coconut, sago and sugar cane. The western islands of Melanesia, especially New Guinea, also had many native species of birds and marsupials—excellent for hunting. The islands of remote Oceania beyond the Solomons were much poorer in biological wealth, having few useful plants and virtually no large land animals. To live here, human settlers had to carry all their domesticated plants and animals (pigs, dogs and chickens) with them in their canoes.

Needless to say, these remote islands were only settled by peoples who already knew the arts of agriculture and canoe construction. Australia and the western Melanesian islands, because of their richer terrestrial resources, were settled thousands of years earlier by hunters and gatherers.

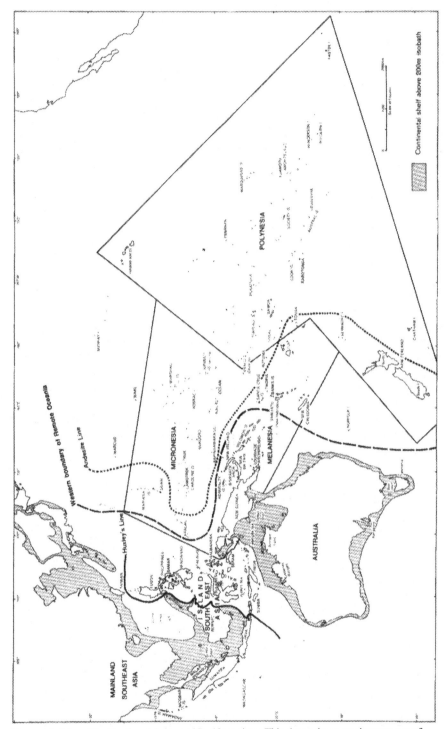

Figure 1.1: Map of the Southeast Asian and Pacific regions. This shows the approximate extent of the continental shelf of Southeast Asia (the Sunda shelf) and between Australia and New Guinea (the Sahul shelf) when they were exposed as dry land 20 000 years ago, and probably for many millennia before this. Huxley's line marks the eastern edge of Sundaland and the limit of continental Asia. The western boundary of Remote Oceania could only be crossed by Austronesian voyagers after 2000 BC. The Andesite Line is a geological boundary that separates the semi-continental large islands of the western Pacific from the true oceanic volcanic islands and atolls to the east.

The Pacific Islanders: biology and language

To understand the prehistory of the Pacific Islands it is necessary to know something of the biological and linguistic variation which occurs in the region at present. Early European visitors quickly realised that the Melanesian islands were inhabited by people who were related to the Aboriginal populations of Australia and who were probably descended from the first settlers of the region. The Polynesians and Micronesians, on the other hand, were seen to be related to the peoples of Indonesia and Southeast Asia and to have arrived more recently. In modern terminology, the former peoples are mainly of Australoid origin, while the latter are mainly classed as Southern Mongoloids. However, some care must be taken here since these two biological groups are not entirely separate either geographically or in physical appearance. In many regions, especially eastern Indonesia and most of Melanesia (except interior New Guinea), there have been millennia of intermarriage between them. Nevertheless, the two basic populations do appear to be of separate origin according to modern genetic and skeletal studies.

The situation with respect to language is rather different from that of human biology. In New Guinea the majority of languages spoken belong to a grouping termed 'Papuan', and some Papuan languages also exist in islands close to New Guinea, for instance, Timor, New Britain and Bougainville. These Papuan languages reveal no clear linguistic relationships with languages spoken elsewhere, although some linguists have claimed that very ancient links might once have existed with the Australian Aboriginal languages. It seems reasonable to assume, in the absence of evidence to the contrary, that the Papuan languages have developed within Melanesia from the languages spoken by the first human settlers more than 40 000 years ago.

The other languages of western Melanesia are termed 'Austronesian'. In New Guinea these are only spoken in pockets around the coast and their speakers clearly arrived long after the island was fully settled by Papuan speakers. This arrival perhaps occurred around 3500–4000 years ago. The Austronesian languages, however, are very different from the Papuan ones in that they are all quite closely related and, prior to 1500, formed the most widespread single language family in the world. Austronesian languages are spoken throughout the Pacific to the north and east of the Solomons: in Vanuatu, New Caledonia, Fiji, and in every island of Polynesia and Micronesia. They are also spoken throughout Indonesia, Malaysia, the Philippines and Madagascar, and were once the dominant languages of southern Vietnam and Taiwan. About 250 million people today speak Austronesian languages over a vast area which extends well over half way around the world, from Madagascar to Easter Island.

The ultimate homeland of the Austronesian languages, that is, the location of what linguists term 'Proto-Austronesian', was located in Taiwan and adjacent southern China about five or six thousand years ago. Austronesian has remote connections with other Southeast Asian languages, especially Thai. Austronesian languages have been carried across the Pacific by colonising populations since 2000 BC, but they clearly did not replace the pre-existing Papuan languages in New Guinea, the Bismarck Archipelago and the Solomons.

The comparative study of languages (presently-spoken ones in the Austronesian case, since very few, except Malay and Javanese, have long traditions of writing) is of immense importance for understanding the prehistoric movements of peoples. In the case of a family as widespread as Austronesian, only population movements via colonisation, rather than trade or cultural contact, can explain the overall distribution. Language studies can also give important information about the way people lived in

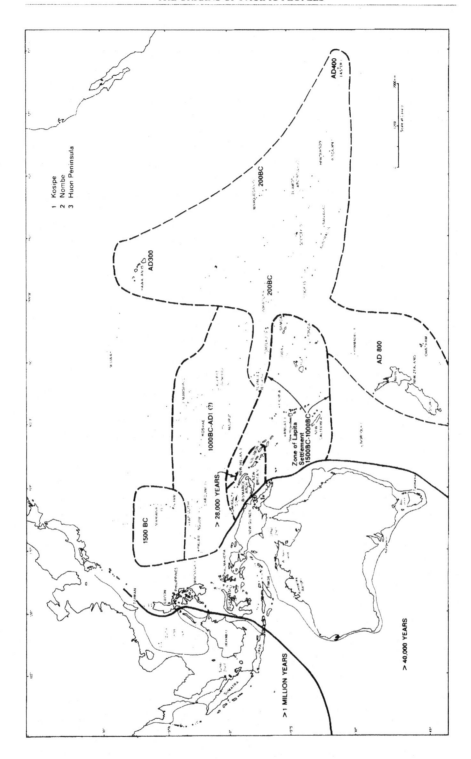

Figure 1.2: Approximate dates of the first human settlements in Southeast Asia and the Pacific. Note how the limits of very ancient settlement correspond with the boundary of Remote Oceania on the previous map. Current data indicate that Australia may have been settled as early as 60 000 years ago.

the past, through reconstructed ancient vocabularies and word meanings. For instance, it is known from the common terminology shared by many Austronesian speakers in Southeast Asia and across the Pacific, that the early Austronesians in the China–Taiwan–Philippine region at about 3000 BC, could build sailing canoes and substantial timber houses, make pots, and make clothing from bark cloth. They could possibly also weave textiles on a loom. They ate the meat of a number of domesticated animals (pig and chicken especially) and grew a range of crops, including rice, millet, sugar cane, yams and taro. They were also skilled fisherfolk. These linguistic observations are very important since they provide details which often do not survive very clearly in the archaeological record.

In addition, linguistic records can also reveal how people of different linguistic origins (such as Papuan and Austronesian speakers) have interacted in the past. This question of interaction is especially important in Melanesia because it is apparent that the patterns of human biology and language here are far more complex than anywhere else in the Pacific. From the summaries of biology and language given above it would be easy to assume that a simple correlation should exist between Papuan languages and people of Melanesian biological appearance, and between Austronesian languages and people such as the Micronesians and Polynesians who are of Southeast Asian physical appearance. While such a simple correlation might have existed to some extent 5000 years ago, it is very obvious that the degree of genetic and linguistic interchange between the various peoples of Melanesia since then has been enormous. Solomon Islanders, Fijians and Samoans all speak quite closely related Austronesian languages yet are very different in physical appearance. Likewise, people who might live in two adjacent lowland New Guinea villages and who are closely related genetically through intermarriage can speak entirely unrelated Papuan and Austronesian languages, as different from each other in their basic structures as English and Chinese.

These examples should illustrate that humanity can behave in complex ways. Many of these observations about interaction have led to scholastic arguments which often continue for decades without clear resolution. For instance, there are some scholars who believe that the Papuan and Austronesian languages do not have separate origins and that both have differentiated from a common ancestor in the western Pacific. I don't agree with this view, but you should be aware that absolute certainty about important aspects of human prehistory can be a very elusive goal.

The origins of the first settlers

Having introduced the Pacific Islanders in terms of biology and language, it is now time to examine the archaeological record left by their earliest ancestors. Twenty thousand years ago the world was in the grip of the last glaciation (Ice Age). So much water was frozen into glacial ice that the sea levels dropped by as much as 130 metres below present levels. New Guinea and Australia were joined by dry land and Sumatra, Borneo and Java were joined to Asia.

These land links were most extensive at this time, but they had been in existence in some form for much of the previous 40 000 years as well. The first humans to reach the Sahul continent (Australia plus New Guinea) arrived about 60 000 years ago and would undoubtedly have been able to take advantage of such land bridges. However, they also had to cross the deep sea passages of eastern Indonesia in order to get from Java to Sahul, and some of these crossings would always have been at least 50 kilometres wide. These are the oldest sea crossings known in human prehistory, although the seacraft remain unknown—perhaps they were rafts.

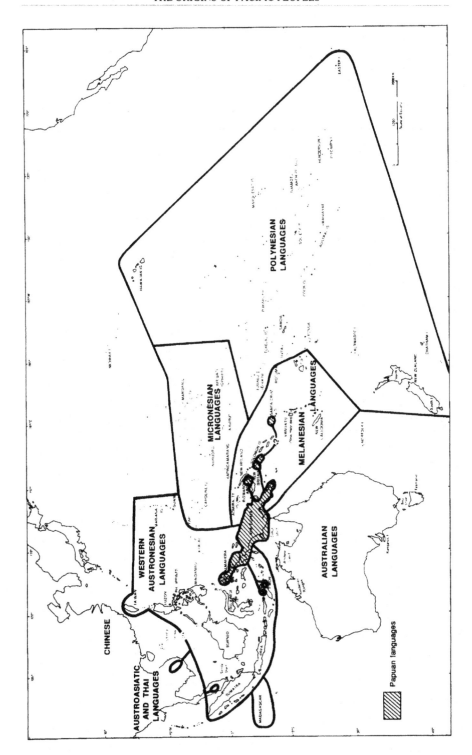

Figure 1.3: The distribution of the Papuan and Austronesian languages in Southeast Asia and the Pacific.

The archaeological record in Australia, New Guinea, New Ireland and Bougainville (the last two islands being reached by further sea crossings more than 30 000 years ago) tells us that these early colonisers lived by hunting, gathering and fishing. They made flaked stone tools, some massive axe-like forms in New Guinea and parts of Australia. They were almost certainly the direct biological ancestors of the present Aboriginal populations of Australia and western Melanesia, and, as noted above, they possibly spoke languages ancestral to present-day Australian Aboriginal and Papuan ones. By 8000 years ago, the sea had risen sufficiently to separate Australia and New Guinea, and after this time a quite remarkable cultural differentiation occurred.

The Aboriginal Australians continued a hunting and gathering lifestyle throughout their prehistory. In New Guinea, however, recent excavations at a site called Kuk in the interior Highlands have shown that people were digging drainage ditches in swamps, perhaps in order to cultivate taro, as long as 9000 years ago. By 6000 years ago these ditches were being dug up to two kilometres long and two metres deep. This is an extremely important discovery, since it shows that the Papuan-speaking peoples of western Melanesia developed agriculture themselves without any transference of ideas from outside.

Agriculture was one of the most important developments in human prehistory because it allowed major increases in the size of shared residential human groups, and in the levels of social and political organisation. Such developments in New Guinea might explain the apparent inability of the more recent Austronesian populations to gain more than small footholds on the island. The situation was entirely different in Indonesia because the newly arriving Austronesian-speaking colonists were able to assimilate their sparser foraging predecessors much more effectively. This major episode of agricultural development in New Guinea provides us with a basic explanation for the great complexity of the region today; both the Papuan- and the Austronesian-speaking populations had evolved high population density cultural systems, such that neither group was able to replace the other in any long-term sense.

The Austronesian colonisations

Around 3500 years ago, the first archaeological signs of human colonisation begin to appear in the islands beyond the Solomons. By 3000 years ago people had reached Samoa, in western Polynesia. Beyond Samoa the rate of expansion appears to have slowed slightly; the first settlements in the Caroline Islands of Micronesia and the Marquesas far to the east in Polynesia date to between 2500 and 2000 years ago, whereas Hawaii was settled about 1600 years ago and New Zealand perhaps only 1000 years ago. Nevertheless, these settlements were all part of the same process of Austronesian colonisation.

The oldest archaeological record of this colonisation in Melanesia, occurring mainly in small coastal locations and not in the Papuan-dominated interiors of the larger western islands, consists of a number of new technological items not previously found in the Pacific. Pottery, elaborately decorated with stamped patterns, is perhaps the most visible feature. It is called Lapita pottery (after a find place in New Caledonia) and occurs in many coastal sites dating to between 1500 and 500 BC, all the way from the Admiralty Islands to Samoa. With it occur shell fish-hooks, polished stone adzes, sharp flakes of volcanic obsidian mined in the Admiralty Islands and New Britain, and remains of domesticated pigs, dogs, chickens and coconuts (soft plants such as yams and taro do not survive archaeologically). This whole complex developed in part amongst ancestral Austronesian-speaking communities in the islands of Southeast

Figure 1.4: Dentate-stamped Lapita potsherds.

Asia (traded New Britain obsidian has even been excavated recently in northern Borneo), but much of the skilful decoration on the pottery might well have been invented in Melanesia itself.

In order to colonise to as far as the Solomons, these Austronesian settlers, like their Papuan forebears thousands of years before, needed only to make short journeys between islands which would have been visible. However, beyond the Solomons lay many much wider gaps, evidently impassable for the simple craft of Ice Age hunters and only navigable for those with the skills needed to build ocean-going canoes and to sail them by observing star rising positions and the directions of ocean currents. The Austronesians had these skills, and over a period of perhaps 2000 years, they were able to use them to reach all the tropical Pacific Islands. They probably reached South America on at least one occasion as well. But just how good were their navigational skills and how did they handle the wind and current conditions of the open Pacific?

These are questions, like those about the relationships between Polynesians and Melanesians, which have exercised the minds of scholars for two centuries. In the central and eastern Pacific, the winds blow for most of the year from an easterly direction; these are called the trade winds. They are sufficiently strong and regular to ensure that the Pacific Islands could not have been settled by unplanned drifters alone; colonising voyages were probably purposeful and well-stocked.

In the western Pacific, especially in Melanesia, winds from a westerly direction occur more commonly during the year; hence perhaps the relative rapidity of the Lapita expansion into Polynesia. However, the strength of the trade winds in the central and eastern Pacific contributed in part to one of the most famous theories about the settlement of Polynesia—that of Thor Heyerdahl. Heyerdahl believed that people must have drifted initially into Polynesia from South America since they would not have been able to sail eastwards into the trade winds from Southeast Asia, and he sailed the Kon-Tiki raft with the winds and currents from Peru to the Tuamotus in 1947 to

Figure 1.5: An Easter Island statue with topknot.   [Photo Diagi Markovic]

demonstrate the feasibility of his views. He also believed that the present Polynesian peoples of the eastern Pacific arrived from the west coast of North America after the first South American settlers, and ultimately replaced them.

The past forty years of research in archaeology, genetics and linguistics have uncovered little to support Heyerdahl's views overall, although it is now accepted that Polynesians and South American Indians were in contact. Polynesians acquired the sweet potato from Peru or Ecuador, for instance. Some of the most interesting discoveries about the settlement of Polynesia have come from studies of weather patterns and experiments with replicas of ancient double canoes. One Hawaiian-style replica, called the Hokule'a, was sailed successfully from Hawaii to Tahiti using only traditional navigational methods, in 1976. Even more importantly, this same canoe was sailed from Samoa to Tahiti in 1986 on a west to east course into what should have been the opposing trade winds. In fact, the winds at the time of sailing (July–August) were mainly from the west during that particular year, and it is now known that Pacific weather patterns are not as unchanging as many earlier authors believed. By waiting for a suitable wind (and Polynesian canoes could sail across or even slightly into the wind) the first Austronesian settlers could and eventually did reach every habitable island in the Pacific.

Pacific prehistory, of course, involved far more than simple colonisation. Each of the hundreds of inhabited islands has had human cultures and populations evolving upon it for periods of between 1000 and 3500 years in the case of the Austronesians, and for upwards of 30 000 years in the case of the Papuan-speakers. All cultures change over time from within as well as due to external influences. As we have seen, some New Guinea Highland cultures underwent very important agricultural changes starting about 9000 years ago. The descendants of the Lapita colonists of Melanesia were eventually transformed in myriad ways into the modern Polynesians, southern Micronesians and Austronesian-speaking Melanesians. The prehistoric Maoris had to make unique adaptations to the temperate environment of New Zealand. (Tropical crops, for instance, were mostly eclipsed by the hardier sweet potato.)

Many of the tropical islanders evolved complex forms of society dominated by powerful hereditary chiefs, and these individuals were undoubtedly the main instigators behind the massive building programs whose remains are still visible on some islands today. Hence the great temple structures and burial monuments, mostly constructed during the 500 years prior to European contact, on islands such as Pohnpei in Micronesia, Tongatapu, Tahiti and Easter Island. The Easter Islanders are famous for their colossal statues, carved of volcanic rock and erected on temple platforms as memorials to chiefly ancestors. The Maoris excelled in the construction of earthwork

Figure 1.6: The Hokule'a under full sail.

fortresses on hilltops. Many of the Melanesian peoples turned their skills towards inter-island trade rather than building works. Remarkable networks for exchanging prestige-giving shell valuables and other products have been reported across the region by ethnographers.

All this cultural evolution can have its negative side as well. Some of the small islands suffered environmental ravages owing to over-population. The prehistoric Easter Islanders, for instance, cut down all their trees and caused such environmental stress that their civilisation collapsed just before Europeans arrived in the eighteenth century. In a frenzy of intertribal warfare all the statues were toppled and the human population evidently decimated. The exact reasons for this are uncertain but one must certainly suspect the involvement of food shortages. Deforestation and the extinction of bird and animal species, whether for food or feathers for cloaks, occurred widely on many islands, including those as large as New Zealand (where many species of flightless moas had vanished by the eighteenth century). Prehistoric peoples did not live in total harmony with nature anywhere in the world, though their capacity for destruction was minimal compared with that of present-day civilisation. Overall, the positive achievements of prehistoric Pacific peoples were far more impressive than their periodic environmental misfortunes.

DOCUMENTS

1 Myths of origin and identity: the predecessors of men— Melanesia

Melanesian cosmological beliefs tend to be vague and unformulated but most Melanesians do conceive of a time 'in the beginning' when mythical beings dwelt on earth. The Dobuans say these *Kasa Sona* are ageless and that they were born with the sun, the moon and the earth, whereas 'We are but newly come!' The Keraki Papuans use the word *Gainjin* to indicate that the first beings were 'larger than life'. In some places these primal beings came from the sky, in other places they emerged from underground or merely came from somewhere else. The world was apparently already in existence but they did play a part in shaping it. Sometimes this included raising the sky. Almost always it included making or releasing the sea. Land-making was widely attributed to these beings but their efforts were usually restricted to a particular piece of land rather than *all* land and almost everywhere spirit beings and culture heroes had strong associations with particular localities, conspicuous landmarks and geographical features which they were often said to have made.

The Iatmul of the Sepik River area say that the dry land was created when a spirit put his foot upon mud. In Buka, two beings, one male and one female, paddled by and when he steered he made the shoreline straight and when she steered she made it indented. Nuga the crocodile of Kiwai cut the rivers of the estuary with the lashing of his great tail when he discovered that his wife had been seduced. Fijian heroes dropped stolen mountains to make islands and widened channels by straddling them and pushing the lands apart.

Beliefs about man's origin were just as various. Some myths say he came into the world fully grown either from the sky or from underground or was released from a tree. Other myths say he was created from clay or sand or was carved from wood or that he developed spontaneously from stones, maggots, sand drawings, blood clots, eggs or plants.

—Roslyn Poignant, *Oceanic Mythology*, Hamlyn, London, 1967, p. 88

2 The origins of mankind—Polynesia

Tuli, the bird messenger of Tangaloa, flew down to earth with a creeping vine to clothe the bare land and provide shade. At first the vine spread; then it withered and decomposed and swarmed with a shapeless moving mass of maggots. Tangaloa took these and fashioned them into human shape. He straightened them out and moulded hand, legs and features. He gave each a heart and a soul and they came alive. This type of myth in which man appeared by a kind of primitive evolution, sometimes aided by a deity, was confined to the western Polynesians.

In the other islands to the east [eastern Polynesia] it was believed that man came into being by a continuation of the process of creation, or rather procreation, which had begun with Atea and Papa. The god Tane was most often considered to be the actual generative agent who impregnated a woman he formed from earth. In Maori lore Tane's procreative power and organ was called Tiki. In other places, including the Marquesas, Tiki or Ti'i (Ki'i in Hawaii) was a separate character who replaced Tane as creator of the first woman.

—Roslyn Poignant, *Oceanic Mythology*, Hamlyn, London, 1967, p. 41

3   Thor Heyerdahl's view

I propose that the East Asiatic element in the Polynesian race and culture entered Polynesia at Hawaii, and with the North-west Coast area as a logical, feasible, and necessary stepping-stone.

—T. Heyerdahl, *Sea Routes to Polynesia*, London, 1968, p. 34

4   The origins of Polynesians

Moreover it is important to stress that the theory differs from many earlier ones which attempted to bring Polynesians through already settled areas of Melanesia according to some particular route, by dismissing the theory of a distinctive Polynesian migration or route within Melanesia. This is replaced with the concept of development within Polynesia itself of the Polynesian racial, linguistic, and cultural patterns which were based on ancestral forms found in Eastern Melanesia and in particular in Fiji.

—R. Green, 'The immediate origins of the Polynesians', in *Polynesian Culture History*, University of Hawaii Press, Honolulu, 1967, p. 236

5   A missionary's view

The original inhabitants of the great Adriatic Islands seem, likewise, before they were driven back from their coasts, to have made very considerable emigrations, although not to distances so remote as those to which their supplanters have been dispersed. The darker race has spread over the vast countries of New Holland and New Guinea, with the adjacent islands of New Britain, New Ireland, and Louifiade, as well as those of Solomon, Santa Cruz, New Caledonia, the chief part of New Hebrides, and the group called Feje. Like the native of Africa, whom in person they generally resemble, they are divided into numerous tribes, and are distinguished by various languages; yet there is a striking sameness in the customs even of those most remotely separated; and they all differ essentially from the nation that occupies the numerous smaller islands of this ocean.

—James Wilson, *A Missionary Voyage to the Southern Pacific Ocean, 1796–1798*, London, 1799

6   Captain Cook's view

The inhabitants of the Sandwich Islands are undoubtedly of the same race with those of New Zealand, the Society and the Friendly Islands, Easter Island, and the Marquesas; a race that possess, without any intermixture, all the known lands between the latitudes of 47° South and 20° North, and between the longitudes of 184° and 260° East ... From what continent they originally emigrated, and by what steps they have spread through so vast a space, those who are curious in disquisitions of this nature, may perhaps not find it very difficult to conjecture ... they bear strong marks of affinity to some of the Indian tribes, that inhabit the Ladrones [Mariana] and Caroline Islands; and the same affinity may again be traced amongst the Battas [Bataks of northern Sumatra] and the Malays.

—Cook, J., and King, J., *A voyage to the Pacific Ocean*, London, 1785, Volume III, pp. 124–5. (This extract, from Cook's first voyage, refers to Polynesians and Micronesians.)

QUESTIONS AND ACTIVITIES

1 To whom is James Wilson (Document 5) referring when he says 'the darker race'?

2 On a copy of a map of the Pacific (see Figure 1.1) colour the locations noted by Wilson in 1799–98. Compare this to Bellwood's map of Pacific languages (Figure 1.3). How might you account for the differences?

3 Against whom do Wilson (Document 5) and Cook (Document 6) compare the people of the Pacific?

4 What evidence enabled Cook to claim that 'undoubtedly' Sandwich Islanders (Hawaiians) were the same as other islanders?

5 On what basis could Cook claim that there was no 'intermixture'?

6 On a copy of a map of the Pacific (see Figure 1.1) colour in the area defined by Cook. What 'race' possessed all the known lands in this region?

7 In what ways do Heyerdahl (Document 3) and Green (Document 4) differ from the opinion expressed by Bellwood in Chapter 1? Your answer should refer to the direction of original migration and the regions passed through.

8 Heyerdahl, Green and Bellwood suggest that Polynesian culture was carried along during migrations from elsewhere, or that it evolved as a unique culture after migrants settled in the Pacific. On the basis of the evidence presented in the extracts, prepare a statement expressing your own opinion on the origins of Polynesians.

9 What is the relationship between Melanesian and Polynesian myths (Documents 1 and 2) and the topography or physical environment of today?

10 Compare these myths to islanders' reactions to European strangers when they began to arrive in the Pacific in the sixteenth to nineteenth centuries. (see pp. 46–7 in Chapter 4)

11 What did Hawaii–Tahiti and Samoa–Tahiti voyages of the Hokule'a prove in the debate over the origins of Polynesians?

12 Further research: Investigate the 'mystery' of the Easter Island (Rapanui) statues.

REFERENCES

Bellwood, P., *The Polynesians: prehistory of an island people*, Thames and Hudson (Revised edition), London, 1984

Gilbert, J., *Charting the Vast Pacific* (Vol. 7 of *Encyclopedia of Discovery and Exploration*), Aldus Books, London, Chapters 1–3

Heyerdahl, T., *The Kon Tiki Expedition: By raft across the South Seas*, Allen and Unwin, London, 1950 (Note: There are many editions and publishers)

Howe, K.R., *Where the Waves Fall*, Allen and Unwin, Sydney, 1984, Chapters 1 and 2

Lewis, D., *From Cook to Mauli*, Doubleday, Sydney, 1977, Chapters 1–3 and 11

Oliver, D.L., *The Native Cultures of the Pacific Islands*, UH Press, Honolulu, 1989

Siers, J., *Taratai: A Pacific adventure*, Millwood Press, Wellington, 1977

Chapter 2
Pre-European Societies in the Pacific Islands

Bronwen Douglas, La Trobe University

In modern popular imagery, pre-European societies in Oceania are often romanticised as idyllic, timeless and unchanging. This essay challenges these and other stereotypes, with particular reference to the geographical regions known as Polynesia and Melanesia—that is, most of the islands in the south Pacific Ocean, plus the Hawaiian chain, north of the equator, but omitting the north Pacific region of Micronesia. These regional names were originally European labels derived from Greek,[1] but now they are used by islanders themselves. Pre-European meant different times at different places, depending on when Europeans first arrived. For example, some islands were visited by Spanish explorers during the sixteenth century. Regular European contacts began in Polynesia in the late eighteenth century, following the 'discovery' of Tahiti in 1767, the voyages of Captain James Cook and the coming of English and American traders and missionaries.

How can we know?

How can we know what Oceanic societies were like before Europeans entered the Pacific? Since writing was unknown in all indigenous Pacific cultures, the sources available to construct such knowledge are mainly products of contacts with the outside world. They include:
- contemporary accounts written by early European visitors
- islanders' oral traditions which, until recently, were mostly recorded by Europeans
- the artefacts and other material remains, which archaeologists study
- the languages, which linguists reconstruct.

Oral traditions and contemporary European descriptions are usually the most numerous and important texts for historians. It must be remembered, however, that oral traditions are not fixed until they are written down. Moreover, like written histories, they are the accounts of the past told by particular persons and are partly shaped by the storytellers' present purposes. Contemporary European texts—for example, Cook's writing on Tahiti—have the advantage that the past they described was recent. However, they also have certain disadvantages: they refer only to the most recent, brief phase of the human occupation of Oceania. By their very nature, they described societies which were already experiencing interaction with the outside world and hence were no longer 'pre-European'. Furthermore, their authors were always ethnocentric, often racist, and had more or less limited understanding of the languages and cultures of the people encountered.

Each kind of text, including the works of professional historians, anthropologists and archaeologists, must be read critically and creatively, rather than literally. We must be alert to the authors' cultures, values and interests, and sensitive to the ways they use language to serve those values and interests.

The most valuable contemporary texts for historians are those that describe what islanders did and said in the past. These 'action descriptions' can suggest patterns, which may be compared with islanders' oral traditions and the works of later anthropologists to form a broad picture of continuities and changes in indigenous cultures and social organisation since the arrival of Europeans. For longer-term evidence of the dynamic and adaptive nature of island societies over hundreds or even thousands of years of human occupation, we must consult the works of archaeologists and linguists.

Common themes

All Pacific societies shared some broad common themes, which mostly also applied to pre-industrial societies in other places and times, including:
- ultimate origin in Asia, spread over many millennia (see Chapter 1)
- non-literacy
- the absence of metallurgy
- subsistence, household-based economies reliant on a mix, where possible, of horticulture, hunting and gathering and fishing
- kinship-based organisation and land-holding
- a stress on exchange of material objects and food in preference to accumulation or storage.

All these societies had religious world views, which meant that people explained human success and failure, as well as natural occurrences, as results of the actions of spirits. Ritual, therefore, was seen as a critical resource. It was used to communicate with the spirits in order to control or influence them, and hence shape the natural and social world.

The most striking aspect of pre-European cultures and societies in the Pacific, however, was their diversity, the bewildering range of variations on common themes which islanders had worked out in particular ecological and human contexts.

Polynesia / Melanesia?

Since only a few valid Pacific-wide generalisations can be made, a more precise focus is needed. Conventionally, Europeans adopted the Polynesia/Melanesia/Micronesia division. However, these labels were not neutral terms which permitted a group of related societies occupying one region to be differentiated on an objective basis from another group of related societies in a neighbouring region. Rather, they partly reflected European prejudices about race, skin colour and degree of 'civilisation'. The inhabitants of the far-flung 'Polynesian triangle' (see Figure 1.1) *did* share a relatively recent common origin, which produced marked similarities in language, culture and physical appearance: the term 'Polynesia' is therefore appropriate culturally as well as geographically. 'Melanesia', however, is a different matter: the very term proposes skin colour as the main basis for linking hundreds of different cultures with little in common beyond the broad themes previously mentioned.

By European (and Polynesian) standards of beauty, the relatively light-skinned Polynesians were far more handsome than 'Melanesians'. Polynesians were seen as more highly civilised than 'Melanesians' because Polynesian societies were to a greater or lesser extent hierarchical and had hereditary selection of chiefs. This was a more familiar mode of government to Europeans than the less stratified, more fragmented societies common in parts of Melanesia. Polynesians were also seen as less

Figure 2.1: The head of a chief: New Zealand.

'savage' than 'Melanesians' because they appeared more receptive to Europeans, their goods and ideas.

The French navigator Dumont d'Urville, who was the first to define and name these three great 'cultural' regions in the Pacific, wrote of 'Melanesians':

> These blacks are almost always grouped in very weak tribes ... Far more debased towards the state of Barbarism than the Polynesians and the Micronesians, they have amongst them neither a regular form of government, nor laws, nor established religions and their intelligence are also generally much inferior to those of the copper-coloured race [the Polynesians].[2]

Such explicit racism has long been discredited. Implications of an evolutionary transition from simpler (Melanesian) to more complex (Polynesian) societies were more tenacious. As late as the 1960s the anthropologist, Marshall Sahlins, wrote of a continuum in Pacific politics, ranging from 'the western Melanesian underdevelopment' to 'the greater Polynesian chiefdoms' and political development. This kind of evolutionism has also been largely rejected. Indeed, European democrats are often attracted by what they see as the egalitarianism of 'Melanesian' societies compared with the more rigid social stratification of Polynesia. The spotlight of European approval seems therefore to have turned full circle. Western political and intellectual fashions, however, remain the criteria for classification and evaluation of non-Western societies.

Alternative perspectives

Given the history of this Polynesia/Melanesia distinction, it is less ethnocentric to describe and differentiate pre-European societies in Oceania on the basis of criteria which partly cut across this regional divide. Such criteria would include differences in natural setting, social scale, social stratification, leadership, power, exchange and gender relations.

GEOGRAPHY, SCALE, STRATIFICATION, LEADERSHIP, POWER

It is clear that the most populous, territorially extensive and elaborately hierarchical social units in the Pacific before European contact were located on larger Polynesian islands (in Hawaii, Tahiti and Tonga), while some of the smallest and least stratified were in New Guinea, within the geographical ambit of Melanesia. These extreme examples became stereotypes: that is, they were taken to be typical of 'Polynesia' and 'Melanesia' respectively. Yet in parts of the New Guinea Highlands there were large, relatively stable political groupings, based on intensive patterns of drainage and horticulture and sometimes controlled by powerful lineages which monopolised shell valuables. In coastal areas in Melanesia, hereditary chieftainship was common, in contrast to the widely-held stereotype that 'Melanesian' leadership was competitively achieved and basically unstable. In degree of political fragmentation, the size of political units, and the relatively limited power residing in chiefly office, the Polynesian Maoris of New Zealand bore more resemblance to the Melanesians of New Caledonia than to Polynesian Tahitians or Hawaiians. The nature and degree of social stratification thus varied widely within Polynesia. Many smaller Polynesian atoll societies functioned similarly to small-scale hereditary chieftaincies in western Melanesia, despite the more recent cultural and linguistic heritage which they shared with other Polynesians.

EXCHANGE, TERRITORY, FIGHTING

The elaborate, genealogically-based territorial hierarchies of Hawaii, Tahiti and Tonga were matched for complexity by intricate exchange networks in parts of Melanesia, such as the lined 'kula ring' and hiri of southeastern Papua and the tee and moka systems in the Papua New Guinea Highlands. Indeed, one reason why 'Melanesians' seemed to Europeans to lack 'regular ... government' was because many societies in Melanesia were structured on the basis of reciprocal exchange 'roads', rather than the permanent territorial entities which Europeans took for granted, Ironically, one

European yardstick of the higher level of civilisation attained by Polynesians was the fact that some of them fought murderous wars to eliminate and dispossess their enemies. 'Melanesians', in contrast, were seen to engage in endless series of limited, localised, not very lethal fights for motives of revenge. Here again, however, the stereotypes were misplaced, since much Polynesian fighting was of the latter type, while wars of conquest were not unknown in Melanesia, particularly eastern Fiji.

GENDER RELATIONS

In gender relations, too, early European stereotypes about the relatively higher status of Polynesian women compared with 'Melanesian' must be reconsidered. Nowhere in the Pacific were women 'equal' to men in political and economic terms, but men and women were widely conceived as complementary in the production of food and material objects and in human reproduction. Throughout Polynesia, women as a category were *noa*, profane, in relation to men, who were *tapu*, sacred, restricted. However, high-ranking women might be *tapu* in relation to commoner men and women by virtue of their class status. Furthermore, in some Polynesian societies first-born women outranked their brothers, while able women of high rank and forceful personality exercised considerable influence, even power, in Hawaii, Tahiti and Tonga. In many New Guinea Highlands societies, men feared women's reproductive powers, which they believed to be weakening and polluting. Male–female relations were thus antagonistic and a high degree of separation of the sexes was maintained. In some parts of Melanesia, however, particularly in matrilineal societies such as the Trobriands of southeastern Papua and the Nagovisi of Bougainville, women enjoyed high status and considerable freedom of action, while male–female relations were benign.

HISTORY, ADAPTATION, CULTURAL INVENTION, CHANGE

Every Pacific society encountered for the first time by Europeans had been shaped by particular processes of adaptation and invention in specific physical and human contexts. This internal dynamic, however, was veiled by European assumptions as to the timeless nature of 'traditional' societies and by the islanders' own tendency to represent their customs as eternal and unchanging. Nonetheless, the prevalence of migration traditions throughout the Pacific hints at the significance of movement as a widespread cultural theme. Recent archaeological and historical research has revealed impressive adaptability and capacity for change in Pacific cultures as widely separated as the New Guinea Highlands, Vanuatu, New Zealand, Tahiti and Hawaii.

In the New Guinea Highlands, the introduction and adoption of the sweet potato during the last three to four hundred years was the latest major episode in a millennia-long prehistory of human readiness to innovate and adapt to changing conditions. In Efate, in central Vanuatu, there were persistent traditions about the revolutionary social impact and prestige of a group of high-ranking immigrants who had arrived several centuries before. These traditions received striking support from archaeological excavation of the grave of one of the new arrivals, a powerful man called Roy Mata, whose corpse was accompanied by those of thirty-nine human beings and a rich assemblage of ornaments: 'the existence of Roy Mata, the details of his burial, the importance of his grave which reflects his legendary prestige and finally the date of the site accord with the tradition'. This dramatic instance of cultural change also contradicted European stereotypes about the absence of marked social distinctions in Melanesia.

Figure 2.2: The collective burial of Roy Mata.

In New Zealand, the Polynesian Maori, confronted with a climate unsuitable for most of their tropical food crops, initially adopted a shifting mode of settlement appropriate to an economy based entirely or primarily on hunting, gathering and fishing. The invention of storage pits for sweet potato eventually enabled its cultivation to be extended far beyond earlier limits and permitted more permanent settlement, focused on earthwork forts. The extension of horticulture compensated for the declining viability of hunting and gathering as a result of man-induced forest and faunal degradation. Whatever the economic context—'primitive' hunter-gatherer or 'advanced' horticulturist—the material culture, art and myth of the Maori were no less rich and creative than their eastern Polynesian forebears.

In Tahiti and Hawaii, the societies encountered by the first European visitors were actually in the throes of dramatic political upheaval. This upheaval caused the hardening of class barriers separating the most highly-ranked members from the rest and the consolidation of larger force-dominated political units. The emergence of 'Polynesian kingdoms' during the early years of European contact in Tahiti and Hawaii has conventionally been attributed to European influence and manipulation; it is now clear, however, that the presence of Europeans, whatever their own presuppositions and intentions, provided no more than contexts and opportunities for the working out of indigenous motivations and tendencies.

Pre-European societies in the Pacific were relatively 'simple' in terms of material culture: since all lacked metal technology, their raw materials comprised plant, animal and natural products, particularly wood, leaves, bark, bone, shell, stone and clay. However a 'simple' material culture and absence of literacy did not necessarily mean a simple culture and society. The intellectual and creative achievements of islanders throughout the Pacific were displayed in myth, genealogy, kinship reckoning, animal and plant classifications, building, painting and carving. Perhaps the most notable were the complex feats of invention and memory involved in the navigational expertise of many Polynesians and Micronesians and the exchange networks in various parts of Melanesia.

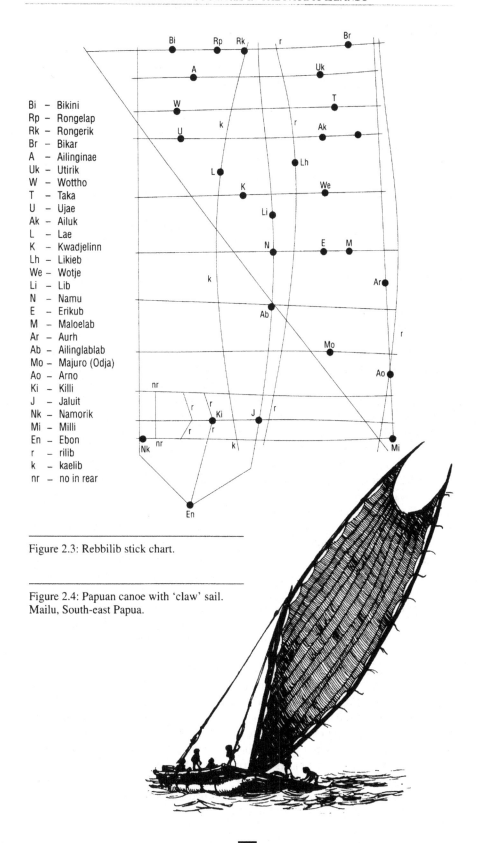

Bi – Bikini
Rp – Rongelap
Rk – Rongerik
Br – Bikar
A – Ailinginae
Uk – Utirik
W – Wottho
T – Taka
U – Ujae
Ak – Ailuk
L – Lae
K – Kwadjelinn
Lh – Likieb
We – Wotje
Li – Lib
N – Namu
E – Erikub
M – Maloelab
Ar – Aurh
Ab – Ailinglablab
Mo – Majuro (Odja)
Ao – Arno
Ki – Killi
J – Jaluit
Nk – Namorik
Mi – Milli
En – Ebon
r – rilib
k – kaelib
nr – no in rear

Figure 2.3: Rebbilib stick chart.

Figure 2.4: Papuan canoe with 'claw' sail.
Mailu, South-east Papua.

DOCUMENTS

1 Barton on the *hiri* expedition in Papua

Every year, at the end of September, or the beginning of October, the season of the south-east trade wind being then near its close, a fleet of large sailing canoes [lakatoi] leaves Port Moresby and the neighbouring villages of the Motu tribe on a voyage to the deltas of the rivers of the Papuan Gulf. The canoes are laden with earthenware pots of various shapes and sizes which are carefully packed for the voyage in dry banana leaves. In addition to these, certain other articles highly valued as ornaments (and latterly foreign made articles of utility) are also taken for barter. The canoes return during the north-west monsoon after an absence of about three months, laden with sago which the voyagers have obtained in exchange for their pots and other articles ...

LEGEND OF THE ORIGIN OF THE *HIRI*

A very long time ago there lived at the Motu village of Boera a man named Edai Siabo. One day he sailed with some other men in a canoe to the islands of Bava and Idiha (small coral islands on the barrier reef off Boera) to catch turtle. They were unsuccessful, and at night the other men went to sleep on the island, whilst Edai Siabo, who was *varo biaguna* ('master' of the turtle net) slept alone in the canoe. During the night a being named Edai, of the kind called *dirava*, arose from the water, seizing hold of him and carrying him under water to the cave among the rocks which was his abode. The *dirava* ... informed him that he had brought him there to tell him about *lakatoi* ... The *dirava* went on to explain how these vessels should be made, and how, if he and his fellows went to the west in a lakatoi, they would be able to obtain plenty of sago to tide them over the season of scarcity ... At last, when all had been told he allowed the [other] men to haul Edai Siabo out of the cave to the surface of the sea, and they placed him in the canoe. He was apparently dead and the men wept sorely over him, but after a while he opened his eyes and revived. His companions asked him what he had been doing, and he told them that he had seen and heard many strange things. When the men asked him what these things were, he told them that the *dirava* Edai had taken him into his rock-cave and instructed him as to the manner of making a *lakatoi* and about the *hiri* (the trading voyage on which the *lakatoi* must sail). The men inquired the meaning of these words and Edai Siabo promised that he would repeat all that the *dirava* Edai had said to him when they had returned to Boera. So they made sail for that place. There Edai Siabo built a model of a *lakatoi* according to all that the spirit had told him, and when he put it upon the sea it sailed along quickly, and all the assembled people exclaimed: '*Inai!* (behold!) who taught you to make such a thing?' and he told them that the *dirava* Edai had taught him thus to make a big vessel, and to sail in it to the west for sago. Then he took the little *lakatoi* to his house, and the men of the village went there to examine it and ask questions. Edai Siabo explained to them how to lash the canoes together, and how to step the mast, and how to make the sail, and so forth. So the people went away and built a *lakatoi*, and they called it *Oalabada* ... When the *lakatoi* was finished it was loaded with earthenware pots ... They sailed for many days into the west until they came to a large village on the banks of a river, and there they stopped. The people received them with great joy inasmuch as they never before had pots in which to boil their sago. The travellers remained until all the pots had been bartered for sago and then the *lakatoi* being loaded they set sail for home ...

Since that time the *lakatoi* have gone every year to the west, and there has consequently been food in plenty during the season of scarcity.

—F.R. Barton, 'The Annual Trading Expedition to the Papuan Gulf', in C.G. Seligmann, *The Melanesians of British New Guinea*, Cambridge University Press, Cambridge, 1910, pp. 96–100 [Captain F.R. Barton was administrator of the colony of British New Guinea, 1904–07.]

2   Captain Cook on Tahiti

Captain James Cook made his third voyage of exploration to the Pacific in 1776–79. The extract relates to the practices of human sacrifice and war in Tahiti in 1777. His comments were made in the context of a ceremony of human sacrifice which he had just observed. Cook's original spelling has been retained in this document.

Whenever any of the Great Chiefs thinks a human Sacrifice necessary on any particular occasion, he pitches upon the Victim, sends some of his trusty Servants who fall upon him and kill him; the King [the highest-ranking *ari'i* or chief on the island] is then acquainted with it, whose presence at the Ceremony, as I was told is absolutely necessary, indeed except the Priests he was the only man that had any thing to do in it. From what we could learn these Sacrifices are not very uncommon, there were in the face of the Morai ['temple'] where this man was buried forty nine Sculls, every one of which were those of men who had been not confined to this place alone. This is not the only barbarous custom we find amongst these people, we have great reason to believe there was a time when they were Cannibals; however I will not insist upon this but confine myself to such as we have unquestionable authority for. Besides the cutting out the jaw-bones of the enemy that is slain in battle, they in some Measure offer their bodies as a Sacrifice to the Eatua ['god'] the day after when the Victors collect all the dead that have fallen into their hands and bring them to the Morai, where with a great deal of ceremony they dig a hole and bury them all in it as an offering to the Gods. But the great chiefs who fall in battle and into the hands of their enemies are treated in a different manner. We were told that the late King Tootaha [one of the most powerful district chiefs on the island who died in battle in 1773; he was not 'King'], Tebourai Tamaida, and another Chief who fell with them were brought to this Morai, their bowels cut out by the Priests before the great alter, and the bodies afterwards buried in three different places, which were pointed out to us in the great pile of stones which compose the most conspicuous part of this Morai. And the Common Men who fell also in this battle were all buried in one hole at the foot of the pile. This Omai, who was present, told me was done the day after the Battle, with much Pomp and ceremony, and in the midst of a great Concourse of people, as a thanksgiving offering to the Eatua for the Victory they had obtained, while the vanquished had taken refuge in the Mountains, where they remain'd about a week or ten days till the fury of the Victors was over and a treaty set on foot …

—James Cook, *The Journals of Captain James Cook on his Voyages of Discovery*, ed. J.C. Beaglehole, vol. 3, *The Voyage of the* Resolution *and* Discovery *1776–1780*, Hakluyt Society, Cambridge, 1967, pp. 204–5

3   Dumont d'Urville on Polynesians and Melanesians

Jules Sebastien-Cesar Dumont d'Urville was an aristocratic captain in the French Navy who led two expeditions to the Pacific and Australia in 1826–29 and 1837–40.

The extract relates to two small islands in the eastern Solomons in 1828: Tikopia, inhabited by Polynesians, and Vanikoro, inhabited by 'Melanesians'.

Astrolabe remained in an almost flat calm three or four miles to the south-west of Tikopia, but the current was perceptibly dragging her westwards. We had been surrounded by natives until sunset. These men, gentle, cheerful and friendly, appeared to me to belong to the same race as the inhabitants of Tonga and Rotuma: they speak nearly the same language and have similar customs. They are mostly tall, well-built, tattooed on the chest and face, wear their hair long and straight to which the application of lime gives a light colour. None of them was carrying weapons ...

The inhabitants of this little place have a very exact knowledge of the various islands for a considerable distance around them. In the east they have clearly indicated to me Rotuma, Fataka (Mitre), the latter uninhabited, Anouda (Cherry Island) inhabited by people of their race, to the nor'-nor'-west, Taumako [Duff Islands] inhabited by people of the same race and two days journey away. To the west and west-nor'-west, Vanikoro ..., Paiou, Vanou and Ocili, occupied by non-cannibalistic blacks, that they collectively call Fidji which is oddly related to the name given by the Tongans to the people of the Viti archipelago. To the west-sou'-west they indicated Natiou and other islands inhabited by the same race; finally, in the south they have cited Warouka (probably Bligh's Banks Island) inhabited by black cannibals; their horror of these people being expressed with graphic gestures and very obvious signs of fear. I was shown a native of Rotuma who had been swept in his canoe by the wind as far as Tikopia, where he found refuge and has to stay ...

Of the four *ariki* or paramount chiefs of the island, three came to pay me a courtesy call, and each offered me a present consisting of three or four coconuts and as many green bananas of poor quality and one or two flying fish. It was a proof of their extreme poverty; I was careful to respond to their courtesies as if their present had been very valuable ...

The whole island of Tikopia contains no more than four or five hundred inhabitants divided under the authority of four chiefs, of whom the paramount chief bears the title *Ariki Tabu*; their prerogatives of office consist mainly in the laws of taboo and tributes on fishing that the people pay them. There is also a priest who came aboard and made me a present similar to those of the chiefs.

The ordinary people only approach these chiefs in a crouching position and they have to prostrate themselves before them. The chiefs themselves when they came before me appeared very nervous; they took my right hand and pressed their noses to the back of it ...

... here [Vanikoro], as in New Holland [Australia], the women are given the hardest and dirtiest work. These women are even uglier than the men, especially as they get older. Their withered, wrinkled and pendulous breasts look like old monks' scrips, and as if they were eager to make their chests more ugly more quickly, they have adopted the custom of binding them tightly with a strap about the breast. Their hair is frizzy and mostly close-cropped.

A short apron covers their private parts, and these poor creatures have for the most part developed a clumsy, misshapen posture from the habit of carrying heavy loads. However hideous these women are, their husbands are extremely jealous and only very reluctantly allow our men to get anywhere near them.

The men, who seem always dressed up, are armed with bows and arrows ... they are so attached to these weapons that they have absolutely refused to hand over a single one of them even for the red cloth which they eagerly covet; to all offers made to them on this subject they merely say that these weapons are taboo like our guns.

We learned today from these men that they are usually at war with the inhabitants of the village situated on the eastern point of Tevai Island, the village that specifically bears the name of Vanikoro. The people there use blowpipes to shoot their arrows, if we correctly understood the gestures of our savages, and they have just lately killed nine men from Tevai ...

Decked out in their war-paint, the men are ridiculously overloaded with rings of white shell or tortoiseshell intertwined and hanging from ears, noses, arms, wrists, knees and even ankles; whereas the women rarely wear any of these ornaments, and then only very few. En masse, like all members of the black race of Oceania [the 'Melanesians'], these people are disgustingly lazy, stupid, savage, greedy and without any good qualities or virtues that I know of. Only our strength inspires their respect, and I think that our existence would be in jeopardy if we were, or they believed us to be, the weaker. It was indeed a cruel fate for our great La Perouse to succumb so tragically as he neared the end of his brilliant expedition; but had he had the time before he perished to get to know the frightful people into whose hands he had been thrown, his shipwreck would have seemed to him ten times more deplorable. Anywhere else, among the people of the Polynesian race, in Tahiti, Tonga, Rotuma, Tikopia, once the first moment of fear and anxiety had passed, he would have been able to treat with them and get from them respect and even help and provisions. The cannibals of New Zealand have sometimes shown themselves hospitable to Europeans wrecked on their coasts. But at Vanikoro, La Perouse's companions must only have found greed, barbarism and treachery. Despite our gifts all we could get from the inhabitants of Tevai were coconuts and a few bananas, so exorbitant were their demands for anything else. As for pigs, they seemed determined not to part with them at any price.

—Jules, S.-C. Dumont d'Urville, *An Account in Two Volumes of Two Voyages to the South Seas by Captain (later Rear-Admiral) Jules S.-C. Dumont d'Urville of the French Navy to Australia, New Zealand, Oceania 1826–1829 in the Corvette* Astrolabe *and to the Straits of Magellan, Chile, Oceania, South East Asia, Australia, Antarctica, New Zealand and Torres Strait 1837–1840 in the corvettes* Astrolabe *and* Zelee, tr. and ed. Helen Rosenman, vol. 1, *Astrolabe 1826–1829,* Melbourne University Press, 1987, pp. 199–201

* In 1772 Polynesian Maoris had ambushed and killed twenty-six Frenchmen at the Bay of Islands in New Zealand. La Perouse was the leader of a French exploring expedition which was wrecked off Vanikoro in 1788. He had previously lost twelve men to an attack by Polynesians in Samoa.

4 Turner on the Tannese

Rev. George Turner was a Scottish Presbyterian missionary who in July 1842 was sent by the London Missionary Society to Port Resolution, on the island of Tanna, in the southern New Hebrides, now called Vanuatu.

At the first glance, one concludes that the Tannese must live in a state of perpetual war. This is actually the case. War is the rule, peace the exception. They were fighting during five out of the seven months we lived among them, and I should think that is a fair average of the way in which they have lived from time immemorial. There is ample proof there that war is the enemy of civilisation and the element of savage life. We were never able to extend our journeys about four miles from our dwelling. At such distances you come to boundaries which are never passed, and beyond which the people speak a different dialect. At one of these boundaries actual war will be going on; at another, kidnapping and cooking each other; and at another, all may be peace, but by mutual consent, they have no dealings with each other. Their fighting is principally bush skirmishing; they rarely come to close hand-to-hand fighting. When visiting the volcano one day, the natives told us about a battle in which one party which was pursued ran right into the crater, and there fought for a while on the downward slope inside the cup! But few fall in their daily skirmishes. Many, however, are cut off after lingering for weeks under fatal wounds.

When the body of an enemy is taken, it is dressed for the oven, and served up with yams at the next meal. Captain Cook only suspected they were cannibals. There is no doubt about the thing now. They delight in human flesh, and distribute it in little bits far and near among their friends, as a delicious morsel. I recollect talking to a native one day about it, and trying to fill him with disgust at the custom, but the attempt was vain. He wound up all with a hearty laugh at what he no doubt considered my weakness, and added: 'Pig's flesh is very good for you, but this is the thing for us'; and suiting the action to the word, he seized his arm with his teeth, and shook it, as if he were going to take the bit out! It is different on some other islands, but at Tanna cannibal connoisseurs prefer a black man to a white one. The latter they say tastes salty! They regard, however, as 'fish' all who come in their way, as the sequel to massacres of white men there has amply proved.

In Eastern Polynesia, the rule has been that in a group of four, seven, or ten islands within sight of each other, we have found but one dialect, and the people having a good deal of intercourse, not only with each other on the same island, but also with the various islands of the group. They had their quarrels and their wars, at times, but they made up matters after a while, and went on again in harmony. In going westward, however, among the Papuan tribes of the New Hebrides, we found ourselves in a totally different region, all split up into the most hostile isolation. Take, for example, four of the southerly islands of the group, viz., Tanna, Eromanga, Futuna, and Aneiteum, all within sight of each other; we find a totally different dialect on each, and books which may be printed for the one will be quite useless to the other. Even on the same island we find two and three different dialects ...

—George Turner, *Nineteen Years in Polynesia: Missionary life, travels and researches in the islands of the Pacific*, John Snow, London, 1861, pp. 82–5

5 Adams on the Tannese

It had been supposed since the time of Cook—when one of his men claimed to have been invited to a cannibal feast—that the Tannese were all anthropophagous. But it was left to Turner to bring a true Ballantynian flavour to the subject, with his portrayal of the Tannese as a hoard of salivating savages, impatiently waiting to pop their next victim into the oven, to be served up with yams at the following meal. 'It would appear that although they invariably eat all slain in war', two visiting L.M.S. missionaries reported in 1858, 'the practice of eating human flesh is from habit, preference and taste and not always merely for revenge but from the mere gratification which they enjoy in eating such food'. Little wonder that the following year poor Paton felt obliged to sit a lonely vigil over his wife's grave, gun in hand, for ten days and nights—or so he claimed—to prevent the Tannese getting at her decomposing remains. In fact, for the whole island there were never more than twenty-eight families with the right to eat human flesh, and they confined themselves to the bodies of fallen enemies—whether to gain their strength or to heap indignity on them is unclear. What confused Paton and Turner was what they saw as a diabolical trade in corpses as they traced a path along ceremonial routes. Turner described their path in 1842:

> The people in our immediate neighbourhood ... when they were in the habit of bringing a victim from inland ... took it to the marum of the district next to their own, and exchanged it for a pig. The people who got it then carried it on to the next marum, and there again exchanged it for a pig, and after being carried through several marums in this way, it reached the district next to the sea, and as they could not carry it further, there it was cooked and eaten.

The dead man's journey ended when the corpse reached such a stage of putrification that the body fluids were breaking through the skin, and when a group which had a family or family line of cannibals decided to keep the body. The acceptance of the body entailed the obligation to send back in exchange one day the body of a killed enemy, following the same route but in the opposite direction. Invariably, it seems, pigs were exchanged for the corpse at each point of its journey. The Samoan teachers who were placed at Port Resolution in 1839 reported that they saw two bodies prepared for the oven, and that 'a compensation was demanded for these 2 lives, and a pig was accordingly given'. William Gill and Henry Nisbet noted in 1846 that a European's body was disposed of in a similar way. Paton reported in 1861 that 'a large fat pig' was given for each of ten bodies received. Years later Paton's son Frank wrote that when two men were killed on the east coast of Tanna their bodies were passed from village to village on the west coast. 'Heathen' attended from far and near, and pieces of the body were sent throughout the missionary's district. By such means alliances were established and confirmed, or repudiated, according to the same principle of reciprocity which underlay other Tannese rituals.

Even warfare, that most characteristic feature of European accounts of Tanna, signifying to European eyes social and even moral chaos, was essentially an exchange ritual. Battles were pre-arranged, depended on suitable weather, and had to fit in with the routine of daily life, such as work in the gardens. They could often be avoided by a gift to the aggrieved party, but failing that, fighting was conducted along what the missionary Gray described as 'well recognised war tactics'. Captain Erskine of the Royal Navy dismissed fighting between two Port Resolution tribes in 1849 as 'a war party marching out daily to the boundary-line to exchange a few spears or stones, without any very serious result'. A decade later, Paton described an altercation on the beach between the harbour tribes and an inland tribe as a grand sort of barbarous Homeric scolding match, where the protagonists exhausted their rage in javelins or reproach. Inglis noted that if one man were killed the battle concluded for the day, to allow the losing side to examine whether any one had breached any of their 'appointed observances', thus provoking the anger of the gods. A battle then, like any other exchange on Tanna, might be viewed as a ritual re-enactment of a theme passed down from the gods, investing reality with its mythic and sacred quality.

We found no such thing as a king or great chief at Tanna. No Thakombau, Pomare, or Kamehameha there ['kings', respectively, of Fiji, Tahiti and Hawaii]. The authority of a Tanna chief does not seem to extend a gunshot from his own dwelling. In a settlement, or village, you find eight or ten families. Their huts are put up, without any rule or arrangement, among the trees; and in this place, which has its village name, you may number a population of eighty or a hundred. There will be at least one or two principal men among them, who are called chiefs. The affairs of this little community are regulated by the chiefs and the heads of families. Six, or eight, or more, of these villages unite and form what may be called a district, or county, and all league together for mutual protection. If a person belonging to one of these villages is injured or killed by the people of another district, all the villages of his district unite in seeking redress, either by a fine or by war and spoliation.

—Ron Adams, *In the Land of Strangers. A Century of European Contact with Tanna, 1774–1874*, Australian National University, Canberra, 1984, pp. 10–12

6 Garanger on Roy Mata

[According to local traditions,] Roy Mata lived long before the Kuwae disaster [a volcanic eruption at the start of the fifteenth century] ...

Roy Mata is a hero who is well known throughout the central Hew Hebrides [Vanuatu]. It was he who would have organised the chiefs' installation ceremonies ... and the dispersal of the chiefs along the Efate coast and in the little islands in the centre of the group. He would also have introduced the matrilineal system into the central New Hebrides and organised the 'Natamvate' feast ...

According to information received at Efate:

A: Roy Mata had asked that after his death he be buried at Retoka.

B: Very ill, he was taken around Efate to the different villages owing him *nasaotonga* [gifts as homage], then into Feles cave at Lelepa, where he died ...

C: The titled people of all the villages who owed him *nasaotonga* gathered ... to go to Retoka for the internment. They had no need of canoes for the sea drew back to make a passage for them.

D: Roy Mata was buried along with several members of his court.

E: Some representatives of different clans were also buried, voluntarily.

F: Some other individuals were buried after having been sacrificed ...

Excavations [on Retoka island] showed that a large area had been laid out, digging the soil out to a depth of about 30 cm (level II), and within it a deeper burial (level III). Roy Mata was buried there along with a couple to his left, a man to his right and a very young woman who was stretched out at his feet at right angles to him.

On the surface of level II lay 33 individuals: 17 females and 16 males, some ... richly adorned. The others, isolated, are much less so or not at all ... Doubtless ... it is a question of the individuals who, according to the tradition, volunteered to accompany Roy Mata to the land of the dead, or of those who were sacrificed ...

The date [based on collagen analysis of a bone sample from Roy Mata] is ... about 1265 AD.

—José Garanger, *Archaeology of the New Hebrides: Contribution to the knowledge of the central islands*, trans. Rosemary Groube, University of Sydney, 1982, pp. 24, 55–6, 71–3. (José Garanger is a French archaeologist.)

QUESTIONS AND ACTIVITIES

1   Ensure you know the meanings of the following terms:

    stereotype   subsistence
    idyllic   horticulture
    indigenous   ritual
    ethnocentric   hierarchical
    racist   stratified
    archaeology   egalitarian
    anthropology   evolutionism
    literacy   genealogy
    metallurgy

2   Ensure you know the location of the following places:

    Tonga   New Zealand
    New Caledonia   Papua New Guinea
    Fiji   Tahiti
    Bougainville   Hawaii
    Vanuatu

3   What do the annual *hiri* expedition and the myth reproduced in Document 1 imply about the leadership of the Motu of Papua New Guinea?

4   What does the myth of the *hiri* tell us about these Melanesians' ideas of the source of important technical knowledge?

5   In what ways does Cook (Document 2) qualify the popular Western image of Tahiti as a 'Paradise' inhabited by 'noble savages'?

6   What does Cook tell us about the significance of religion to Tahitians?

7   In what ways did racial preconceptions shape Dumont d'Urville's descriptions of Tikopians and Vanikorons (Document 3)? Look for examples where his choice of words reflected his double standards regarding Polynesians and Melanesians, especially in relation to personal appearance, demeanour, assumed motivations and gift exchanges.

8   What information does Dumont d'Urville provide about the similarities and differences between the people of Tikopia and Vanikoro?

9   What examples of European ethnocentrism and cultural stereotyping exist in Turner's account (Document 4)?

10 Compare Turner's and Adams' (Document 5) interpretations of cannibalism and fighting on Tanna.

11 In what way could a historian writing on Tanna use Turner's text?

12 Who was Roy Mata (Document 6)? When did he live? What did he do? How do we know?

13 In what ways do local myths and archaeological data complement and confirm one another with relation to Roy Mata?

REFERENCES

Bellwood, Peter, *Man's Conquest of the Pacific: The prehistory of Southeast Asia and Oceania*, Oxford University Press, New York, 1977

Garanger, José, *Archaeology of the New Hebrides: Contribution to the knowledge of the central islands*, trans. Rosemary Groube, University of Sydney, 1982

Golson, Jack, 'The Ipomoean Revolution Revisited: Society and the sweet potato in the Upper Wahgi Valley', in Strathern, Andrew (ed.), *Inequality in New Guinea Highlands Societies*, Cambridge University Press, 1982

Howe, K.R., *Where the Waves Fall: A New South Sea Islands history from first settlement to colonial rule*, George Allen & Unwin, Sydney, 1984

Kuykendall, Ralph S., *The Hawaiian Kingdom*, University of Hawaii Press, 1968

Oliver, Douglas L., *Ancient Tahitian Society*, Australian National University Press, 1974, vol. 2, pp. 1121–32

Oliver, Douglas L., *Native Cultures of the Pacific Islands*, University of Hawaii Press, 1989

Sahlins, Marshall, 'Poor Man, Rich Man Chief: Political types in Melanesia and Polynesia', in Vayda, Andrew P. (ed.), *Peoples and Cultures of the Pacific: An anthropological reader*, Natural History Press, New York, 1968

NOTES

1. Polynesia: from the Greek *poly-*, + *nesos*, island; Melanesia: from *melas*, black, a reference to the generally darker skin tones of the inhabitants; Micronesia: from *mikro-*, small, a reference to the tiny size of the islands.
2. Jules Sébastien-César Dumont d'Urville, 'Sur les îles du Grand Océan', *Bulletin de la Société de Géographie*, 17 (1832):11 (tr. B. Douglas).

PART TWO
EUROPEAN 'DISCOVERY'
OF THE PACIFIC

INTRODUCTION

What world view did Europeans carry with them into the Pacific? What was the impact in Europe of the discovery of hundreds of islands and atolls scattered across the vast Pacific ocean? What did Europe make of the people who were living there? What impact did the first explorers' reports and published journals, 'scientific' observations and images conveyed in early art works have on Europeans setting out later to visit, trade or settle in the islands?

What impact did stories of 'strangers' and even stranger language, tools and possessions, have on islanders when they first met Europeans in a face-to-face encounter and then later on a regular basis?

Chapters 3 and 4 offer answers to these questions by introducing a range of evidence. How did the attitudes of the salon, forecastle and lower deck shape behaviour when islanders and Europeans first met on the deck, beach or village clearing? Was Omai a noble savage? Why did Europeans name Palau, Niue and Fiji respectively the Islands of Thieves, Savage Island and the Cannibal Isles? What did Mangaians think of Cook's visit? This evidence also draws attention on the use to be made of oral history.

Adams and Quanchi point to a range of tactics—violence, appeasement and reciprocal exchange—used to control the 'other' when they first met. How did Europeans judge and record the behaviour of the islanders? How did islanders portray these strangers in their stories, dance, song or art? Were they returning ancestors, ghosts, providers of new and wonderful goods, political allies or enemies? How did the meeting change both islanders and Europeans?

Chapter 3
European Discovery
or Multiple Discoveries

Ron Adams, Victorian University of Technology

Other people: other histories

We know that the islands of the Pacific had been sighted, explored and settled, in many cases thousands of years prior to European contact. But as the historian Oscar Spate has commented, in one sense there was no such thing as 'the Pacific' until Magellan traversed and named the huge expanse of water in 1520–21. In the sense of placing on written or graphical record the existence and position of the newly-found lands and seas—and making knowledge of them available to seamen, merchants and scholars round the world—the 'discovery' of the Pacific, suggests Spate, was essentially a European achievement.

But even in this limited context the question remains: what did Europeans in the great era of Pacific discovery between 1521 and 1792 in fact 'discover'? To what extent did they see and experience what they already expected, or wanted, to discover? To what extent did they record, in written and pictorial form, what they assumed that others expected or wanted them to record? To answer these questions it is necessary to understand the attitudes and beliefs (and the social structures in which these attitudes and beliefs were located) which Europeans carried with them on their voyages of discovery. It is also necessary to continually pose the further question: to what extent were these attitudes and beliefs changed in the encounter with other people and other places?

The constant challenge of history is the attempt to comprehend attitudes, beliefs and social structures different from our own. Each and every society constructs its own understanding of reality according to the conceptual frameworks available to its members. Reality may include witches, ancestral spirits, viruses, magical stones, Jehovah, the theory of gravity, or the notion of progress. What is 'real' in one society need not be 'real' in another. The difficulty for the student of history attempting to uncover another society's 'reality', is that much of what constitutes the 'reality' passes without comment, precisely because in the normal course of events what is real is taken for granted, and requires no further explanation or justification.

Fortunately for the student of culture contact in the Pacific, the early European voyages were not in 'the normal course of events'. Within the artificial confines of shipboard life, and in the first encounters with strange people and alien environments, Europeans were often moved to reflect upon, to explain and to justify, their own attitudes, beliefs and sustaining social structures. Not the ordinary seamen—most of whom lacked the education, and possibly the inclination, to record their thoughts for posterity—but the officers and gentlemen of the upper-deck, whose attitudes, beliefs and social structures will tend to be those of a more privileged class. This obviously limits how far we can generalise on European attitudes, beliefs and social structures.

Nonetheless, there is often a certain succinct clarity in the expressions of attitudes, beliefs and social structures in the journals, essays and books which the early voyagers wrote. This results from the degree of economy which Europeans (upper or lower deck) had to exercise in what they carried with them on their voyages of discovery. As Arnold Toynbee has commented in *A Study of History*:

> ... overseas migrations have in common one and the same simple fact: in transmarine migration the social apparatus of the migrants has to be unpacked again at the end of the voyage. All kinds of apparatus—persons and property, techniques and institutions and ideas—are subject to this law. Anything that cannot stand the sea voyage at all has to be left behind, and many things—not only material objects—which the migrants do take with them, have to be taken to pieces, never perhaps to be reassembled in this original form. When unpacked, they are found to have suffered a 'sea change into something rich and strange'.

According to Toynbee's Law of transmarine migration, it should be easier to detect the attitudes, beliefs and social structures of the European voyager compared with the European who stayed at home. At the same time, there is the added complication that the voyager's attitudes, beliefs and social structures might well have suffered (as Toynbee puts it) a 'sea change into something rich and strange'.

The packing and unpacking to which Toynbee refers characterised every encounter between islander and European, and every account of the early voyages of discovery provides rich evidence of the process at work. A particularly extravagant example of how Europeans imported what we might term (following Toynbee) their 'cultural apparatus', and of how that apparatus suffered a 'sea change into something rich and strange', is provided by the 1605–06 voyage to Espiritu Santo by Pedro Fernandez de Quiros.

Quiros had been Chief Pilot on an earlier (1595) expedition to the Solomon Islands, and his aim when he sailed from the South American port of Callao in December 1605 was to rediscover the Solomons. But it was in the north of what is today Vanuatu that Quiros landed five months later, on the island he christened Austrialia del Espiritu Santo in honour of the Spanish King, who belonged to the Royal House of Austria. To mark his discovery, Quiros created the Order of the Knights of the Holy Ghost, comprising every member of the expedition, all of whom were given a cross of blue taffeta to wear across their breast. It was, the old Franciscan friar on the voyage commented tongue-in-cheek, a marvellous diversity of Knights: 'negro-knights and Indian-knights and knights who were knight-knights'. But for Quiros—in the grip of a religious mania—it was a totally serious business, as he set about his elaborate preparations for taking formal possession of the island.

Try to picture the scene on Espiritu Santo Island on 14 May 1606—the day of Pentecost. The infantry fired off their arquebuses (guns), the ensigns leavened their flags, the Father Commissary (head priest) kneeling on the beach with his five barefoot monks, received from the admiral a large wooden cross, made specially for the purpose from a tree which grew on the island. The cross was carried with all due solemnity and reverence to a pedestal in a makeshift church built the day before. (Camp gossip had it that Quiros planned to replace the makeshift affair with a church of solid marble, to rival St Peter's Church in Rome.) Then, amidst sprinklings of holy water and with the chords of the *lignum* ringing in his ears, Quiros took formal possession of the island.

> Be witnesses the heavens, the earth, the waters, with all their creatures, and those who are present be witnesses how I, the Captain Pedro Fernandez de Quiros, in these parts, which until now have been unknown in the name of Jesus Christ, son of the Eternal Father and of the Holy Virgin Mary, truly God and man, set up this sign of the Holy Cross on which His person was

crucified, and on which He gave His life as a ransom for the whole human race, being present as witnesses all the officers of marine and war on the day of Pentecost, the 14th of May, 1606. In these parts of the south, until now unknown, where I am, and have come with approval and licence of the Supreme Pontiff, Clement VIII, and by order of the King our Lord Philip III, King of the Spains, despatched by the Council of State I, Pedro Fernandez de Quiros, in the name of the Most Holy Trinity, take possession of all these islands and lands newly discovered, and that I shall discover as far as the Pole.

I take possession of these parts of the south as far as the Pole in the name of Jesus, Saviour of all people, however unknown they may be ... And I take it with the intention and object that all the natives in all these parts should have the Holy Evangelist preached to them zealously and clearly...

I take possession of all the parts of the south as far as the Pole in the name of John of God, and of all the professed brethren of his Order: that they may found, administer, and maintain their professed charity in all the hospitals there may be in all these parts; it being so necessary that the natives may become acquainted with all our procedure, and feel the devotion and love that our sufferings for them, and the curing of their infirmities, and the other good things we do for them, so justly merit.

I take possession of these parts of the south as far as a Pole, and of all the rights that His Holiness and His Majesty may determine lawfully to pertain in regard to the divisions of the lands and the services of the natives, to the discoverers, settlers, defenders, and conservers, which are all the military belonging to the Order of the Holy Spirit; having the obligation, without pay, to take the duties of all the royal and public offices, and all the Divine and human control of the natives, with profession of all the rest that the constitutions of the Order lay down.

Finally, I take possession of this bay named St Philip and St James, and of its port of Santa Cruz, and of the site where is to be founded a city which is to be named New Jerusalem.

—Clements Markham (ed.), *The Voyages of Pedro Fernandez de Quiros, 1595 to 1606,* 2 Vols, London, 1904

Later the same day, Quiros proclaimed a municipality and distributed civil offices among the new colonists. There was an accountant, a treasurer, a factor (a kind of business manager), a registrar of mines and nineteen magistrates. There were ten Judges of the Peace, who between them divided up the offices of: attorney to the municipality, sworn executor, secretary to the municipality, chief constable, royal constable, general purveyor, storekeeper and custom house guardian. In many respects it was a standard Spanish municipality, a political arrangement which, by recreating institutions with which they were familiar, enabled the Spaniards to establish the cultural boundaries of their new colony by distancing it from the alien world they confronted. The process is suggested in the wording of the pledge of loyalty made by each official on the assumption of office: with a promise to carry out his duties 'in these remote parts, in the midst of so many barbarians'.

Eleven days after the proclamation of the municipality, the cross, the royal standard and all the other flags were again brought out, for the celebration of the feast of Corpus Christi. Across the beach and into the jungle was fashioned a street, framed by a canopy of branches, palms and flowers. Along this pathway into the barbarian heartland marched the officials of the new city, led by the General bearing the cross. The priests recited masses, the Father Commissary celebrated a High Mass, and the magistrates carried candles or flags. Then followed a sword-dance, with all the dancers dressed in silk, and another dance by young Spanish boys (again, dressed in silk) who sang in praise of the Holy Sacrament.

The election of the city officials, the building of the makeshift church (and the anticipated building of a marble cathedral), the elaborate processions and celebrations, capture something of the entire history of culture contact in the Pacific. As historian Greg Dening has noted, the critical advantage of cross-cultural history 'is that the cultures in their exposure to one another lay bare their structures of law, of morality, their rationalisations in myth, their expressions in symbolism and ritual'. Despite the sufferings and privations endured on the voyage out from Callao, despite the deaths and murmurings of rebellion alluded to in the accounts of the voyage, each voyager still carried in his head an understanding of what was proper and what was improper, what was natural and what was unnatural.

The boundaries between proper and improper, natural and unnatural, may have shifted in the encounters with 'natives', but never to a point which seriously questioned the division of the world into civilised and savage. In terms of this division, it was neither improper nor unnatural to set 'natives' to flight, to enter their homes and raid their gardens, to steal their pigs and kidnap their children, and to shoot their men.

We can only guess at what the islanders made of the actions of the Spanish. From the various accounts it would seem that they were terrified at times, enraged and defiant at others; that they were curious, amazed, grateful and puzzled. The Spanish commentators noted quite unselfconsciously how three boys they kidnapped wept for their fathers, how they in turn begged for the return of their sons, how the people rejected an offer of goats for the children, and how one of the boys cried bitterly to be returned to shore. 'Silence, child! You know not what you ask', was the reply. 'Greater good awaits you than the sight and the communion with heathen parents and friends.' At the material level, the 'greater good' included a costume of silk, emblazoned with a cross on the breast. (Quiros liked to think that the sight of the cross elevated the barbarian boys' minds, even if they did not understand its significance.)

Two of the boys (what happened to the third is not clear) were taken back to Mexico when New Jerusalem was abandoned. Baptised Pedro and Pablo, they were taught to recite four prayers in Spanish and to make the sign of the cross. In broken Spanish they thrilled audiences with their accounts of heathen practices and delighted their spiritual mentors with their simple questions about religious faith. How was it, asked Pablo after observing the burial at sea of the Father Commissary, that the weighted body went to the bottom of the sea, whereas he had been told at his baptism that believers went up to heaven when they died? The answer that only the soul went to heaven reportedly left him 'doubtful'. Pedro is presented as less sceptical. On entering a church in Mexico and seeing many crucifixes, he asked how there could be so many gods when he had been told there was but one. To the answer that they were all representations of the true Christ, Pedro is said to have 'appeared satisfied'.

The accounts of the expedition tell us a good deal about the attitudes and beliefs of a man in the grip of religious mania, and a little about the actions of the choir boys, the negro cooks and the rest of the expeditionary force. But they tell us nothing of events from the perspectives of 'Pedro' and 'Pablo'. It is a general problem. Given the absence of contemporary first-hand accounts, how can we gain access to the meaning and significance which islanders have attached to their early encounters with Europeans?

A number of historians have turned to non-written sources of information, such as stories and songs, as a partial solution to this problem. To understand the significance for the Maori of Captain Cook's visit to Mercury Bay in 1769, for instance,

J.C. Beaglehole featured an account by Te Horeta Taniwha, who was a young boy at the time of Cook's visit. Taniwha's story was first taken down at Lieutenant-Governor Wynard's direction during the gold field negotiations with the Maori at Coromendel in 1852, that is, more than seventy years after the event. According to the version used by Beaglehole (Document 1b), Cook's men were perceived by the local Maori as *tupua*, or 'goblins', though when they were seen to eat food it was realised that they were 'not goblins like the Maori goblins'. Nonetheless, Taniwha recalled how he and his two boy-companions were afraid of being bewitched by the strange visitors.

For Beaglehole, it is at this level of general impressions that Taniwha's account is of historical value. It is of least value in matters of detail which are contradicted by the written European accounts. Thus the fact that the episode recounted by Taniwha is not mentioned by Cook or the naturalist Banks makes it, according to Beaglehole, 'extremely unlikely that it happened'. Similarly, Taniwha's confusion of Banks with Gore is described as a 'blot on Te Horeta Taniwha's reminiscences'.

Such a comment suggests that the value and significance of Taniwha's account of Cook's visit was assessed by Beaglehole in terms of the extent to which it conformed to the European accounts. A problem with this approach is that it assumes that both the written and the oral (or originally oral) accounts are evidence for essentially the same thing. But there are fundamental differences in the ways of 'managing' knowledge in oral and literate cultures. The difficulty for people such as Beaglehole (and ourselves!) is that writing has so removed us from oral cultures 'that it is very difficult for us to conceive of an oral universe of communication or thought except as a variant of a literate universe'.

For oral peoples the significance of words lies in their actual *utterance*, with all the accompanying gestures, vocal inflections and facial expressions which help to achieve empathetic and communal identification between speaker and audience. At this level, the significance of Taniwha's story lies in the personally interactive world created by the story's telling and retelling. And it is in the telling and retelling of a story that historical knowledge is given expression in an oral society. In such a society, the past exists only to the extent that it speaks to the present; for if stories fail to say something relevant to the present they will not be retold, and the history they express will be lost. While we cannot recreate the interaction which existed between storyteller and audience, we can try to imagine in what ways a particular story might have been relevant to them, which might in turn provide us with an insight into the meanings which the episode held for the original participants.

The ability to distinguish between Banks and Gore, while significant for Beaglehole (as the foremost historian of Cook's various voyages), did not hold any similar relevance for Taniwha and his audiences. And why should it have? What appears to have been more relevant as the story was recounted down the years was Taniwha's testimony that Cook had presented two handfuls of seed-potatoes to an 'old chief' of the Nga-ti-pou tribe, who was thus the first Maori to cultivate the new food. According to Taniwha, after the potatoes had been planted for three years,

> ... and there was a good quantity of them, a feast was given, at which some
> of the potatoes were eaten, and then a general distribution ... was made
> among the tribes of Waikato and Hauraki.

Taniwha goes on to state that the assertion of the Nga-puhi tribes that they were the first in New Zealand to have the potato is a fiction.

What was the relevance of the potatoes to Taniwha and his audiences, which ensured that the information was recounted down the years? Possibly it was a way of asserting the pre-eminence of the Nga-ti-pou tribe vis-a-vis the Nga-puhi. It might have been a reminder to *all* Maori of the debt owed to the old Nga-ti-pou chief who had the foresight to accept and nurture the gift of what was to become an important food source. Perhaps it was also conveying an important message to succeeding generations of the need to conserve food supplies. Possibly the reference to the distribution of seed potatoes among the Waikato and Hauraki tribes was making a political point in favour of exchange rather than warlike relations. It may well be, then, that the significance and meaning of Cook's visit lies in the creative ways in which the Maori were subsequently able to use the new circumstances offered by the addition of a new source of food, rather than in the immediate awestruck response highlighted by Beaglehole (cf. Document 1c).

In a similar way, in the history which I wrote on early European contact with the island of Tanna in southern Vanuatu, I missed an important element in establishing the significance of Captain Cook's visit in 1774. In my account I detailed what could be gathered from the various written records made by the company on board HMS *Resolution*, concluding with the marine Wedgeborough's fatal shooting of a young Tannese man. I contrasted Cook's lament that the Tannese would look upon the British as 'invaders', determined to impose their will through superior weapons (Document 2a), with the local Tannese understanding of the event as related to a resident British missionary sixty-eight years later (Document 2b). For me, the later account was important as evidence of the way in which the Tannese attached meaning to their encounter according to a cultural framework fundamentally different from the European. In their terms the shooting signified *their* control over the British, rather than the reverse (Document 2c).

In my analysis of their story, I concluded that the Tannese reference to two 'kangaroos' (that is, Tahitian dogs) left by Cook did not have any real significance in the encounter between the Tannese and the Europeans. However, on reflection, I think it is important to examine the relevance of the dogs which ensured that this piece of information was still being recounted nearly seventy years after the event. The people of Port Resolution telling the story were possibly making the claim (perhaps directed to the missionaries, perhaps to other Tannese) that a special relationship between themselves and the British had been initiated by Cook's gift. From this point of view, it may well be that the 'kangaroos' constitute the story's key element, rather than merely an anecdotal aside, as I had previously assumed.

But as well as asking in what way a particular item of information might have been sufficiently relevant to justify its retelling, it is also important to ask precisely for *whom* the information was relevant. Clearly, to talk of 'the Tannese', or of 'the Maori', or of 'the people of Espiritu Santo', is to talk at a very generalised level. Just as written sources with which historians work represent particular interpretations, so too oral sources are, ultimately, particular individuals' representations of events. It is true that they might accurately reflect how an event is generally perceived by a wider audience, such as the people of Port Resolution or the Nga-ti-pou tribe. But 'cultures' are not homogeneous, and it would be a mistake to assume that all of the people of Port Resolution, or of the Nga-ti-pou tribe, shared the same interpretation of events as represented in the surviving accounts.

To acknowledge these limitations in the usefulness of the recorded statements of islanders is to acknowledge that other people at other times have had other histories, to which we are largely denied access. But by acknowledging that 'culture' ultimately is comprised of people and relationships between people, we are also brought closer to a real understanding of the history of culture contact in the Pacific.

DOCUMENTS

1a   An encounter: Captain Cook's view [original spelling]

[November, 1769]

While we were making these observations five Canoes came along side of the Ship, two large and three small ones, in one were 47 people but in the others not so many. They were wholy strangers to us and to all appearance they came with a hostal intention, being compleatly arm'd with Pikes, Darts, Stones &c however they made no attempt and this was very probable owing to their being inform'd by some other Canoes (who at this time were along side selling fish) what sort of people they had to deal with. At their first coming along side they begun to sell our people some of their Arms and one Man offer'd to sale an Haahow, that is a square pice of Cloth such as they wear. Lieut Gore, who at this time was Commanding officer, sent in to the Canoe a piece of Cloth which the man had agreed to take in exchange for his, but as soon as he had got Mr Gore's Cloth in his posission he would not part with his own, but put off the Canoe from along side and then shook their paddles at the People in the Ship. Upon this Mr Gore fired a Musquet at them and from what I can learn kill'd the man who tooke the Cloth, after this they soon went away. I have here inserted the account of this affair just as I had it from Mr Gore but I must own that it did not meet with my approbation because I thought the punishment a little too severe for the Crime, and we had now been long enough acquainted with these People to know how to chastise trifling faults like this without taking away their lives.

—James Cook, *Journals*, 1769

1b   An encounter: Te Horeta Taniwha's view

In the days long past, when I was a very little boy, a vessel came to Whitianga. Our tribe was living there at that time. We did not live there as our permanent home, but were there according to our custom of living for some time on each of our blocks of land, to keep our claim to each, and that our fire might be kept alight on each block, so that it might not be taken from us by some other tribe.

We lived at Whitianga, and a vessel came there, and when our old men saw the ship they said it was a *tupua*, a god, and the people on board were strange beings. The ship came to anchor, and the boats pulled on shore. As our old men looked at the manner in which they came on shore, the rowers pulling with their backs to the bows of the boat, the old people said, 'Yes, it is so: these people are goblins; their eyes are at the back of their heads; they pull on shore with their backs to the land to which they are going.' When these goblins came on shore we (the children and women) took notice of them, but we ran away from them into the forest, and the warriors alone stayed in the presence of those goblins; but, as the goblins stayed some time, and did not do any evil to our braves, we came back one by one, and gazed at them, and we stroked their garments with our hands, and we were pleased with the whiteness of their skins and the blue eyes of some of them.

These goblins began to gather oysters, and we gave some *kumara*, fish, and fern-root to them. These they accepted, and we the women and children began to roast cockles for them; and as we saw that these goblins were eating *kumara*, fish and cockles, we were startled, and said, 'Perhaps they are not goblins like the Maori goblins.' These goblins went into the forest, and also climbed up the hill to our *pa* at Whitianga. They collected grasses from the cliffs, and kept knocking at the stones on the beach, and we said, 'Why are these acts done by these goblins?' We and the women gathered stones and grass of all sorts, and gave to these goblins. Some of the stones they liked, and put them into their bags, the rest they threw away; and when we gave them the grass and branches of trees they stood and talked to us, or they uttered the words of their language. Perhaps they were asking questions, and, as we did not know their language, we laughed, and these goblins also laughed, so we were pleased. The warriors and old men of our tribe sat in silence and gazed at these goblins. So these goblins ate the food we had presented to them, with some relish they had brought on shore with them, and then we went up the Whitianga River with them. Now, some of the goblins had walking-sticks which they carried about with them, and when we arrived at the bare dead trees where the shags roost at night and have their nests, the goblins lifted the walking-sticks up and pointed them at the birds, and in a short time thunder was heard to crash and a flash of lightning was seen, and a shag fell from the trees; and we children were terrified, and fled, and rushed into the forest, and left the goblins all alone. They laughed, and waved their hands to us, and in a short time the bravest of us went back to where the goblins were, and handled the bird, and saw that it was dead. But what had killed it? Our old people waited in suspicion, and went back to the settlement, as also did the goblins. We were now at quiet and peace with them, and they gave us some of the food they had brought on shore with them. Some of this food was very hard, but it was sweet. Some of our old people said it was *punga-punga* from the land from which these goblins came. They gave us some fat food, which the same old people of our tribe said was the flesh of whales; but the saltiness of this food nipped our throats, and we did not care for such fat food ...

I and my two boy-companions did not walk about on board of the ship—we were afraid lest we should be bewitched by the goblins; and we sat still and looked at everything we saw at the home of these goblins. When the chief goblin had been away in that part of their ship which he occupied, he came up on deck again and came to where I and my two boy-companions were, and patted our heads with his hand, and he put his hand out towards me and spoke to us at the same time, holding a nail out towards us. My companions were afraid, and sat in silence; but I laughed, and he gave the nail to me. I took it into my hand and said '*Ka pai*' ['very good'], and he repeated my words, and again patted our heads with his hand, and went away. My companions said, 'This is the leader of the ship, which is proved by his kindness to us; and also he is so very fond of children. A noble man—one of noble birth—cannot be lost in a crowd.' I took my nail, and kept it with great care, and carried it with me wherever I went, and made it fit to the point of my spear, and also used it to make holes in the side-boards of canoes, to bind them on to the canoe. I kept this nail till one day I was in a canoe and she capsized in the sea, and my god was lost to me.

The goblin chief took some of his own things and went with them to our old chief, and gave him two handfuls of what we now know were seed-potatoes. At that time we thought they were *parareka*, and we called them by this name, as the things he gave to the old man were not unlike the bulb of the *parareka*, or like the lower end of that fern, at the part where it holds to the stem of the fern-tree.

The old chief took the gift and planted it, and we have partaken of potatoes every year since that time. These things were first planted at a place in the Wairoa called the Hunua, half-way between Drury and the Taupo settlement, east of the entrance of the river Wairoa, opposite the island of Waiheke: and the old chief to whom the potatoes were given was of the Nga-ti-pou tribe, who occupied the Drury district at that time.

After these *parareka* had been planted for three years, and there was a good quantity of them, a feast was given, at which some of the potatoes were eaten, and then a general distribution of seed *parareka* was made amongst the tribes of Waikato and Hauraki.

The Nga-puhi tribes say they had the potato before any other tribes of New Zealand. This assertion is a fiction: we, the tribes of the Thames, first had potatoes, as we can show that even at this day the potato grows of its own accord in the Hunua district, from the fact that in the days of old the *pa* at the Hunua was attacked by a war-party, the *pa* was taken, all the people killed and eaten, their bones were broken and knocked like nails into the posts of the store-houses at their own home, and the place was sacred for a long time, not any one daring to go there, and was quite forsaken for years, but potatoes continued to grow there of their own accord on the banks of the streams, where the soil is carried by the freshes in the creeks, and potatoes are to be obtained there at this day ...

One of our tribe was killed by the goblins who first came to Whitianga. We—that is, our people—went again and again to that ship to sell fish, or mats, or anything that we Maori had to sell; and one day one of our canoes, in which were nine persons, paddled off to the ship but one of that nine was a noted thief, and this man took a dogskin mat to sell to the goblins. There were five of them at the stern of the canoe and four in the bow, and this thief was with those in the stern. When they got alongside of the ship, the goblin who collected shells, flowers, tree-blossoms, and stones was looking over the side. He held up the end of a garment which he would give in exchange for the dogskin mat belonging to this noted thief; so the thief waved with his hand to the goblin to let some of it down into the canoe, which the goblin did; and, as the goblin let some of it down into the canoe the thief kept pulling it towards him. When the thief had got a long length of the goblin's garment before him, the goblin cut his garment, and beckoned with his hand to the man to give the dogskin mat up to him; but the thief did not utter a word, and began to fold up the dogskin mat with the goblin's garment into one bundle, and told his companions to paddle to the shore. They paddled away. The goblin went down into the hold of the ship, but soon came up with a walking-stick in his hand, and pointed with it at the canoe which was paddling away. Thunder pealed and lightning flashed, but those in the canoe paddled on. When they landed eight rose to leave the canoe, but the thief sat still with his dogskin mat and the garment of the goblin under his feet. His companions called to him, but he did not answer. One of them went and shook him, and the thief fell back into the hold of the canoe, and blood was seen on his clothing and a hole in his back. He was carried to the settlement and a meeting of the people called to consult on the matter, at which his companions told the tale of the theft of the goblin's garment; and the people said, 'He was the cause of his own death, and it will not be right to avenge him. All the payment he will obtain for his death will be the goblin's garment which he has stolen, which shall be left to bind around his body where it is laid.' His body was taken and put into one of the ancient cave burial-places. Not any evil came from this death, and we again went to barter with the goblins of that ship, and the goblins came again and again on shore, nor was there one evil word spoken, or any act of transgression on our part for that death.

—Te Horeta Taniwha, in John White, *Ancient History of the Maori*, Vol. v, Wellington, 1889

1c   An encounter: a historian's view

He [Cook] and Banks were not the only curious observers. The people were tenacious of memory; more than eighty years later, when Cook's countrymen had come to New

Zealand as settlers, an ancient chief, Te Horeta, a man of blood in many wars, told them of the great happening of his childhood. The ship had come, it seemed a supernatural thing, and its men supernatural beings, for they pulled their boats with their backs to the shore where they were to land—had they eyes at the backs of their heads? They pointed a stick at a shag, there was thunder and lightning and the shag fell dead; the children were terrified and ran with the women into the trees. But these *tupua*, goblins or demons, were kind, and gave food: something hard like pumice-stone but sweet, something else that was fat, perhaps whale-blubber or flesh of man, though it was salt and nipped the throat—ships bread, or biscuit, salt beef or pork. There was one who collected shells, flowers, tree-blossoms and stones. They invited the boys to go on board the ship with the warriors, and little Te Horeta went, and saw the warriors exchange their cloaks for other goods, and saw the one who was clearly the lord, the leader of the tupua. He spoke seldom, but felt the cloaks and handled the weapons, and patted the children's cheeks and gently touched their heads. The boys did not walk about, they were afraid lest they should be bewitched, they sat still and looked; and the great lord gave Te Horeta a nail, and Te Horeta said *Ka pai*, which is 'very good', and people laughed. Te Horeta used this nail on his spear, and to make holes in the side boards of canoes; he had it for a god but one day his canoe capsized and he lost it, and though he dived for it he could not find it. And this lord, the leader, gave Te Horeta's people two handfuls of potatoes, which they planted and tended; they were the first people to have potatoes in this country. There are other traditions, brief lights: none as circumstantial as this.

—J.C. Beaglehole, *The Life of Captain James Cook*,
Hakluyt Society, London, 1974, p. 206

2a   Captain Cook and the Tannese: Cook's view

[August 1774]

Monday, 15th. In the PM I made an excursion in company with Mr Wales on the other side of the harbour, where we met from the Natives very different treatment [from what] we had done in the morning, these people, in whose neighbourhood lived our friend Paowang, being better acquainted with us than those we had seen in the morning, shewed a readiness to oblige us in every thing in their power: here was a little Stragling Village consisting of a few houses which need no other description than to compare them to the roof of a thatched house taken of the walls and placed on the ground, the figure was oblong and open at both ends, some indeed had a little fence or wall of reeds at each end about 3 feet high, some seem'd to be intended for more families than one as they had a fire place near each end, there [were] other mean and small hovels which I understood were only to Sleep in, in one of these which with some others stood in a Plantation but separated from them by a fence, I understood was a dead Corps, they made Signs that he slipt or was dead, circumstances sufficiently pointed out the latter. Curious however to see all I could I prevailed on an elderly man to go with me within the fence which surrounded it, one end of the hut was closed up the same as the sides the other end had been open but now shut up with Matts which he would not suffer me to remove, he also seem'd unwilling I should look into a Matted bag or basket which hung to the end of the hut, in which was a piece of roasted yam and some kind of leaves all quite fresh: thus I was led to believe that these people dispose of the dead some thing in the same manner as at Otahiete. The Man had about his neck fastened to a String two or three locks of human hair and a Woman present had several; I offered some thing in exchange for them but they gave me to understand this could not be done as they belonged to the person who laid in the hutt.

As I had nothing to do I went on shore with them and found a good number of the Natives collected about the landing place as usual, to whom I distributed all the presents I had about me and then went on board for more. In less than an hour returned, just as our people were getting some large logs into the board; At the same time four or five of the Natives steped forward to see what we were about, and as we did not allow them to come within certain limmits unless it was to pass along the beach, the sentery ordered them back, which they readily complied with. At this time I had my eyes fixed on them and observed the sentery present his piece (as I thought at the men) and was just going to reprove for it, because I had observed that when ever this was done, some or another of the Natives would hold up their arms, to let us see they were as ready as us, but I was astonished beyond measure when the sentry fired for I saw not the least cause. At this outrage, most of the people fled, it was only a few I could prevail upon to remain; as they ran off I observed one man to fall and was immidiately taken up by two others who led him into the water, washed his wound and then led him off. Presently after some came and described to us the nature of his wound, which I now sent for the surgeon to dress, as I found the man was not carried far. As soon as the Surgeon came I went with him to the man, which we found expiring; the ball had struck his left arm, which was much shattered, and then entered his body by the short ribs, one of which was broke. The rascal who perpetrated this crime, pretended that a Man had laid an arrow a Cross his bow and was going to shoot it at him, so that he apprehended himself in danger, but this was no more than what they had always done, and I believe with no other view than to shew they were armed as well as us, at least I have reason to think so, as they never went further. What made this affair the more unfortunate, it not appearing to be the man who bent the bow, that was shott, but another who stood by him. This unhappy affair threw the Natives into the utmost consternation the few that were prevailed on to stay ran to the plantations and brought Cocoa nutts &c and laid [them] down at our feet, so soon were these daring people humbled.

—James Cook, *Journals*, 1774

(Cook's original spelling has been retained in this document.)

2b   Captain Cook and the Tannese: a Tannese view

They (the Tannese) were terrified for him (Cook), especially when he fired upon them, and supposed that he was more than human. Seven, they say, were wounded, two of whom died and five recovered ... They say that he went up to a marum and saw a chief very ill and surrounded by people wailing over him, and on being told that certain persons were burning his rubbish and causing all the sickness he sought them out and fired upon them! ... They point to one or two places and say 'there Kuke stood and talked'. They also point to a mountain where he cut an ironwood tree. They also say that he left them two Kangaroos and show us where they lived for some time. Bye and bye they became annoyed by the howling of the animals—and then they killed them and eat them.

—George Turner (1842–43), *Journal*, New Hebrides,
London Missionary Society, South Seas Journals, No. 143, p. 13

2c   Captain Cook and the Tannese: a historian's view

The transformation of Tahitian dogs into kangaroos proves something of an anecdotal aside on the process of culture contact (though it also carries a serious lesson on how oral tradition is not chrono-logic). The more profound element in the myth is the presumption that Cook sought out and killed the *nahak* sorcerers responsible for the chief's illness. It sums up, with an economy of words that comes from the absence of scepticism, the gap between what contact signified to the Tannese and what it signified to the Europeans … From his knowledge of funeral rites in Tahiti and New Zealand, Cook concluded that the person in the hut was dead; going by the oral tradition he was, rather, 'very ill'. It would have been clear to the Tannese that Cook took an interest in the matter; and when, four days later, one of his men fired upon and killed a warrior—quite possibly from the west side of the bay—it would have seemed that Cook, an ancestor, had sought out and punished the offending sorcerer. Perhaps it was the purpose of his visit for, the next day, after conferring with Paowang, Cook departed whence he came.

—Ron Adams, *In the Land of Strangers*, Australian National University Press,
Canberra, 1984, pp. 31–2

2d   Captain Cook and the Tannese: a historian's view

Adams argues that the Tannese saw Cook and his party as returned ancestors or gods (1984: 25–9). While it is impossible to recover the Tannese interpretations with certainty, what the contemporary texts indicate is the diversity of Tannese reactions, which strongly suggests that a number of interpretations were current, none of which were final. This is apparent in incidents such as the attempts by some to cheat in exchanges and make off with equipment from the ship, the attempted seduction of sailors and the sheepishness of the Tannese on discovering that the sailors were men, not women, and in the varied and changing responses of defiance and friendliness, cowardice and hostility.

—Ron Brunton, *The Abandoned Narcotic: Kava and cultural instability
in Melanesia*, Cambridge University Press, Cambridge, 1989, p. 148

QUESTIONS AND ACTIVITIES

1   According to the Journal entry (Document 1a), what significance did Cook attach to the shooting of the Maori warrior at Mercury Bay?

2   According to Te Horeta Taniwha's account (Document 1b), what significance did the Maori participants attach to the shooting?

3   Using Dening's observation on cross-cultural history (page 35), what 'structures of law [and] morality' and what ideas on property, fair exchange and authority influenced Lt Gore in shooting a Tanna man?

4   Reread the section on the Spanish attempt to settle on Espiritu Santo (pages 33–4), and list the structures of law and morality that the Spanish seem to have operated with. What myths, symbols and rituals did they use to rationalise their attempts to impose these structures?

5   In terms of Cook's movements, as recorded in his Journal (Documents 2a, 2b), what led the Tannese to believe that Cook was exacting revenge on the sorcerer presumed to be making their chief ill? ['Burning rubbish' refers to the sorcerer's ritual for making his enemies ill.]

6   What does Adams say about the Tannese belief that Cook's actions were an act of revenge?

7   Could it be argued that both Brunton and Adams are correct in their interpretations?

8   On page 37 it is suggested that only relevant information is retained in oral accounts. The reason for the reference to the gift of the dogs in the Tannese version of Cook's visit is that it proves that Cook initiated a special relationship with the people of Port Resolution. Can you suggest what might have been the relevance of the reference to the cutting of the ironwood tree?

9   Using examples from the documents, write an account of the double-sided nature of culture contact in the Pacific.

REFERENCES

Adams, Ron, *In the Land of Strangers: A century of European contact with Tanna, 1774–1874*, Pacific Research Monograph Series, No. 9, ANU Press, Canberra, 1984

Beaglehole, J.C. (ed.), *The Journals of Captain James Cook on his Voyages of Discovery*, 3 Vols, Cambridge University Press for the Hakluyt Society, 1955, 1961, 1967

Dening, Greg, 'Review of Hugh Laracy's *Marists and Melanesians*', *New Zealand Journal of History*, 12 (1978)

Markham, Clements (ed.), *The Voyages of Pedro Fernandez de Quiros, 1595 to 1606*, 2 Vols, London, 1904

Ong, Walter J., *Orality and Literacy: The technologizing of word*, Methuen, London and New York, 1987

Spate, O.H.K., *The Spanish Lake (The Pacific Since Magellan*, Vol. 1), ANU Press, Canberra, 1979

Chapter 4
Being Discovered:
Perceptions and Control of Strangers

Max Quanchi, Queensland University of Technology

For Pacific Islanders the 'discovery' period was characterised by the first, unexpected arrival of strangers, a subsequent phase in which visits were common though still irregular and brief, and a third phase in which European vessels began to stay longer and some marooned or ship-jumping men lived briefly with island communities. This 'discovery' and first-contact period stretched over a hundred years, though on some islands it was compressed into a few decades. For centuries islanders had confronted, killed, turned away, welcomed or absorbed strangers and invaders from other islands, but the *papalangi* (white men) were different. Attitudes towards the Europeans involved more than responding to their physical presence. It included responding to the technology left behind when they departed. It included responding to different ideas on life, death, manners, behaviour, property, leadership and male–female relationships.

These first perceptions and responses did not occur just in a defined 'discovery' or initial exploration period. They were attitudes formed during the overlapping presence of traders, whalers, missionaries, scientists and settlers. They were attitudes developed during meetings with a range of quite different Europeans and usually in quite different sequences of contact.

What attitude did islanders adopt towards European presence, technology and ideas and what was their attitude towards the knowledge Europeans possessed about things which had previously been outside or beyond their known worlds and experiences?

The discovery period

Islanders had to deal with strangers long before Europeans ventured into the Pacific. Islanders had knowledge of their region and knew sailing directions to hundreds of near and distant islands, but successive waves of migration, or storms, had delivered strangers or new settlers to places as far as apart as Hawaii and New Zealand. This settling and migration phase was over by the time Europeans started to arrive. Conquering fleets of warrior-laden canoes also came regularly from over the horizon, though inter-island imperialism had also waned by the time of increasing European exploration and presence. Strangers continued to appear in canoes unexpectedly after being blown thousands of kilometres off their original course. Throughout the 'discovery' period, Micronesians from Kiribati and the Caroline Islands, for example, were often found in Melanesia or the Philippines. Annual trading exchanges, often with people thought of as strangers, also linked many widely dispersed parts of the Pacific. Yapese, for example, may have voyaged as far south as New Guinea to stockpile produce to trade later when they sought stone from the quarries on Palua in western Micronesia. But all these meetings with strangers, whether friendly, accidental or conquering in nature, were with men and women similar to themselves. The white man and woman were different.

In 1602, one of the first Spaniards to describe the Chamorro people of the Mariana Islands, noted that they were hard working, compassionate, gentle with children, practised feasting, speech making and joke telling, were boastful and enjoyed games and trials of strength. A century later, in 1722, another Spaniard, Juan Antonio Cantova, was the first to describe the nearby people of the Caroline Islands to the south of the Marianas. Cantova wrote that these people also tested their strength and skill in spear and rock throwing contests, performed dances and feasts, bathed three times a day, and while men fished, farmed and built canoes, women cooked, planted crops and made sails from palm leaf mats, and young men were taught astronomy and navigation. These domestic, recreational and ritual activities continued for another hundred years as the Spanish made occasional voyages and brief visits. Elsewhere in the Pacific, although French, British, Dutch, German, Russian and American ships began arriving regularly, the daily round of domestic activities also altered very little in the early contact period.

Visits by Europeans in the 'discovery' period often occurred decades apart. Penrhyn Atoll (Tongareva) was first visited in 1788 by the British trading vessel *Lady Penrhyn* but not again until a Russian scientific expedition led by von Kotzebue visited in 1816. A child born at the time of one European visit might grow up knowing of *papalangi* but might not experience their presence until well into adolescent or early adult years. That is, during a week-long visit in the early contact period, the 'strangers' could create enormous turmoil, consternation and a prolonged state of excitement. People's daily routines, rules and established customs of behaviour were probably turned upside-down. This turmoil passed when the strangers departed, not to return for months, years or often decades. Although each of the early meetings was usually quite short, by the time of subsequent visits, hours of discussion, re-enactments and story telling had shaped a more permanent and prescribed set of attitudes towards *papalangi*.

In the era of European 'discovery' of the Pacific, several changes of attitude were noticeable among islanders and Europeans in the initial contact phase. These changes of attitudes were gradual, from initial awe and wonderment through manipulation or reserved stand-offish positions and eventually to disregard and contempt.

The attitude of the European officers and crews in the discovery period was less susceptible to change, despite their 'new' experiences bartering on the decks of ships, trading on palm-fringed beaches, taking guided tours of temples and gardens or meeting 'others' in the privacy of cabins and shady nooks. Most European officers, crew, artists and scientific observers retained the values and opinions of their shipboard life or of their European intellectual, agricultural and industrial background. Most early European visitors 'discovered' in the Pacific what they had already thought was there. Their attitude towards Pacific Islanders was based on a vision of romantic, idyllic freedom later to become cemented in the form of two theories, of the good or noble savage and of fatal impact.

Modern historians suggest that these early European visitors had adopted an exploitive, dominant and culturally superior relationship with the island people they met, an attitude perhaps set before they arrived in the Pacific. This suggests that Europeans tended to maintain a set of preconceived attitudes throughout the period of initial contact. In contrast, Islanders went through several stages of differing responses and attitudes to the presence of 'others'.

Attitudes—forming and changing

Changes in attitude towards the 'other'—European towards islander and islander towards European—took place at different times in different parts of the Pacific. The Spanish–

Chamorro relationship in the Marianas lasted for two hundred years, but the Spanish had virtually destroyed the Chamorro culture and people within a century of establishing their rule in 1670. There were fewer than two thousand of the estimated 100 000 Chamorro remaining by 1790. At the other extreme, trembling and shaking at meeting the 'ghosts' of their ancestors as they first thought, it was not until well into the twentieth century that most highland tribes of Papua New Guinea saw Europeans. Nor was the initial reaction to the arrival of strangers uniform. On Niue, Islanders were unwilling to even show themselves in 1774 to James Cook on the *Endeavour*, the first white man to land on their island. In contrast, Sonsorol Islanders in 1710 had demonstrated immediate friendship and a willingness to trade with Francisco Padilla on the *Santissima Trinidad*. The Sonsorolese kissed and embraced the Spaniards and later on shore put on a huge feast, performed songs and dances and presented the visitors with mats as gifts.

In Fiji in the 1830s an early European beachcomber, William Diaper, noted that young girls 'would scream as though they were going into fits' if they were brought near to him, but on other islands females willingly traded sexual favours for the manufactured products offered by sailors, beachcombers and traders. In contrast to the Niueans who remained in hiding during Cook's visit, only showing themselves later to hurl spears and stones, in the Gilbert Islands, an ambitious chief had his warriors kill all European traders and beachcombers in his domain. He immediately gained a monopoly of trade and control over his people's access to the desired European goods the visiting ships and traders had introduced.

The more common attitude across the Pacific, rather than aggression, was that chiefs and leaders were quick to acknowledge that long-term access and control of trade was best achieved not by warlike and violent acquisition but by negotiation and compromise with the new strangers.

Secretive observation with a later dash of bravado by Niueans, bloody encounters between Chamorro and Spaniards in the Marianas, a friendly welcome on Sonsorol and a shaking, trembling fear by New Guinea Highlanders only partly hint at the range of initial reactions. In the initial response to 'others' some common reactions can be identified. Despite the differences of place and time, one common attitude was that the strangers were regarded as gods or spirits. Their bodies, as well as the clothing, food and material possessions they carried with them, were regarded as mysterious, politically or spiritually powerful and probably supernatural.

Attitudes changed quickly as misunderstandings were cleared away. Europeans did not eat fire, but smoked tobacco; they were not eating men but watermelons and biscuits; they were not immortal but bled and groaned when hit; they were not spirits but normal men who soon demonstrated quite familiar habits of toilet and sexual liaison. European attitudes were affected in similar ways. What Europeans first judged on the basis of a fleeting glimpse, as free love, benevolent leadership, harmony and natural abundances was seen by some, when contact became more regular, as cruel, rigid, hard rules and a society poorly balanced between limited resources and deprivation.

How could island people control the 'other'? What tactics could they use to exclude, integrate or manipulate when strangers next appeared in their midst? In the second contact phase, characterised by greater numbers of Europeans and their permanent settlement, how much did Islanders' attitudes change?

Tagging the 'other'

A problem in answering the question of how one group controlled the other in the contact relationship, is that the records of the moment when islanders first confronted

European strangers and of the subsequent period in which the two began to establish regular contact, are nearly all written by European scientists, traders, missionaries or naval captains. Some accounts of early contact were even further removed from the actual event, being 'ghost' written by romantic dreamers and philosophers in Europe relying on a scrappy notebook brought back from the Pacific by a former trader, beachcomber or castaway. In 1789 George Keate, for example, wrote *An Account of the Pelew Islands* based on the journals of a Captain Wilson who had been marooned on Palau (Pelew or Beleu). One modern historian has described this work as a 300-page 'illusion'. Yet for more than a hundred years it was considered a reliable and reasonably accurate account of the relationship which existed between Europeans and Palauans. James Cook and Joseph Bank's descriptions of the Pacific were similarly altered by John Hawkesworth when he edited and published Cook's journal of his first voyage. These three volumes, although now containing Hawkesworth's ideas on the Pacific as well as Cook's, were immediately popular and were republished many times in several languages. To ensure that an accurate account of his next expedition to the Pacific reached the public, Cook published his own journals of the second voyage.

The written European versions of 'contact' reflected European opinions and values. When Francis Drake visited one island in 1578 he called the people thieves because they pretended to trade while stealing all they could lay their hands on. The name 'Islands of Thieves' or *Ile de Ladronnes* remained in use as a stereotype for quite some time. James Cook, leaving under sail after a failed attempt to meet the 'natives' of a then uncharted island (Niue), noted that it should be known henceforth as 'Savage Island' due to the brief rock and spear throwing exchange he had with the islanders. This name stereotyped Niueans in the same way that Fiji for a long time was known as the 'Cannibal Isles'. In contrast, Cook named Tonga the 'Friendly Islands' and the Frenchman Louis de Bougainville tagged Tahiti *Nouvelle Cythera* in recognition of the new paradise he had discovered. Francisco Padilla's journal, by the Spaniard who first visited Sonsorol Island, compared the friendly reception of Sonsorolese to the unfriendly welcome he got from Palauan Islanders just to the south. These tags tended to be passed around the wharves and harbourside taverns of ports on world trade routes and were officially recorded in ships' logs and appeared later in books published by returned captains and explorers.

Islanders also used tags. In Polynesia variations of the word *Papalangi*, which apparently meant men who burst down from the sky, were common. The meanings of *Pakeha* in New Zealand and *Haole* in Hawaii are obscure but are probably related to the view that the strangers were gods. In Kiribati the phrase for Europeans, *I matang*, meant men from the west, the mythical ancestral home of the first Kiribati people. In the first phase of contact, these tags were not demeaning, though as islanders quickly came to regard the exploitation, treachery, drunkenness and licentious behaviour of Europeans in less favourable light, these phrases took on a derogatory tone.

Gaining an advantage

Both the strangers passing through and the owners of the land, water, animals, fruits and timber had something to gain from an exchange. After the first hostility, fear or amazement had passed, it was to both sides' advantage to engage in a friendly barter, trade or exchange of products. Europeans wanted details of exploitable resources and sailing instructions to nearby islands, to restock water and fresh food, to repair rigging and scrape ships' hulls in a safe anchorage, opportunities for officers and crew to take shore leave, to observe exotic scenes and displays of culture, to collect curios and artefacts and to enjoy the company of women. The islanders wanted the strangers' exotic technology, some of it because of its immediately apparent superior uses, but mostly because it was symbolic of new and powerful forces. So the sailors collected shell scrapers and stone axes (of no use to them) and islanders collected clocks, buttons and leather-bound books of no use to them. But there were advantages to be gained. The European strangers gained a safe haven and greater knowledge of the 'new world' while islanders gained iron tools and items of great prestige to be used in traditional trading, marriage and military or spiritual exchanges. The islanders gained what often seemed insignificant to the European but which was of great value in a local island or atoll context. The European also gained what often seemed insignificant to the islander, for islanders did not immediately understand the value Europeans placed on certain minerals, timbers, fish from the lagoon, carvings, tools and shells.

In this exchange of material possessions the islanders held the upper hand, for without appropriate 'trade' they could refuse to supply the strangers with essential pigs, chickens, water, fruit and vegetables. In a later period of regular shipping and trade for island produce such as sandalwood or bêche-de-mer, the need to offer products the islanders wanted became even more crucial. The desirability of goods on offer determined the success or otherwise of a speculative trading voyage out of Sydney, Hobart or Valpariso. Faced with an islander's reluctance to barter because of poor quality axes, tobacco or cloth, a ship's captain had no choice but to sail on in search of more hospitable and less astute entrepreneurs.

Aggressive, violent attitudes

There were many violent incidents in the initial contact period. Europeans and islanders were equally brutal and gratuitous in their excessive use of force against 'others' who refused to trade, who borrowed (stole) what they could or who offered insults and showed little respect for established manners and customs. Islanders displayed brutal and aggressive attitudes when they felt their laws had been infringed, their status insulted, their possessions taken without recompense or that, like all strangers before, the *papalangi* must also be met with force. In similar situations, Europeans were equally brutal.

The failure of both sides to understand the language, values and moral viewpoint of 'others' was probably a cause for much of this conflict. For example, in the Marquesas Islands understanding the meaning of the word *tapu* (taboo) was a key mechanism in the fear and violence which governed relationships between *Te enata* (Marquesans) and *Te Aoe* (outsiders) and between *Te enata* themselves. For example, between 21 July and 5 August 1595, the first Europeans to visit the Marquesas, killed 'easily and massively', leaving two hundred *Te enata* dead. The officers, sailors and marines of the Mendana expedition killed to control 'others', because not knowing the language or knowing the place of *tapu* in *Te enata* culture, they could not understand the personal, political and spiritual relationships in which they had become entangled.

The breaking of *tapu* (rules regarding access, contact usage, ownership, status and behaviour) was the cause for much European–Islander violence in the Marquesas. The breaking of *tapu* has also been suggested as an explanation for other incidents, such as Cook's death in Hawaii in 1789, missionary John Williams' death on Eromonga in 1839 and missionary James Chalmers' death in the Gulf of Papua in 1901. It is also true that common theft, personal insult, brutish aggression and uncontrolled thuggery also caused many tragic incidents. Misunderstanding the behaviour of 'others' led to violence in the contact period, but generally this violence was not premeditated.

Violence occurred (unexpectedly to both European and islander victims) because striking out was a defensive response to a situation which went outside normal rules of behaviour.

In the discovery and the first contact period, most encounters were amicable. For example, of five hundred recorded visits by whalers—the first regular European contact in the Gilbert Islands—only ten or so violent incidents occurred. In writing a history of Kiribati and Tuvalu, Barrie Macdonald concluded from this evidence that 'there were in reality very few cases of theft, deception or violence, partly because basic conventions of behaviour for both parties were well established in the early years of the trade'. The first phase of contact was therefore of considerable importance because it was during this discovery phase that these 'basic conventions of behaviour' were established.

These basic conventions were derived from the values and morality of each culture. In practice, they were balanced against what islanders and Europeans were willing to tolerate in order to gain a specific advantage in trade, knowledge or material possessions. Once established, the ground rules for negotiations, gift exchanges, bartering, access and sexual liaisons were broken at the cost of losing the advantage each side sought.

Control mechanisms

A number of strategies or control mechanisms were employed to maintain these basic conventions. The declaration of the beach as a safe, neutral or 'de-militarised zone' where sides could meet, was one of these conventions. Captains fearful of losing their ship were reluctant to allow swarms of 'savages' to run free over their vessel, just as chiefs, leaders and spiritual leaders were loath to let powerful strangers enter the places on shore that they considered sacred or meaningful. Each tried to control the other by choosing the place where exchanges could take place.

Misunderstanding of the values of 'others' was significant in the formation of initial attitudes. Tongans, for example, thought that what Europeans called bravery was instead recklessness. As Tongans believed that to fight then run away to fight another day was appropriate behaviour, to die in the European manner in what Tongans thought was a vain quest for glory was simply foolish. Polynesians were amazed, for example, at the whipping punishments dealt out to sailors for petty crimes. Europeans were similarly amazed at islanders' use of the death penalty for what the Europeans saw as trifling misdemeanours.

For the Europeans there was one law, supposedly inviolate and applicable to all. For islanders laws were perhaps more expedient. Punishments were determined more by an individual's status, kinship and the complexities of political, military and spiritual obligations and relationships. Polynesians might consider, for example, that a sailor breaking a *tapu* by walking through a temple, was excusable because sailors were poorly educated men of rough manners and customs. Had an officer acted in this way it might have been interpreted as a deliberate act of intervention or calculated disrespect and a reaction would have been immediate and probably violent. European law allowed far less for such circumstantial factors. It must be noted that for many Europeans entering the Pacific, both officers and crew, violence was widespread in the social relationships from which they came. Indiscriminate, inhumane behaviour, destroying property and killing men, women and children wantonly and without regret was a reflection of the society they came from as much as of the circumstances they found in the islands.

The ability to supply or boycott ships, to withdraw inland or alternatively to stockpile produce on the beach in anticipation, was a major control mechanism. Islanders withheld supply to gain an advantage, but also to demand better quality, certain brand names, or increasingly more exotic paraphernalia. Any steel axe was acceptable the first time, but once trade and bartering became regular, a failure to offer superior quality axes would quickly terminate a ship, beach or trade store negotiation over the supply of a cargo of sandalwood. Hawaiian chiefs often placed value on European products not because they could use them, but just because they had them as symbols of their chiefly status. To trade with Hawaiian chiefs, a supply of different and new items had to be continually shipped in because once having, for example, material of one colour, only another colour was then desirable as a symbol of their chiefly status.

Withholding the supply of their own island produce and withholding labour, hospitality, information or access was a means of gaining an advantage. There is no doubt that withholding or alternatively making sexual liaisons freely available was a common bargaining tactic. Withholding labour was an equally powerful tactic since the visiting strangers had to rely on islanders to cut and carry timber, harvest and carry crops and collect coconuts.

The forming of temporary alliances between Europeans and villages, clans or tribes in their wars against long-time opponents was also a mechanism for establishing control and advantage. Europeans could offer marines, muskets and cannon in favour of one side in a local war, but ships' captains could equally withhold this symbolic and threatening military power if a bargain was not struck to their satisfaction. Ambitious Pacific Island leaders were quick to appreciate the value of a temporary military alliance with a well armed visiting ship. Knowing this could give them victory in a struggle not otherwise within their grasp, they made sure that their harbour was where ships anchored, that their village was the first in a trading exchange or that they developed a personal friendship with regular visiting captains.

Attitudes towards, and the manner of association with, the 'other' were based on advantages and opportunities. For their part, islanders could attract beachcombers or marooned sailors to stay in their village, offer crews and pilots to under-staffed vessels or bestow symbolic, traditional titles and names to long-standing friendly captains. Through these associations an advantage could be gained and an opening made for further strategies to be employed. Historian Ian Campbell's study of the early contact period led him to conclude that 'Polynesian history shows unremitting calculation and determination to seize whatever advantages circumstances offered'. In Micronesia, and to a lesser extent in Melanesia, allowing for significant differences in time and duration, this conclusion is applicable to a great many meetings in the discovery and first contact period.

Figure 4.1: Inhabitants of Penrhyn (Tongareva) greet von Kotzebue in 1816.
[British Library, London]

Figure 4.2: '*Resolution* and *Adventure* at Moorea 1772' by James Cleverly.
[Mitchell Library, Sydney]

Figure 4.3: 'A View of Moorea'.
[National Maritime Museum]

Figure 4.4: Captain Cook's death in Hawaii, 1779.
[Mitchell Library, Sydney]

Figure 4.5: The Reverend and Mrs Creed landing at Taranaki, New Zealand.
[National Library of Australia]

Figure 4.6: Captain Cook landing at Mallicolo (Malekula, New Hebrides).
[Mansell Collection]

Figure 4.7: Marquesan women entertaining the French crew of *Zelee*, c. 1837–40.
[British Library, London]

Figure 4.8: Easter Islanders entertain the French crew of *La Venus*, 1838.
[Pitt Rivers Museum]

QUESTIONS AND ACTIVITIES

1. Compare Figure 4.1 (Penrhyn) and Figure 4.2 (Moorea). How is a peaceful contact suggested in the Penrhyn scene? How is a peaceful contact suggested in the Moorea scene?

2. The scene at Moorea (Figure 4.2, a pencil sketch by James Cleverly) was later copied by his brother, John Cleverly (Figure 4.3), but it contains several differences. List these differences and explain why you think the changes were made.

3. Compare the artist's portrayal of Cook's death (Figure 4.4) with Mr and Mrs Creed's arrival at Taranaki (Figure 4.5). In what way are these two scenes similar?

4. In the sketch of Cook's landing at Malekula (Figure 4.6), how has the artist suggested that friendly relations were being established?

5. Compare Figures 4.4, 4.5 and 4.6. Is there a standard format for this type of scene? How are the islanders' reactions to the arrival of the 'strangers' portrayed in these scenes?

6. Describe one of the dancing scenes (Figure 4.7 or 4.8). Read your paragraph to your classmates and ask if they can identify which scene you have described.

7. Why are these dance scenes portrayed on board ship rather than ashore in a village, building or temple?

8. On the basis of all the figures in this chapter, arrange a panel to debate or discuss the assertion that 'Artists on voyages of discovery portrayed for audiences back home an impression of exotic, friendly, noble island peoples'.

REFERENCES

Campbell, I., 'Polynesian Perceptions of Europeans in the Eighteenth and Nineteenth Centuries', in *Pacific Studies,* Vol. 5/2, 1982, pp. 64–80

Campbell, I., *A History of the Pacific Islands*, Queensland University Press, Brisbane, 1990

Dening, G., *Island and Beaches*, University of Honolulu Press, 1980

Hardy, J., and Frost, A. (eds), *Studies from Terra Australia to Australia*, Australian Academy of the Humanities, Canberra, 1989

Hardy, J., and Frost, A. (eds), *European Voyaging towards Australia*, Australian Academy of the Humanities, Canberra, 1990

Hezel, F., *The First Taint of Civilization*, University of Honolulu Press, 1983

Macdonald, B., *Cinderellas of Empire: Towards a history of Kiribati and Tuvalu*, Australia National University Press, Canberra, 1982

Munro, D., Iosefa, S., and Besnier, N., *Te tala o Niuoku: The German plantation on Nukulaelae Atoll 1865–1890*, University of the South Pacific Press, Suva, 1990

Scarr, D., *The History of the Pacific Islands*, Macmillan, Sydney, 1990

Spate, O.H.K., *Paradise Lost and Found: Vol. 3, The Pacific since Magellan*, Pergamon Press, Sydney, 1988

PART THREE
ISLANDERS AND EUROPEANS IN THE NINETEENTH CENTURY

INTRODUCTION

During the nineteenth century, islanders and Europeans met on the beach, exchanged valuable products, offered their labour in each other's service and adopted each other's dress, food, clothing, customs and beliefs. Some travelled widely through strange new lands and waters and created new communities and settlements. Why did they cross frontiers into the territory of 'others'? What did they gain from these interactions?

Chapters 5–8 address these questions by introducing a range of evidence. The evidence will suggest answers to specific questions: What was the difference between 'refreshment' trade and the mining of forests in the sandalwood trade? What did missionaries hope to achieve by creating model Christian societies among Polynesians? Why did Kororareka boom and bust? What did three moons in Mackay mean to Malaitans? What did the Hawaiian Boki hope to gain by heading off into Melanesia? What did island men and women do with the spare time available because of the use of new western technology?

The answers to these specific questions will in turn suggest some more general explanations of the meaning of religious ideas, economic transactions and labour roles as islanders and Europeans entered each other's territory. In frightening, unexpected and radically different settings, these ideas, transactions and roles can be traced through the actions of individuals—planters, missionaries, traders, beachcombers, whalers— or by tracing their impact on islanders' social, economic, political and cultural organisation. In what ways had islanders reacted to these ideas, transactions and roles by the end of the nineteenth century? How have European portrayals of these interactions and these frontiers changed over time?

Chapter 5
Trade Interactions

Marion Diamond, University of Queensland

Traditional Pacific islander societies were based on subsistence agriculture and fishing in which trading was usually limited to customary visits between neighbouring island groups. During such visits the islanders exchanged local products for reasons of ritual and friendship rather than for economic necessity. When European ships began to visit, from the end of the eighteenth century, the islands were gradually absorbed into wider cash economy trading contracts with the outside world.

The first trade between Europeans and Pacific islanders began in the eighteenth century; during the next 150 years, trade developed from an occasional, almost casual arrangement which had only a minimal impact on the islanders, into a more regular pattern of mutual dependence. For many islanders, the shift was from self-sufficiency to dependence on outside commodities which changed their lifestyle irrevocably. For Europeans, the shift was from barter-gatherer style trading opportunities, to a sustained trading pattern made possible by the exploitation of renewable resources in the islands.

For Europeans and islanders alike, the pattern of trade gradually changed over time. The early European traders were rather like traditional hunter-gatherers, relying on the exploitation of natural resources. They hunted for whales, and gathered exotic island products such as sandalwood and bêche-de-mer, establishing an erratic and uncertain trade with the islands. This emphasis on crude exploitation of products, often to the point of extinction, gradually changed with the development of a more stable and sustained trade based on renewable resources, such as plantation-grown cotton and coconuts.

For the islanders, the pattern of trade also changed over time. It began with a casual demand for commodities such as nails and beads, highly desirable, and easily incorporated into the traditional economic framework, but gradually changed to a more sustained demand for consumption products, such as woven cloth and guns, which were eventually to change the islanders' whole economic and social system.

Casual shipping contacts

Europeans first moved into the Pacific in the second half of the eighteenth century, when both France and England sent out explorers such as Bougainville and Cook, who visited island groups in the course of the voyages. The first form of trade between Europeans and islanders was the supply of these sailing ships with what was known as 'refreshment', that is, with water and fresh foodstuffs, and sometimes involving a trade in sex. This early trade was based on barter, and European ships commonly carried trade goods such as nails and other metal cutting tools, woven cloth, and nicknacks such as mirrors and beads which captains quickly learned were attractive to the islanders.

The trade was limited, sporadic and unpredictable. Ships arrived randomly, and the demands of the shipload of sailors could impose great pressures on the people of an island, whose resources were not great, who could not predict when the next ship would arrive, and who had no way of storing a surplus of foodstuffs in anticipation of such visits. Traditional societies based on hospitality and reciprocal exchange were placed

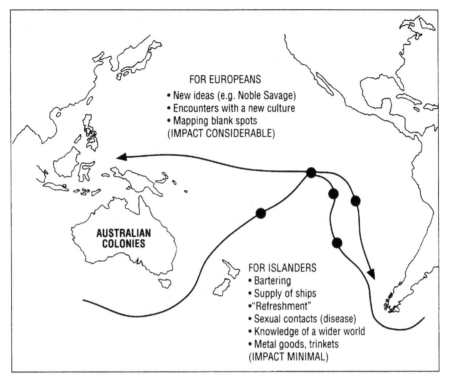

Figure 5.1: Exploration.

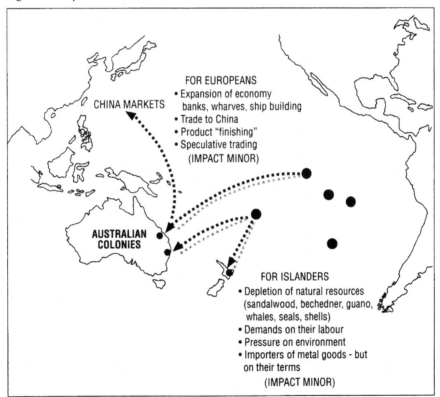

Figure 5.2: Hunting and gathering.

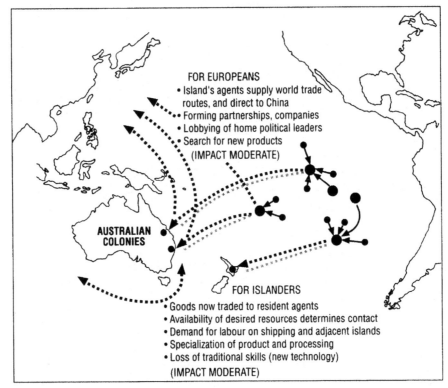

FOR EUROPEANS
- Island's agents supply world trade routes, and direct to China
- Forming partnerships, companies
- Lobbying of home political leaders
- Search for new products
  (IMPACT MODERATE)

AUSTRALIAN COLONIES

FOR ISLANDERS
- Goods now traded to resident agents
- Availability of desired resources determines contact
- Demand for labour on shipping and adjacent islands
- Specialization of product and processing
- Loss of traditional skills (new technology)
  (IMPACT MODERATE)

Figure 5.3: Warehousing and beach communities.

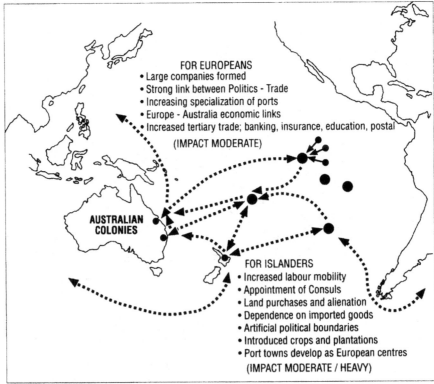

FOR EUROPEANS
- Large companies formed
- Strong link between Politics - Trade
- Increasing specialization of ports
- Europe - Australia economic links
- Increased tertiary trade; banking, insurance, education, postal
  (IMPACT MODERATE)

AUSTRALIAN COLONIES

FOR ISLANDERS
- Increased labour mobility
- Appointment of Consuls
- Land purchases and alienation
- Dependence on imported goods
- Artificial political boundaries
- Introduced crops and plantations
- Port towns develop as European centres
  (IMPACT MODERATE / HEAVY)

Figure 5.4: Plantations and partition.

under great strain. An all-male crew added extra pressures because of their sexual demands on the local population. The lack of women on the ships made it very difficult for the islanders to visualise what European societies could be like if, as far as they could tell, these societies had no women of their own!

As long as ships arrived to trade only sporadically, the European trade goods probably only had a marginal impact on the indigenous culture. The new metal tools improved the productivity of agriculture and building. They also made warfare more dangerous, because a metal axe could cut down a man as well as a tree. Since European ships were not very happy places, some sailors chose to escape, becoming amongst the first white people to settle in the Pacific. Single men were relatively easy to incorporate into an island's society, where they sometimes became important figures. Beachcombers or castaways could be valuable advisers for the islanders, helping them to deal with European technology, such as the guns that were sometimes traded in return for ships' supplies.

The explorers were followed by whalers from England, France, Russia, America and Australia, who moved into the Pacific about the beginning of the nineteenth century. Whalers also stopped at the islands in search of refreshments, bartering coconuts, fish, vegetables and firewood from the local inhabitants. As well as buying indigenous food, the visitors introduced new crops, such as watermelons and pumpkins, and new animals, such as pigs and poultry, which were to have an enormous effect on the island economy and ecology.

The whalers had often sailed very long distances from their European or American ports and, by the time they arrived in the Pacific, they were often short-handed. It therefore became a common practice for young men from the islands to work aboard the whalers during the killing season. They were paid a share of the catch—though usually not as large a share as the white sailors—and so became accustomed to selling their labour in return for European goods. Working on board ship also offered much more opportunity to learn about new languages and cultures. Language was particularly important as a means of drawing islanders into the wider world, and also a means by which they could negotiate on more equal terms with that world.

Beach communities

The first European settlements in the Pacific began when trading patterns began to stabilise, with ships visiting particular island ports on a regular basis. A mixed community of Europeans and islanders began to congregate along the beach at these ports, to serve the shipping and whaling trade. These early beach communities included sailors, escaped convicts, missionaries and traders' agents, together with their local wives and mixed race children. Such beach communities developed, for instance, at Honolulu in Hawaii, Apia in Samoa and Levuka in Fiji, Papeete in Tahiti and Kororareka (Bay of Islands) in New Zealand.

As trade became more regular, islanders near these port towns or on regular well used trade routes acquired a taste for the items that the traders brought. As their demand for trade goods grew they began to initiate economic activity, rather than just responding to casual contacts with the outside world. For this reason, they were actively involved in the creation of beach communities, which were sometimes controlled by a local headman or chief. Such a chief could acquire wealth and authority through his ability to negotiate with the traders, to control the sale of local commodities, or to organise local labour, for instance in preparing cargoes of sandalwood for export.

Sandalwood trade

The early traders concentrated on the exploitation of naturally occurring resources, such as sandalwood, whaling and tortoiseshell. They were interested in quick profits rather than a steady, sustainable trade, and so they harvested these products to the point of exhaustion. The sandalwood trade is a case in point. The trade began as an offshoot of the China tea trade. In Australia there was a strong demand for tea, which everybody then drank, and which formed part of the rations of convicts and free labourers. But Australia had few products to sell to China in return. Fortunately, the traders discovered that the Chinese liked sandalwood, a sweet-scented wood which grew in outcrops throughout the Pacific, and which was burnt in religious ceremonies in China.

American traders found sandalwood in Hawaii at the end of the eighteenth century, and the Australian ex-convict, Simeon Lord, discovered more groves in Fiji in 1804. Soon a number of Sydney traders were involved in the trade. The usual pattern was to find a suitable grove, recruit local labour to cut it down and load the ship with the wood, then sail to China with the cargo. The profits could be very high, up to 100 per cent, but it was an erratic trade. The first ship to arrive in Canton might sell its cargo for a very good price, but if a number of ships arrived in port close together, the limited demand for sandalwood was quickly satisfied, a glut developed, and the price collapsed. In a desperate bid to cover their costs, the sandalwood traders of the 1810s cut down all the sandalwood they found, completely destroying the groves in Fiji and Hawaii—and destroying their trade in the process.

A generation later, in the 1840s, a new wave of sandalwooding began when new groves were discovered in Melanesia. This time the trade was organised through large trading firms, and was more stable. The traders put their agents in the islands to supervise the collection of sandalwood from the neighbouring islands and to prepare it for export. An agent like Captain Paddon, who worked for Jardine, Matheson of Hong Kong, could save the traders time and money by having the supply ready when a ship arrived from Sydney. The traders then sent it to China at a steady rate, so that prices in the market remained more stable.

The impact of regular trade

The sandalwood trade involved more social interaction with the islanders than the 'refreshment' trade. The traders needed a large local labour supply to harvest the groves, and for this they depended on finding a local leader who would organise labour for them in return for payment in trade goods. This arrangement could establish the political power of a local chief. In Hawaii, in the early 1800s, Kamehameha I organised labour for the American sandalwooders, who paid him with ships and guns that he then used to extend his authority throughout Hawaii. When the groves began to fail at home, the Hawaiians themselves tried to enter the sandalwood trade, sending out an expedition to Melanesia in 1829 in search for new groves. This expedition was a failure, but it shows how, once islanders acquired a taste for European goods, they began to initiate trading ventures of their own.

As the islanders learned how valuable their labour and their island products were to the traders, they became more particular about what they wanted in return: Robert Towns' list of trade goods illustrates how carefully he had to meet the demands of his consumers. However, economic values are relative to social norms. The Europeans thought they were getting a bargain by trading trivia for sandalwood. The bargain was also good from the islander's point of view, exchanging sandalwood, which was just another firewood, for new goods which were of immense value to the island economy.

At first, the trinkets of the traders had no great impact on the island society and the islanders, and islanders could manage perfectly well without beads and mirrors if they were no longer available. Other items affected the society much more significantly.

Some new goods, such as metal axes, metal fish hooks and woven textiles, replaced their indigenous equivalents of stone or shell or bark. As the substitutes became common, they lightened the workload of the people—usually men—who traditionally made them. But there was a cost to this trade, too, for the traditional skills that went into making these items were lost, and this left the islanders vulnerable if the supply of these goods later dried up, and dependent on the traders for a continued supply. The trade items had less impact on the work of the people—usually women—who were the gardeners responsible for maintaining the food supply. In fact, the pressure to provide foodstuffs to sell to the traders may even have increased their workload.

There was a limit to what a small and static society could absorb in the way of trade goods. After a while, local demand was satisfied, and the traders had to find something new. What the traders wanted was some tradeable item that could be sold, and would be used up quickly, so that demand for the item was constantly renewed. In China, that item was sandalwood—or opium; in Australia it was tea. In the Pacific, the consumer items that provided a constantly renewed demand were alcohol and tobacco. Tobacco became so commonly used that sailors were able to tell if the islanders had seen white men before by seeing whether or not they knew how to use tobacco.

A steady trade

Until the mid-nineteenth century, the Europeans remained little more than hunters and gatherers of exotic items. From the sea and shore they took whales, whales teeth, seals, pearls, pearl shell, bêche-de-mer and tortoise shell; from the land they took sandalwood, timber for firewood, coconuts, 'refreshments' and some minerals, particularly guano (bird-droppings) for fertiliser. There was little value added to any of these items, which were collected and bundled on to the ships, which then sailed away to the markets, and there was little heed paid to the possible exhaustion of the resource through over-harvesting.

However, both the islanders and the traders had an interest in developing a more predictable and stable trade. This meant the development, on the one hand, of a regular and permanent demand amongst the islanders for trade goods such as tobacco, and on the other hand, the development of renewable resources from the islands which could be traded permanently. The first regular trade of this kind was developed by British missionaries in Tahiti, who introduced pigs, taught local islanders to make salt pork, and began a trade with Sydney which lasted from 1801 to 1826. The profits of this trade were estimated at about 20 per cent, much less than the profits which were possible in the sandalwood trade, but with less risk of failure too.

Missionaries were important throughout the Pacific in the shift to a money-based economy, partly because they were keen to convert their congregations to a European way of life, but partly also because Christianity brought with it demands for new consumption items—clothes, for instance. They also tried to introduce the work ethic, and to set a value on labour: in Tahiti and Tonga, for instance, missionary regulations used enforced labour as a punishment for breaking their moral code, and this involved the new idea of measuring labour by the hour.

Plantations

By the 1860s, there was an expansion of white settlement in several island groups, as the beach communities consolidated. Although the whaling trade was in decline, and early products like sandalwood and tortoiseshell were largely worked out, other products took their place in the export trade. Sugar and cotton were introduced and, together with coconuts, became the staple cash crops of plantation agriculture in Hawaii, Samoa, Fiji, and New Britain.

The products of the plantations—sugar, cotton, coconut oil and copra—were unlike earlier island products in their impact. They depended, first, on the availability of land. While there had often been small land purchases from the islanders amongst the beach communities, it was the growth of plantations that saw the first large-scale transfers of land to Europeans, and its removal from traditional patterns of use. Security of tenure was necessary for the planters, who wanted to be sure that no one would challenge their ownership of crops which might, as in the case of coconuts, take several years to harvest. But land purchases were often troubled by the conflicting notions of property held by the buyers and the sellers. Was a piece of land bought for all time, or for a limited period? Could it be bought or inherited by a third party? Disputes were common, and might involve the intervention of naval officers or consuls.

Unlike the earlier productions of the islands, which were exported in a raw state, plantation products were refined before export. Sugar-cane was crushed and converted into molasses or raw sugar, cotton was ginned, and coconuts were transformed into oil and copra. This added value increased the profits for the planter, but required a greater input of labour, as did the harvesting of the crops. Since labour could not always be found locally for plantation work, the expansion of these crops often led to the importation of workers from other islands.

All these factors made plantations expensive to establish, often beyond the capacity of individual settlers. Many of the plantations were therefore developed and controlled by companies, such as the Australian companies Burns Philp and Colonial Sugar Refineries (CSR), the German company Godeffroy's of Hamburg, the British firm Lever, J.S. Macfarlane of New Zealand, or many island-based companies such as Hennings of Fiji and the short-lived Union Plantation and Trading Company in the Solomon Islands. The development of company investments was another stage in the gradual stabilisation of trade, allowing for capital formation on a larger scale. But it also had political implications, for these were much more powerful organisations than the early firms had been, and they had both the power and the motivation to influence government policy with regard to the Pacific.

The Pacific islands and the world economy

By the end of the nineteenth century many Pacific islands were becoming integrated into the global economy, just as they were also being absorbed into colonial empires. Exports were regular and sustained, based on the renewable resources of plantation crops, while imports were equally regular, meeting demands amongst the indigenous population for metal, tobacco, cloths and canned foods which had been unknown and unimagined a hundred years before. Where Europeans and islanders met, for trade or for labour, barter had given way to a money-based economy, and the old ways of reciprocal gift-giving were being marginalised from the market place.

If European goods were increasing in importance in island society, the products of the Pacific also had a place in the wider world. The first exports of the islands, such as sandalwood, bêche-de-mer and pearlshell, were luxury items aimed at the Asian market. However Pacific products were used by the new technologies of the industrialising West as well. Whale oil, for instance, was the main lubricant which literally kept the wheels of industry turning. Cotton was a necessary raw material for the textile mills of the industrial revolution, and 'sea island cotton', which was considered particularly fine, was especially important when production in America was interrupted by the Civil War during the 1860s. Coconut oil and copra were used in the production of soap and candles from the 1840s. Guano from the Pacific provided the nitrogenous fertilisers that made possible an enormous expansion of agricultural production in Europe, Australia, New Zealand, Japan and America from the 1870s.

This integration into the wider world brought greater wealth to the islands, a greater variety of foodstuffs and consumer items, and an expanded knowledge of the world.

The profits of the new economic system could improve the lot of many, or they could be dissipated on alcohol and tobacco, or used to buy the guns and metal axes that made traditional warfare more deadly. In short, trade with the outside world brought new wealth to some, but not always to the people most responsible for creating it, the plantation labourers, or those most disrupted, the people whose land was sold to new settlers.

There could be no going back once the islands were linked to world markets. Their integration made them much more vulnerable to economic changes, especially since most islands were dependent on just a few export products. In the 1850s, petroleum was discovered in America, and thereafter whale oil was gradually superseded by petroleum products. The demand for guano dropped when a new process for making artificial phosphate (superphosphate) was discovered in Germany just before the First World War. Coconut oil was gradually replaced by cheaper palm oil in many soap products, while candles gave way to gas and electricity. Gradually the wealth which had been linked to plantations during the late nineteenth century declined in the twentieth, without any comparable decline in the demand by islanders for imported goods.

DOCUMENTS

1   Jargon of the western Pacific

mana a Polynesian word which covers all the supernatural powers involved in wizardry, the influence of the god embodied in a man and equally in inanimate objects.

man-o'-war hawk the frigate bird.

mary all women are so called generically. Established in New Zealand before 1815, according to Nicholas.

mary belong Malekula man.

him fella Adam him want'm mary.

mast two fellow mast: a schooner or ketch.

master big fellow master: captains, traders, etc.

small fellow master: sailors, etc.

big fellow master too much: governor.

big fella master belong blackman: chief.

god big fella master belong white man.

one fella master belong god: angel.

match that fellow break (to light) plenty match.

me object.

he tell me takeum cutter big fellow hospital Ambrym.

I think you give me big fellow tobacco.

belong me: my.

meat kaikai meat along butcher.

he all bone got no meat: to be thin.

mebbe maybe, perhaps.

suppose you killum killum plenty too much mebbe he die finish.

medicine you give him medicine belong him.

milk like milk inside.

misinari

1. missionary.

he make bad for misinari.

2. that fine product known to Exeter Hall and the monthly concert as 'the native Christian.'

missi Miss.

missis big fellow missis.

The differentiation of these two items is not regarded with precision, the estate being invisible and in the islanders' eyes not particularly holy; that any distinction appears in our material may be due to the fact that missi is reported by a maiden lady.

money he put money, you kitch him money belong you.

moon month.

very good you speak three moon.

more wantum one fellow water, two fellow water, we give; no wantum more.

more better you come out.

more good you me two fella we eat'm this fella apple.

make no more cry: to comfort.

mother father, mother he no wild.

move (of emotion felt).

>   bal belong him he move he no sileep.

much see *too much*.

>   how much you pay?

musket he give this fella master belong god one big fella musket.

pappa pappa belong me he go finish yes'er day.

peasoup, pisupo

>   This is the designation of all foreign foods which are preserved in tinned
>   drums. Its origin is in fact less simple than might appear, for in the dietary
>   schedule of the whalers pea soup was not put up in tins but freshly prepared
>   in the galley when needed. 'Soup and bully' was the only tinned food of such
>   voyages. The term now covers all foods that come in round flat tins; beef is
>   the staple article under this designation, for mutton, whether fresh or pre-
>   served, is generally repugnant to the Islander's palate. Salmon is an exception
>   to the peasoup classification, being known as samani.

pickaninny child. Found in New Zealand in 1815 by Nicholas.

>   pickaninny belong me.
>
>   pickaninny stop along him fella: an egg.

>   —William Churchill, *Beach-la-Mar: The jargon or trade speech of the Western
>   Pacific*, Carnegie Institute of Washington, 1911, pp. 46–7

2 Governor King on trade

Governor King to Earl Camden
(Despatch marked 'Separate No.2,' per H.M.S. Investigator; acknowledged by
Viscount Castlereagh, 21st November, 1805.)

Sydney, New South Wales
30th April, 1805

In a former Letter I had the honor of stating the General and Individual inconvenience
that attended the Americans not only occupying Fishing Stations in and about Bass's
Straits but frequenting this port, from which they have drawn several useful People, and
in fact depriving the Inhabitants of the only Staple hitherto acquired. How far this may
or may not be allowable I have not taken upon me to decide, but have requested
Instructions thereon. I also stated the Circumstances of a small Vessel belonging to an
Individual being sent in quest of the Beche-de-Mer. That Vessel is returned, and altho'
they failed in that Object, yet they acquired another of not less Value, namely, Sandal
Wood, which is in such great Request with the Natives of India and China. It has long
been known, from the intercourse with the Friendly Islands, that Sandal Wood was a
production of some of the Feejee Islands, which are a Group hitherto not much known.
The proprietor of this Vessel was induced to make the Trial from the information of a
person who professed a knowledge of the place where it was to be obtained, but who,
unfortunately with several others, were cut off at Tongataboo, one of the Friendly
Islands. After going to several of the Feejee's, and finding much difficulty and not a
little apprehension for the safety of their small Vessel from the Natives' attack, they
accomplished their Object by procuring Fifteen Tons of Sandal Wood in exchange for
pieces of Iron at an Island called by the Natives Vooie. Whether it is plentiful or not
is doubtful, as the people belonging to the Vessel could not land, and that carried on
board by the Natives was in small Quantities, however, should it prove abundant and
become more easy to obtain, it may hereafter be an advantageous Object of Commerce
with China.

Of late Years there has been a great intercourse with Europeans with the Society and Sandwich Islands, which has not only furnished them with abundance of Firearms, but has also been the means of a number of Europeans continuing on those Islands, among whom are some of indifferent, not to say bad, Characters, mostly left from Ships going to the North-West Coast of America, Whalers, and several from this Colony, who have gained much influence with the Chiefs whom they have assisted in their Warfare.

— 'Governor King to Earl of Camden, 30 April 1805', in *Historical Records of Australia*, pp. 320–3

3   W. McGown on trade

William James McGown, sworn and examined at Sydney, 9th October 1916.

I am Secretary of the Malaita Company Limited, who are coconut-growers in the British Solomon Islands; we operate on the Islands of Malaita, Guadalcanal, and Russell Islands, but principally on Malaita. The company controls about 15,000 acres of land all told, which is practically all freehold. We have been engaged in plantation work since 1909, and the trees are only just beginning to bear. There are about 4,200 acres planted, and are now in various stages, from recently planted to bearing, but none yet in full bearing. The company was formed in 1909, with a capital of £50,000, which was later increased to £150,000—£140,000 worth of shares have been allotted, on which £134,000 has been paid. They are £100 shares. The registration of the company was the 13th July, 1909. It started clearing almost immediately. I can say that I am quite familiar with the planters' side of the work, although I have not been living on the plantations. I have lived for twenty-five years on sugar plantations which had Kanaka labour, and the conditions there were very similar, so that I am quite conversant with them. The sugar plantations I refer to were very similar, so that I am quite conversant with them. The sugar plantations I refer to were in Queensland. With regard to German trade before the war, we were not affected by that at all, because we are purely planters, and not traders. We have always sent down our supplies from Sydney by Burns, Philp, and Company and Lever Brothers' steamers, and have never shipped anything to the islands excepting by those two companies. The steamers from Sydney do not call at Malaita; our head-quarters are at Aola, a small island of 5½ acres, about half-a-mile off the coast of Guadalcanal, opposite one of Lever Brothers' properties, which is called Aola, and is situated between Guadalcanal and Malaita. The island is known as Aola. I think it took that name from Lever Brothers' property opposite. That, however, is our main port of call from Sydney. The boats also call at Russell Island, which is another point of the company's properties; it is about 70 miles from Aola, and just adjoining another of Levers' plantations on the same island. The steam-ship communication at present is quite satisfactory. It is a monthly service, and answers our requirements. When the plantations, of course, get more freely into bearing, along with others, I expect the present ship-owners will extend their service and put on larger boats. Dealing with the labour question on Malaita, we have greater difficulties there than planters on any of the other islands in the Solomon group, because of the warlike conditions of the natives. They are more warlike on Malaita than on any other island in the group so far as I know. The company first started on Malaita, and then, later on, purchased Captain Pope's properties. We have had a good deal of trouble with the natives on Malaita, because, when they are brought to the coast where the coconut-growing is done, should they commit any offence, they simply break away into the bush, and that is the end of it. We are obliged to bring natives from other islands to do the work on Malaita, although the population of that island is greater than on any of the others. We have not been able to break them in. In fact, the natives from the other islands are afraid of the bush natives of Malaita, and consequently the former do not make a practice of bolting into the bush. They do not mix at all. We have had a lot of trouble with Malaita natives, and have had them fire on our employees several times. Very often sniping is done there now, and we are required to keep an armed sentry on guard practically all the time. I should have brought with me a photo showing the armed natives standing there guarding the property. We have sometimes had several of our friendly natives armed. That sort of thing does not exist, I understand, on the other islands. We really have never had sufficient protection against the outrages of the natives—I mean sufficient Government protection; which, as pioneers of Malaita, we have always considered we are justly entitled to ...

The natives do not require much to live on, and they are not a thrifty class of people, the more money you give them for their produce the less copra you will get. They do not cultivate the coconut, they get the copra from natural groves. They gather nuts and make copra themselves and sell it mostly to the traders. There are various traders operating there. We do not do general trading; we used to, but dropped it; the natives do not do much trading through us for ordinary supplies, excepting when we are recruiting, and then we have to give them certain articles in the way of tobacco, &c.

—William McGown, evidence to the Commission investigating British and
Australian trade to the South Pacific, presented to Parliament of the
Commonwealth of Australia, 25 April 1918

4   Jardine Matheson Papers

LETTER FROM CAPTAIN PADDON (IN VANUATU / NEW HEBRIDES)

Captain Paddon announces that he is sending a cargo of sandalwood to Jardine Matheson in the Alfred.

I am forced to ship this wood on Thacker & Co's account in consequence of being left here by Mr Heejeebhoy Rustomjee without any assistance for upwards of two years.

... I cannot get any returns from New Zealand for the cargo left there: one settlement has been turned down by the Natives at which I had left goods, and at another the Agent for the sale of the goods left has failed; others write that in consequence of the state of the country they are unable to remit any proceeds at present; had Mr Rustomjee sent me any assistance I could have shipped sandalwood from this Island at from £6 to £8 per ton, but as I have had to leave the Islands and take the wood to Sydney in a small vessel of 40 tons, (the only vessel I have had, and she mortgaged to more than her value), to pay interest on money and leave my business, I am unable under the circumstances to ship it in Sydney under from £12 to £14 per ton.

... The China men I send up in the Brig say they will return in her, if you could forward them to me in any manner or send me any other Chinamen you would render me a great assistance, they are by far the best people I could have amongst the Islands. If you could give me any information about the quality of sandalwood or Bêche de Mer you could much oblige me as I have not had a line from Heejeebhoy Rustomjee since I left China and did not know any thing about the matter when I left.

—Jardine Matheson Papers. James Paddon, Annatam [Anateum], New Hebrides,
to Jardine Matheson & Co, Hong Kong,
8 November 1845. Unpublished papers, Mitchell Library

LETTER FROM THACKER AND CO.

... Captain Paddon's Brig 'Governor' has arrived from Anatam, and by her we had letters from Captain Davis of the 'Arabia' in which he informs us of the very precarious state of Captain Paddon's health ... his death may be expected at any moment—and he cannot be induced to return to Sydney.

In the event of his death, we fear from the disposition of the persons, by whom he is surrounded, his property would go to destruction, and that it would be almost impossible for us, who in fact are his only Creditors, to recover any part of it. Under these circumstances we think it advisable to show you how we stand with him, and to solicit your kind exertions on our behalf, in the disposal of the Sandal Wood Cargoes we have in China to the best advantage, for upon the result of their sale every thing depends.

... for your information and guidance, we beg to state that there are but two Sandal Wood establishments now in the Pacific, namely Paddon's and Towns'—Paddon's may be considered as virtually at an end, or at all events suspended for a length of time for he has not now the means to prosecute the Trade to any extent, and what little wood he may collect will be sent to us here, whilst Captain Towns informs us that he has given positive directions to his party to retain the wood at the Isle of Pines, and that he does not intend to ship it to China, till the Market there is relieved of its present large Stocks. We think therefore a rise in price may be anticipated, and we understand from Captain Johnson of the 'Regia' that that was the opinion of Mr. Dallas when he was there in January last, but you on the spot will be the best judges, and we must leave it to you to act as you may deem most to our advantage.

—Jardine Matheson Papers, In-Correspondence. Australia. Unbound letters. Thacker & Co. to JM & Co., 29 April 1850. Unpublished papers, Mitchell Library

5   Exploiting the islands

The geographical position of Sydney, the superiority of its harbour, and the enterprising spirit of its merchants, have raised it, even at this early period of its existence, to the rank of a great commercial city. There can be little doubt that it is destined to become the London of the southern hemisphere. But enterprising as its merchants are, there are many sources of wealth around them of which they have not yet taken advantage.

To draw attention to one field for commercial enterprise, almost limitless in extent, is the object of the writer ... The Islands of the Pacific afford a sphere for exertion which has as yet been but little heeded by the Australian merchants. There has indeed been some traffic with these islands, but it has been of a very partial and superficial nature. No attempt whatever has been made to develop their latent resources. The trade has been chiefly conducted by small merchant vessels which have gone from place to place trusting to Providence and to the temptations of hardware and trinkets for their cargo. There has been no settled principle of exchange—no definite arrangements for a continuous supply—but the trading masters have driven the best bargain at each place, utterly reckless of the future. The general conduct, too, of these persons, and of their men, as will afterwards be shown, has been such as to inflict most serious injury upon the general interests of commerce, and to retard the progress of civilisation.

A glance at the Map will show that the position of Sydney is peculiarly favourable for commercial intercourse with these groups. Stretching from the north-eastern coast of New Holland across the broad expanse of the Pacific, almost to the shores of South America, is a perfect chain of Islands, in number almost too great to count, which produce spontaneously some of the most valuable articles of commerce. Most of the groups are sufficiently near each other to afford great facility for inter-communication. In fact there has always been an intercourse between several of the principal groups, even by means of the frail canoes of the natives. A few stations or factories therefore, in positions judiciously selected, would at all times secure the possession of accurate intelligence as to the state of affairs in the surrounding groups, and the speed with which merchants of the Australian metropolis could communicate with these places, and act upon the information thus obtained, would give them such commercial advantages as would enable them to defy competition.

... although there are abundant proofs that in former times these islands have been inhabited by a far more numerous and more civilised race than their present occupants; ages of barbarism, desolating wars, and the almost universal practice of infanticide, have left but a small population. There is ample room, therefore, for the exercise of European industry. Millions of acres of the most fertile land in the world are wholly untilled, and such of the islanders as are left, are without profitable employment. Such employment can only be afforded them by the aid of their civilised brethren. It is from the merchant that this aid must come. There are tens of thousands now living in forced and profitless idleness who might be made the producers of wealth.

It is by the formation of permanent establishments upon the islands of the Pacific, that the merchant would derive the greatest and most certain profit. By establishments is not meant merely trading stations, but the settlement of small parties of Europeans, under whose superintendence the labour of the natives could be directed to the production of such articles as would meet with a ready sale in the European markets. Take cotton as an example ...

But there are many other articles, and some of them, perhaps, still more profitable than cotton, which could be produced in this way, to almost any extent. Such establishments would, at the same time, increase and render steady, the traffic already carried on in these quarters. The occupants of the trading stations, which are from time to time formed among the Islands, are, after all, mere birds of passage. Their object is simply to obtain from the Islanders as large a quantity as possible of their sandal-wood, their tortoiseshell, and their cocoa-nut oil; and upon the lowest possible terms. They care not although they should 'kill the goose which lays the golden egg', for they can remove elsewhere. It is no object with them to raise the Islander in the social scale, or to increase his resources. Their interests are rather of a contrary nature. So long as he remains in a state of barbarism, he is more at the mercy of the white trader than he would be in an improved condition, with a means of permanent employment ...

—Charles St Julian, *Notes on the Latent Resources of Polynesia*,
Kemp and Fairfax, Sydney, 1851, pp. 1–8

QUESTIONS AND ACTIVITIES

1   In which phase of trading contracts might the language described by Churchill (Document 1) have been created?

2   Why did slang-hybrid-English develop as a 'trade' language? Why didn't traders learn and use the language of the island where they traded? Why didn't islanders learn and use English?

3   What trading 'advantage' with China was Governor King referring to (in Document 2) when he reported the discovery of sandalwood in Fiji?

4   As early as 1805, Governor King refers to a 'great intercourse with Europeans'. What was the extent of European contact with Hawaii and Tahiti up to 1805? Is Governor King warranted in using 'great intercourse' to describe these contacts?

5   With a partner, take either a European or Fijian role, and compose an answer in response to the statement: Fifty tons of sandalwood was fair exchange for a 'few pieces' of iron.

6   Why is it significant that Mr McGown (Document 3) stresses his company's land is 'all freehold'?

7   Despite Mr McGown's claim, in what ways might conditions on Queensland sugar plantations be different to copra plantations in the Solomons?

8   Why might the people of Malaita not have been enthusiastic about entering a cash economy by establishing plantations and seeking regular paid work?

9   What commodities was Mr McGown referring to when he reported, 'trading through us for ordinary supplies'?

10 List the problems faced by traders in the islands, using as a guide Thacker and Company and James Paddon's letters to Jardine Matheson and Company (Document 4).

11 Why is there no reference to labour (casual or indentured Pacific Islanders) in these letters? Describe in your own words the relationship between labour, natural resources, market price (in China) and trader's or company profits.

12 What did St Julian (Document 5) mean by the phrase 'a few stations or factories'?

13 How would James Paddon and Thacker and Company, knowing their own fortunes to be declining in the Solomon Islands in the late 1840s, have responded to St Julian's 1851 suggestions of boundless unrealised profits?

14 Is St Julian's phrase, 'of a very partial and superficial nature', an acceptable description of trading contacts in the Pacific up to 1850?

REFERENCES

Campbell, I.C., *A History of the Pacific Islands*, Queensland University Press, Brisbane, 1990

Hainsworth, D.R., *The Sydney Traders*, Melbourne University Press, Revised Edition, 1982

Hainsworth, D.R., *Builders and Adventurers*, Cassells, Sydney, 1968

Howe, K.R., *Where the Waves Fall*, Allen and Unwin, Sydney, 1984

Oliver, D.I., *The Pacific Islands*, University of Honolulu Press, Revised Edition, 1988

Ralston, C., *Grass Huts and Warehouses*, Australian National University Press, Canberra, 1977

Scarr, D., *The History of the Pacific Islands*, Macmillan, Sydney, 1990

Shineberg, D., *They Came for Sandalwood*, Melbourne University Press, 1967

Young, J.M.R., *Australia's Pacific Frontier*, Cassells, Sydney, 1968

Chapter 6
Religious Interaction

Andrew Thornley, Newington School

The rise of missionary activity

The movement of Christianity into the Pacific had its origins in the European fascination with the newly discovered land masses and islands of the Oceania region. Roman Catholic priests had accompanied Spanish explorers in the western Pacific in the sixteenth century with some impact in the Marianas but negligible contact during their stay in the Solomons and Vanuatu. At the end of the eighteenth century both Protestants and Roman Catholics were inspired and motivated to action by the accounts of Pacific explorers such as Cook, Wallis, Bougainville and La Perouse.

Scientific and liberal opinion in Europe believed that the 'noble savage' should be left in an unspoilt state but zealous evangelical religious groups were not of similar mind. They argued that the pure condition of Pacific society had already been corrupted by the earliest traders, whalers and adventurers who had shown little or no interest in promoting Christianity. In Great Britain and France particularly, religious renewal such as Wesleyanism and Roman Catholic revival sponsored the development of missionary movements directed by the biblical command, 'Go Ye into all the world and preach the gospel to every person'.

Two missionary organisations were founded in England: in 1795 the interdenominational London Missionary Society (LMS), which began its work in Tahiti, and in 1817 the Wesleyan Methodist Missionary Society, which started in New Zealand. In America, in 1810, the Congregational Church formed the American Board of Commissioners for Foreign Missions, whose work was to focus on Hawaii. The Roman Catholic Church in France had been terribly fractured during the Napoleonic era but following the restoration of the monarchy in 1815, Catholic revivalism took over the missionary role in the Pacific formerly initiated by the Spanish. In 1825 Pope Leo XII devised a plan to send French missionaries to the Pacific and shortly after Pope Pius implemented the Mission d'Oceanie program, carried out by two French orders, the *Societé de Picpus* for eastern Pacific islands and the *Societé de Marie* for islands in the west.

Background and attitude of missionaries

Roman Catholic missionaries were initially almost exclusively ordained priests who tended to transport to the Pacific their reclusive way of life and their sacramental practice of Christianity. Their reluctance to use local islander converts as mission agents inhibited the rapid spread of Catholicism. Protestant missionaries did not all have the lengthy training of Catholics. The LMS and Wesleyan agents were mainly from the lower middle classes and only a minority were clergymen; the remainder were artisans and 'godly mechanics' who, by bettering themselves in the service of God could bestow useful civilising skills upon their converts. In the words of one influential mission sponsor, Rev. T. Haweis, one of the founders of the LMS:

A plain man, well read in the Bible, full of faith and of the Holy Ghost, though he comes from the forge or the shop, would, in my view, as a missionary to the heathen, be infinitely preferable to all the learning of the schools; and would possess, in the skill and labour of his hands, advantages which barren science would never compensate.

—cited in: Neil Gunson, *Messengers of Grace*, Oxford, 1978, p. 37

The evangelism of these early missionaries was based on the primacy of the Bible, the superiority of Christian culture and the virtues of strict morality. They were to show little respect for indigenous cultures. True conversion and spiritual rebirth were the principal objects of all revivalist missionaries and they were driven by a sense of urgency to bring about the salvation of all nations in order to prepare for the eventual coming of Christ's kingdom.

As missionaries came into contact with Pacific Island society they were horrified by certain customs. In their eyes they saw sins abounding and named them according to European standards as infanticide, human sacrifice, sexual promiscuity and homo-sexuality, cannibalism, widow strangling and murder. It is true that many of these activities shocked European beachcombers and traders; but whereas early beachcomb-ers and traders largely conformed to islander ways, the missionaries were the first white people who deliberately aimed at changing the customs of the land. Their overall attitude to Pacific Islanders was shaped by the moral repulsion they felt. In essence, they believed in the complete depravity of the 'heathen' (their term for non-Christians). This depravity, it was alleged, had resulted from the progressive degradation of natural man, arising from his abandonment of belief in one God. Hence missionaries saw themselves as engaging in a spiritual war against absolute evil where compromise was unthinkable.

Missionary–islander interaction

It was not a straightforward matter for missionaries to settle among the Pacific Islands; the existence of a mission station did not immediately signify success. In many islands missionaries were preceded by whalers and sandalwood buyers who had introduced European diseases, rifles and liquor. As an example, the principal cause of the failure of the first Protestant missions to Tonga and the New Hebrides (Vanuatu) was the widely held belief that the missionaries and their countrymen were the bringers of disease. A further problem stemmed from the association of missionaries with the various naval ships that cruised the Pacific Islands. As messengers of peace, it was ironic that Protestant missionaries in Fiji and many other islands had to rely on the support of British and American naval power to help secure their foothold. The Catholics were also associated with French gunships, such as in 1848 in the Solomon Islands, when a French warship sent a punitive expedition inland to avenge the murder of missionaries.

The activities of traders in Melanesia had raised the indigenous people's expecta-tions concerning European wealth. On the Banks Island group between the Solomon Islands and Vanuatu, Bishops Selwyn and Patterson of the Melanesian Mission were forced to give presents of beads, fish-hooks and calico to the leading men of each village in order to secure friendly relations with the islanders. The result was to create an association between the mission and the hope of material gain while the message of Christianity was quietly ignored.

To a significant extent, missionaries were only able to establish contact with Pacific Islanders by seeking the favours of prominent leaders. In Tahiti, Tonga and Fiji, the

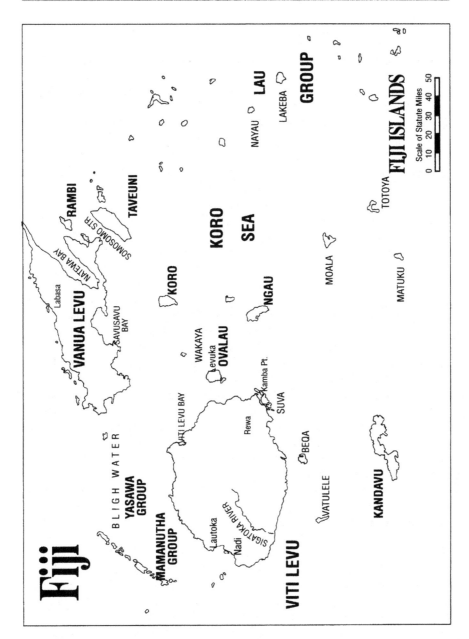

Figure 6.1: Fiji.

support of respective powerful chiefs—Pomare, Tupou and Cakobau—was essential for the mission to survive and then expand. Naturally the chiefs stood to benefit from this arrangement if by doing so they could harness the new technology and ideas of the Europeans. Involved in this arrangement was a risk the missionaries took of alienating permanently the enemies of the mission's patron chiefs and thus becoming party to the traditional rivalries of each island group. The earliest attempts of the Catholics in the Solomon Islands were thwarted because the priests steadfastly refused to go to war in support of one tribe against another.

When the Wesleyan missionaries first settled in Fiji, they were obliged to seek the patronage of the chief of the Lau islands, Tui Nayau. He was anxious to warn them that their survival could not be guaranteed because stronger chiefs resident on the main island might well challenge the missionary presence. The Wesleyans survived in Fiji because they were sponsored from Tonga and had the support of the recently converted Tongan Christian chief, Tupou. By that stage in the 1840s a power struggle had erupted in Fiji between the chiefly kingdoms of Bau and Rewa on the main island of Viti Levu. The Wesleyan Mission at Rewa had been evicted. The war raged intermittently for a decade and was only resolved when Tupou intervened militarily with 2000 Tongan warriors in support of the Bauan leader, Cakobau (pronounced Thakombau), at the Battle of Kaba in 1855. Cakobau showed his gratitude by adopting Christianity. He subsequently espoused the cause of British colonialism in Fiji and was a leading chief when the island group became part of the British Empire in 1874.

Following its adoption by Cakobau, the way was opened for rapid expansion of Christianity in Fiji. Cakobau's chiefly rival on the island of Taveuni, Tui Cakau, displayed his independence by welcoming Roman Catholic missionaries into his sphere of influence. Likewise, in the interior regions of Viti Levu, chiefs who resented the increasing power of Cakobau directed their people to either Catholicism or the more recently arrived missionary agents of the Seventh Day Adventist church. But the major role of evangelisation in Fiji was taken by the Wesleyan Tongan converts under the patronage of Ma'afu, a high chief of Tonga who, frustrated by restricted ambitions in his homeland, used his countrymen to spread his power and with it, the new religious order, throughout the islands and coastal provinces of Fiji. The peaceful intentions of Christianity were frequently compromised by the warlike operations of Tongan adventurers as they plundered the villages of Fiji.

Religious interaction in the Pacific was not always as violent or as overtly political as in Fiji but the major characteristics of European power on the one hand, combined with local rivalries on the other, were generally present. Once Christian missions became established, the process of interaction assumed a different perspective. Priority was given to learning the local language so the Bible could be translated by missionaries. Rudimentary schools were established on mission sites to teach literacy skills. Medical assistance proved an immediate means of outreach. Carpentry and associated trades were taught. Agricultural pursuits were encouraged. Missionaries attempted to make their settlement a model of European civilising influences.

Missionary life had little of the romantic notions associated with living in the Pacific. Supplies for the mission stations had to be transported from Australia or New Zealand and were irregular, ships often not being sighted for intervals of a year or more. Skilled medical help was virtually non-existent; disease and sickness were of constant concern. Education facilities for missionary children were inadequate and many families were separated for long periods when children were sent to colonial boarding schools. Missionary wives were obliged to lead an isolated existence while their husbands spent months travelling throughout the islands.

Figure 6.2: Tutors' residences at the mission seminary, Malua.

Missionaries identified one of their major priorities as gathering together a group of students who could be trained as catechists and sent out to live and work in the many villages which required assistance both in learning about the new religion and in teaching young children. Because they were an important source of labour in their own district, aspiring catechists required the permission of clan or family leaders to leave their village and travel to the mission station where they would be tutored for two or three years and sent out as catechists. If they performed their job well, they then might be considered as probationary ministers. With the growing influence of Christianity, these pastors occupied positions of prominence in the community and so careers in the church provided an opportunity for men from the lower ranks of society to improve their status.

Christianity was constantly a force for social change and social mobility. From the point of view of traditional chiefs and big men in whom political authority resided, the church was seen as both a support and an aid to secular power. It was also a challenge to the time honoured routines of society in the sense that the church was a means by which western ideas filtered into the island community. Traditional leaders therefore sought to influence, if not control, church structures. While changes in local leadership and authority did take place, rank and position in the church usually occupied a secondary place to rank and position in the traditional hierarchy.

The meaning of conversion in islander societies

An important and controversial change involved in missionary interaction with Pacific Islanders was that of conversion: the renouncing of traditional beliefs and an acceptance of Christianity. So much of pre-European culture in the islands was bound up with religious customs that even the external act of Christian baptism was to result in a changed outlook. Traditional religions involved a complex relationship between ordinary people and a range of supernatural deities who possessed influence and power in most aspects of everyday life. Acting as intermediaries for these deities were the men and women with special powers. Priests fostered a close relationship with the secular

Figure 6.3: Classroom at Malua, and cottages of the students.

and used the powerful *tapu* (or rules of access and behaviour) to separate the different levels of society. Although this was an enforced system of control, it did help society maintain its cohesiveness.

Missionaries appreciated the close links between traditional religion and society; in order to bring about effective change they believed that society itself had to be transformed. Thus they campaigned vigorously against activities such as cannibalism, wife-strangling and infanticide and in many cases successfully reduced their incidence, though this 'success' was often part of an inflated story of their own influence. But the existing order did not simply give way when these practices were reduced. While islanders were prepared to be influenced by Europeans in changing some of their customs, they did not automatically attribute those changes to the influence of the Christian God. In the eyes of many islanders, Jehovah was regarded as the particular god of the white people, existing independently of all their own deities.

It has already been suggested that one of the missionaries' greatest assets was their association with the spread of European influence. Many missionaries sought to deny this factor but it was almost impossible for them to isolate themselves from their background. The Europeans' access to new and seemingly limitless resources was most appealing to the islanders. The missionaries contributed to this process. A particularly powerful example is the printing press, which was first used in the Pacific by missionaries as they endeavoured to make the Bible available to their converts. The impact of the written word was considerable and the desire of the islanders to become literate must be regarded as an important factor in explaining the conversion of Pacific Islanders.

Access to European technology in its many and various forms became an important channel for arousing initial interest among potential converts and evidence of the intense desire to get hold of European goods was the high incidence of stealing from mission premises. Every mission station confronted this problem and at times it led to considerable friction. In the Solomon Islands the indigenous people ignored the Catholic priests partly because they refused to tolerate any such theft. However it remains a fact that a missionary's relationship with the islander was helped by their possession of goods and technology. Islander attitudes can best be summed up by the powerful Fijian chief of Taveuni, Tui Cakau who made a special trip to a rival district to request the missionaries to come and reside in his kingdom in 1837. When questioned about his response to the truth of Christianity, he replied: 'True— everything is true from the white man's country; muskets and gunpowder are true and your religion must be true.'

In Papua New Guinea and the nearby islands of Melanesia, this identification of Christianity with European power resulted in the concept of 'cargo' and the development of so-called cargo cults or religiously influenced movements arising from the response of islanders to European contact. The anthropologist Peter Lawrence recorded the following observation by a local informant, which neatly highlights the link between European 'cargo' and Christianity:

> Everything we have was created by its own particular deity: taro, yams, pigs, slit-gongs. If we want to grow taro we perform rituals to the taro goddess. You white men come with your goods and we like them, so that we ask ourselves, 'Who and where is the god of cargo.' Then the missionaries and tell us about Jehovah and we assume that he is the key to our problem.
>
> —R.J. May and H. Nelson (eds),
> *Melanesia beyond Diversity*, ANU Press, 1982, pp. 58–9

This was a natural enough assumption given that the islanders were so far removed from the actual means of production of the white man's goods. The result was that the motivation and the meaning of conversion was both economic and socio-political. People wanted the new wealth for its obvious utility but also as a prestige symbol allowing them relationships of equality with the Europeans.

It can be seen that reasons for conversions were very complicated, involving social, economic and political factors. Missionaries were just as overwhelmed in trying to discern motivation and they rather predictably resorted to a two-tier religious explanation. They claimed there were two types of conversion: there was the experience of heart acceptance or true faith (see Document 1) and then there was outward acceptance or nominal conversion. Most converts fell into the latter category. But nominal acceptance was a break with the past and involved an eagerness to learn about new

Figure 6.4: Training institution, Tonga.

Figure 6.5: Wesleyan mission premises, Neiafu, Vavau—erected 1833.

ideas. Nevertheless, belief in the old deities remained. As the missionary John Hunt wrote about Fiji in the 1840s, 'when Fijians renounce paganism, they were not so much convinced that their gods were false as that ours is true'.

The experience of Christian conversion, as seen in Fiji, involved elaborate ceremony. After a number of villages, usually linked by tribal affiliation, had resolved to convert, their chief would send a message to the nearest European missionary requesting as many teachers as could be given, if possible one for each village under the chief's influence. The arrival of teachers was marked by a solemn feast at which priests of the old order would formally farewell their gods; although relegated, they might be recalled if the new religion was unsatisfactory. Following this ceremony, tangible links with past beliefs and practices would be severed:

- villagers would reduce their sizeable heads of hair and wrap two yards of calico or native cloth around their waists
- cannibalism where it had been practised would cease
- murder was forbidden
- infanticide was regarded as a crime
- all but one wife was renounced, and
- war was prevented wherever possible.

In addition the traditional *tapu* concept was now applied to the Sabbath to symbolise the break with the old order. Children were sent to school and family worship was conducted every day. The declaration of adherence to Christianity produced significant change.

Role of islander missionaries

As Christian interaction proceeded throughout the Pacific, European staff were unable to provide the day-to-day requirements of existing mission stations or adequately contribute to new mission areas. The solution lay in using indigenous converts. Accordingly, Tahitians were used in Tonga and Fiji; Tongans were used in the Fijian islands; and Fijians, Samoans and Cook islanders were among the first to go as missionaries to Papua New Guinea. For islanders who worked as village pastors, the principle of self-sufficiency was introduced and each village was expected to support its pastor by providing food and cash resources. Contributions were usually made annually and this activity stimulated the exchange of goods and the development of a rudimentary western-style cash economy. Villages were encouraged to compete with each other in raising the greatest contributions in support of the church. While missionaries applauded this development, they were less enthusiastic about sponsoring indigenous control of missions. The more enlightened clergy recognised that they had to prepare for this eventuality.

The impact of Christianity

In the process of religious interaction, missionaries brought about considerable social and political changes. The diminishing of traditional beliefs contributed to the undermining of structures which those beliefs had helped to support. The chiefs in Polynesia appreciated this fact and responded by exercising a careful supervision of the new directions to which Christianity and westernism pointed. In Melanesia the effects of Christianity, especially the emergence of cargo cults and millennial movements, had a wide-ranging impact since traditional leadership was more broadly based and thus more open to the influence of new ideas.

In the early part of the nineteenth century, missionaries were criticised by other European settlers for their over-zealousness in condemning activities such as traditional dances and kava drinking. At times the missionary impact on culture was more serious; for instance, on the island of Mangareva in eastern Polynesia, the Roman Catholic demands for labour for church building depleted the human resources necessary for traditional gardening and fishing. In addition female vows of chastity did not help the replenishment of a population already reduced by European diseases. In

Figure 6.6: Cottage of Nisbett and Turner at Tanna in 1842.

other places Christian influence could be of assistance in coping with European contact. On the island of Ponape in Micronesia, legislation enacted by the local rulers with missionary advice offered protection against problems of drunkenness and venereal disease.

Religious interaction helped to enhance the status and role of women. In New Caledonia the LMS missionaries strenuously opposed what they interpreted as trading in sex by chiefs and the failure of chiefs to punish husbands for domestic violence. In Papua, institutions for girls saved from infanticide were established, and women considered to be former sorceresses were trained in medical work. The wives of European missionaries acted as gender models for indigenous women by teaching in schools, working as nursing sisters and developing craft work as well as leading various church activities, such as Bible classes. In Fiji, women formed a majority amongst church members and gradually assumed responsibility within the local church.

The educational impact of missionaries was extensive and brief mention here cannot do justice to their significant impact and contribution. We have seen earlier that the urgent priority of the Christian missions was to teach their converts to read and write so as to bring about independent Bible study and the reading of other books considered morally uplifting, such as *Pilgrim's Progress*. The task of education was largely left to missionaries in the early years of contact; teaching was mainly carried out in the vernacular language though where resources were available, students judged by the missionaries to be more 'capable' were sent to central schools where they could learn advanced subjects and study English. When the island societies were annexed by various European powers, colonial authorities satisfied their educational responsibilities by continuing to leave the mission with the primary responsibility for education and they were given financial assistance to help pay for new school buildings and the salaries of qualified teachers.

Conclusion

By 1900 Christianity had emerged as a major influence in the contact between Europeans and islanders. Missionaries and island converts had in many places initiated and in other islands reinforced the abandonment of traditional structures and the selective assimilation of European ideas. Religious interaction had brought about the presence of Christian churches centrally located in each village. Attending these churches was a committed group of active church members who met regularly throughout the week, surrounded by a larger number of nominal believers for whom religious adherence was nevertheless an important social requirement. The wider influence of the missionaries had been felt in areas such as education and social welfare. A new generation of island church leaders was being trained on home soil and within a relatively short space of time would assume a large responsibility in religious and secular affairs.

DOCUMENTS

1 A Samoan man's account of his conversion

My father was a wicked old man. The Christian religion was set up in our village but he was an enemy of it and we, the children, had to comply with his wishes. As I grew up, it seemed to be my very trade to lie and steal; and the Sabbath I generally spent in hunting wild pigs. Then it happened that I was taken very ill. My father and all the family was crying and concluded I was dying. In my distress it occurred to me, as a last resort, to call upon God, and for the first time I prayed to the true God. Next morning I felt better, and continued to recover. I now determined to give up heathenism, and serve the Lord. About that time I heard Mr. Hardie preach and well remember his saying, 'Make haste and repent; for if you do not, death will come, and then you can never obtain eternal life'. This made me all the more anxious to follow Christ. After a time war broke out. My father did all he could to get me off to the war. He first tried to coax and flatter me, praising my bright sharp eyes, which would make me the beauty of the corps, but this did not do. He then tried anger, and at last went off in a rage. My mind was made up. I was determined to hold on to Christ. Instead of going to war, I got up, put on a decent cloth, and joined a party of Church members and steady people who were going off to remonstrate and try to prevent fighting. For a long time I did not make it known formally to the teacher what a change had come over my mind. People wondered and talked about it. They saw that I had begun to pray, attend school on the weekdays, and on the Sabbath just like a church member, and yet I was not one. By and by I opened my mind to the teacher and, after a year or two, was received into the church. I am greatly delighted to add that my old erring father seems now to be turning to the Saviour too.

—Quoted in Rev. G. Turner, *Nineteen Years in Polynesia*, John Snow, London, 1861, pp. 148–9

2 A European observer comments on Fiji (1859)

I shall probably be accused, by those versed in Fijian affairs, of an undue partiality for the Wesleyan missionaries by viewing their conduct in the light I do, and endeavouring to separate the doings of the missionaries from those of the barbarous hordes who overran the country. I admit that the latter is a matter of no slight difficulty. Christianity had early root in Tonga; and when, in 1835, the Wesleyans in that group determined to extend their operations to Fiji, they naturally fixed upon Lakeba, and those parts where a strong population of Tonguese was already established, and where they could use a language familiar to them until Fijian had been learnt. Tongamen were found extremely well qualified for acting as pioneers in teaching the rudiments of the Christian faith; and during the whole period that the Wesleyans have been labouring for the conversion of Fiji, they have employed a large number of them. They were spread over the whole country, and unfortunately, became in Maafu's hand, ready instruments for the execution of his plans. They supplied him with reliable information about the quarrels, weaknesses, and resources of the different territories, were never tired of praising their great chief, and ever ready to prompt the Fijian rulers to apply to him in cases of dispute and war. All these facts cannot be gainsaid; and those must be strangely ignorant of the working of the Polynesian mind, who fancy that doctrines of so recent a growth as those of Christianity would ever induce a native of subordinate position to remain indifferent to the wishes and orders of his chief. When King George (Tupou) visited Fiji, it was in the mission vessel 'John Wesley', and it was on board of that vessel the arrangement relative to the subjugation of Kaba was concluded. Finally, nothing was said by the missionaries whilst Maafu achieved his conquest, and it was only after great atrocities had been committed that a letter of remonstrance was sent to him.

—Quoted in Berthold Seemann, *Viti: An account of a Government mission to the Vitian or Fijian Islands in the years 1860–61*, London, 1862, pp. 253–4

3 Bishop Patteson explains his mission in the Solomon Islands (1866)

We start with the fullest belief in the capacity of these races; and with a very strong conviction that we must by our treatment of them and life with them prevent their acquiescing in the idea of their inferiority, inability to help themselves etc. ... I always regard them as the permanent, ourselves as the transient element in the mission, and try to raise them to the consciousness of their being called and intended by God to be the evangelists of their own people. We aim at a practical teaching of the truth 'God hath made of one blood, etc.' And this is done by making no distinction whatever between whites and blacks as such; by eliminating all that is conventional etc. in us and does not belong to us as Christians but qua Englishmen with English notions of civilisation etc. We don't aim at making Melanesians Englishmen but Christians; and we try to think out the meaning and attitude of the Melanesian mind and character—not to suppress but to educate it.

—Quoted in John Garrett, *To Live Among the Stars*, World Council of Churches, 1989, pp. 184–5

QUESTIONS AND ACTIVITIES

Document 1

1 What other information is needed before judging the validity of this source?
2 What influence led the narrator to ignore Christianity?
3 What factors made him change his mind?
4 Why might the father resist Christianity more resolutely than the son? From your reading of this chapter, why might Christianity appeal more readily to the younger generation?
5 In what way is the narrator's attitude to war a sign of changes brought about by religious interaction?
6 What activities differentiated a church member from other people in the community? Why would these activities have appealed to people?

Document 2

7 To what extent can this source be considered a fairly reliable interpretation of missionary activity?
8 According to Seemann, what is the problem in assessing the achievement of the missionaries in Fiji?
9 Why did the missionaries in Fiji begin their work at Lakeba? (Check the position of Lakeba on a map of Fiji.) From your reading of this chapter, are there other reasons why Lakeba was chosen?
10 How was the cause of Christianity damaged by the activities of the Tongans? Were there any positive results from these activities?
11 What allegations are made about missionary collusion in the Tongan involvement?
12 How do you think the missionaries might have defended their actions?

Document 3

13 In what ways is Patteson criticising the nature of European interactions with the Pacific Islanders?
14 According to Patteson, how is he going to avoid the normal pattern of European–Islander interactions?
15 What biblical support does Patteson quote for his argument? Try to locate the more complete text of this quote in the Bible. (You will probably need a concordance.)
16 Explain what Patteson means by differentiating between Christian attitudes and the attitudes of Englishmen.
17 What is Patteson's vision of a Melanesian church?
18 Was Patteson ahead of his time in expressing these ideas? Why?

Illustrations

19 In the illustrations in this chapter, what general impression have the artists tried to convey to readers in Europe?
20 What characteristic common in housing in Europe can be seen in the illustrations from Tonga, Tanna (Vanuatu) and Malua (Western Samoa)?
21 Does the 'mission' architecture indicate particular cultural attitudes on the part of the missionaries?
22 What impression would Samoans have of Christianity as they walked past the Malua school and dormitories?
23 If you did not read the caption for the Tanna illustration, in which country might the scene be set?

REFERENCES

Davidson, J.W., and Scarr, D. (eds), *Pacific Island Portraits*, Australian National University Press, Canberra, 1970

Garrett, John, *Footsteps in the Sea: Christianity in Oceania to World War II*, World Council of Churches, 1992

Garrett, John, *To Live Among the Stars: Christian origins in Oceania*, World Council of Churches, 1982

Gunson, Neil, *Messengers of Grace*, Oxford, 1978

Kent, Graeme, *Company of Heaven*, A.H. Reed, 1972

Laracy, Hugh, *Marists and Melanesians*, Australian National University Press, Canberra, 1976

Scarr, Deryck (ed.), *More Pacific Island Portraits*, Australian National University Press, Canberra, 1978

Schutz, Albert J. (ed.), *The Diaries and Correspondence of David Cargill*, Canberra, 1977

Lawrence, P., 'Madang and Beyond', in May, R.J., and Nelson, H. (eds), *Melanesia beyond Diversity*, Vol. 1, Australian National University Press, Canberra, 1982

Chapter 7
Labour Recruiting and Indenture

Clive Moore, University of Queensland

Early labour recruiting

Imagine yourself standing on the beach of your tropical island. Your island is small, but it is almost your whole world. You know that there are other islands nearby but they are inhabited by strangers and frightening spirits. As you look out to sea something that looks like an island appears, but it is moving. You run back to your village shouting, 'An island is coming here!', and quickly the people gather on the beach to watch the approach of the first European sailing ship they have seen. When the inhabitants of this floating island come ashore, your small world ceases to be isolated. The island is a ship, a big canoe with sails like wings. The crew are mainly white skinned, though some are like you but from some other island. They all speak a foreign language and communicate through gestures and by offering presents of axes, knives, cloth and tobacco. They want you to come away with them. Your mother is frightened and tries to stop you, but your father is eager to get the wondrous new goods and is willing to let you go, with your uncle and several other young men from your village.

Kidnapping and force

The description of the ship mistaken for an island comes from Buka island, adjoining larger Bougainville island, part of Papua New Guinea. This is the type of first contact scene that often confronted the earliest Pacific Islanders to enlist as labourers on plantations in Queensland, Fiji and Samoa, and elsewhere within the islands. Often the first labourers were obtained by trickery and violence. Also at Buka, in 1871 the crew from a ship named the *Carl*, operating out of Fiji, attracted curious people in their canoes out to the ship, smashed the canoes and forced them into the ship's hold. Frightened, mixed up with strangers in the dark, they tried to escape, rioted and were shot by the crew.

The voyage of the *Carl* is often quoted as if it were typical; it was not. During the second half of the nineteenth century and in the early years of this century, there were thousands of voyages involved as Europeans tapped into the vast reserve of labour in the Pacific. Most were uneventful. Historians have concluded that there was an early phase of kidnapping in most areas, for about a decade. This varied depending on the prior contact the people had with the outside world. If they were on a major shipping route, or in an area where whalers, pearlers, bêche-de-mer or sandalwood gatherers had worked, or on islands with missionaries or early European trading or government settlements, they were at least partially aware of what was being asked of them in terms of going away to plantations. The labour trade, as it is usually called, went on for several decades. Generation followed generation onto the decks of the schooners and brigs that passed through the islands recruiting labour. Whilst there can be no doubt that kidnapping occurred, it was not the normal situation. Islanders met European recruiters on the beaches, usually at passages through the surrounding reefs. Beyond the fringe of beach was impenetrable jungle. Curiosity and under-estimation of Europeans often lured them into danger once, but seldom twice. We lack respect for the intelligence of the people of the Pacific if we think they allowed themselves, for half a century, to be kidnapped off their own beaches by a handful of white men in rowing boats.

'Labour reserve' is a term used to describe the Pacific Islanders available for employment as labourers, as if they were a reservoir of human labour waiting to be tapped by capitalism. Pacific islands labour reserves emerged from early labour markets and networks of European expansion. In the second half of the nineteenth century there was heightened competition for labour in the South Pacific, particularly after the establishment of sugar plantations in Fiji and Queensland and copra plantations on most major islands.

The statistics on contracts, ages and movements indicate the complex nature of the labour trade. Ninety-five per cent of the labourers were males, aged from sixteen to thirty-five. The figures for each colony vary, depending on the period over which the labour migrations took place and the number of labourers, but close to one million indentured labour contracts were entered into by Pacific Islanders between 1850 and the beginning of the Pacific War in 1942.

Asian labour migration

It should also be noted that labour migration involved more than just the indigenous people of the Pacific: 600 000 Asian labourers migrated to the Pacific between the 1850s and the 1940s; 377 251 Chinese, Japanese, Korean and Filipino labourers were employed in Hawaii between 1852 and 1929. Fiji received 60 965 Indian labour migrants between 1879 and 1916, many of whom remained in Fiji. New Caledonia received approximately 47 400 Indian, Indo-Chinese, Japanese and Javanese labour immigrants between 1892 and 1939. Smaller numbers contracted or migrated freely to French Polynesia, the New Hebrides (Vanuatu), New Guinea and Samoa. For instance, 6984 Chinese went to Samoa between 1903 and 1934. Asian indentures decreased and disappeared after the First World War, the exceptions being the Japanese Mandated Territory of Micronesia, where Japanese labour was used, and Nauru. Although this chapter concentrates on indigenous labour recruiting, the indenture process was also used to bind Asian labourers to work in the Pacific Islands. Many were also on 'circular labour' contracts, meaning that they were recruited from their home countries and returned there after the period of work. But sufficient numbers of Asian labourers remained behind to be extremely significant forces in the populations of Fiji, New Caledonia and Hawaii.

The moving labour frontier

One element common to labour recruiting in the Pacific is movement of the recruiters over time, northwards on a water and island frontier quite like the land frontier in Australia. Since Europeans first settled in the Pacific, islanders had worked for traders, bêche-de-mer and sandalwood gatherers, or missionaries, but not in large numbers or through any organised and regulated system of labour recruitment. The first islander labourers to work in Australia came from southern Melanesia, briefly in the 1840s, then solidly on from the early 1860s. Recruiters moved north in search of labour, reaching the central Solomon Islands at the beginning of the 1870s, moving north to the archipelagoes off New Guinea in the late 1870s and 1880s. There was also a movement of the frontier from the coast to the inland on all of the islands. As Papua New Guinea was explored further and its colonial administration established, slowly, under German and British control from 1884, recruiters worked their way around the huge island of New Guinea, along the north and south coasts late in the nineteenth century and early this century. The densely populated New Guinea Highlands were not opened up by the colonial administration until after 1930. They became a focus for recruiting from the 1950s onwards, but even there the labour frontier gradually shifted west and south. This moving frontier rolled on for more than a century and in general terms the experiences of villages in the New Hebrides (Vanuatu) in the 1860s have quite a lot in common with those of the New Guinea Highlands in the 1960s, when faced with circular labour migration.

Health and mortality

The labour migrations were generally circular (that is, they came to work and then returned home), though the Asians tended to remain, as with the Indians in Fiji, or move on, as with Asians in Hawaii who moved to California. Most labourers from the South Pacific left their islands to work for a number of years, then returned home. One consequence of this was high mortality rates. The more isolated a human community, the more unique its disease environment is likely to become. The Pacific islands were isolated from the outside world and from each other. Labourers circulating from one area to another had little immunity from exposure to new diseases. Between the 1860s and 1900s in the Queensland labour trade, the average death rate was around 55 per 1000. The death rates for European males of a similar age (sixteen to thirty-five years old) in Queensland over a similar period was around 9 or 10 per 1000. The major killers were bacillary dysentery, respiratory tract infections such as tuberculosis, pneumonia, bronchitis and pleurisy. The next most important causes of death were other diseases of the gastro-intestinal tract, infectious diseases (particularly measles), and fevers.

The normal annual death rate among labourers in the Papuan gold fields in the early 1900s was about 100 per 1000 but occasionally went higher when epidemics struck. Other figures from Papua New Guinea in the 1920s and 1930s average out at around 15 to 30 per 1000 workers. Death rates fell after the Second World War with the introduction of modern drugs, but over the whole period of labour migration one of the saddest aspects of the labour migrations was the enormous costs in human lives.

The indenture system

Labourers were legally bound by indenture agreements, based on the much older master–servant relationship from Europe, under which they were obligated to work for a number of years (usually two or three but sometimes as many as five) at a set wage rate and set conditions. Usually the indenture agreements also included the arrangements to recruit the labourers from their villages and return them home at the end of the contract. A question often asked is whether indenture is the same as slavery? Slaves are owned as property and can be bought and sold. Entry into indentured employment was voluntary (in theory at least) and the system contained provisions to protect the labourers, as well as penal provisions to control them. But justice was pretty rough and ready in the colonies and on Pacific islands last century and early this century. The indenture system was certainly exploitative, in favour of the employers, and one historian has called it a 'new system of slavery'; but if we are strict with our definitions and not just dealing in rhetoric, it was not slavery.

Although the workers seldom chose to confront their employers directly, there is evidence that they resisted employers in various ways. Malingering and working slowly were typical ways of resisting, as were pretending to be ill, and sabotage to machinery, crops and work animals. Desertion was also common, and strikes did occur, such as a famous strike in Rabaul in 1929. Resistance did not always occur at work, nor was it always directed at employers. Fighting between groups of labourers was sometimes a way of releasing aggression that should probably have been focused on an unfair employer.

Cultural kidnapping

This raises other questions. If the majority were not kidnapped and were indentured labourers rather than slaves, does this make labour recruiting and indenture acceptable? Certainly the Europeans involved had a more global knowledge, were part of colonial capitalist societies and were taking advantage of people from small-scale societies in the islands. They had a cultural advantage and although physical kidnapping may have only been a brief phase, the phrase 'cultural kidnapping' has been used to describe the way in which the labour recruiters took advantage of the islanders' naiveté over the value of their labour and the low value of their wages and the goods with which they were paid.

Using 'cultural kidnapping' expands the simple division between labour recruits who were 'kidnapped' and those who enlisted voluntarily. By using this third category, we can more easily explain what occurred. It was usually not just a simple division between recruiting by deception and voluntary enlistment. The Pacific Islanders were being taken advantage of because of the cultural differences: relating first to the actual recruiting process, but also on the plantations in master–servant relations, and in the high value islanders placed on such cheap European manufactured goods as axes, guns, tobacco and cloth.

The only way to judge the motivations of the labourers is in terms of the value they attached to European goods within their own societies. To a person using stone tools and weapons, a steel axe was of enormous value, probably comparable today to replacing a handsaw with a chain saw, or replacing a wheel barrow with a truck. The comparison may seem extreme, but the difference in technology was very great.

The effect on island societies

Labour recruiting involved much more than just introducing new technologies at a village level. By the 1890s in Queensland, more than a quarter of the new recruits had already previously worked as labourers in Queensland, Fiji, Samoa or New Caledonia. Travel for exchange and trade was a way of life in the Pacific; by sea, such as the Kula trade of the Massim area in the islands to the east of Papua New Guinea; or by land in salt trading networks or Moka ceremonies in the New Guinea Highlands. The labourers incorporated travel to the plantations and mines into patterns of pre-contact mobility. Their behaviour while away was governed by the need to maintain links with their island homes and their families.

The returning labourers had an enormous impact on their own societies. A Solomon Islander who went to work in Fiji, Samoa or Queensland in the 1880s or 1890s and came home again had a box of European goods to distribute. In Melanesia possessions are not owned in the same way as Europeans conceive of property. Island societies work around displays of and distribution of wealth, and reciprocal gift exchanges and obligations. By going away to work and returning with valuable possessions, a male labourer was able by distribution of gifts to buy his way into the favours of his elders, who would be responsible for collecting the traditional bride wealth to exchange with another family to obtain him a wife. He would also progress socially much faster than his brother who had stayed at home. He would also be more worldly wise, particularly in future negotiations with Europeans. Today the process is less regulated but the majority of males in Vanuatu, the Solomon Islands and the Papua New Guinea Highlands, still migrate long distances to work over a period of years, then return to their villages.

Village leaders have often cooperated to make the migrant labour system operate effectively. But local men singled out by European labour recruiters to help in recruiting were not always of traditional importance. These men were more likely to have been labourers themselves, have some knowledge of what was required and have some knowledge of English, German or French, depending on the colony. They began to amass wealth, which was distributed in the usual way. The result was that within a generation of contact, the power base of local leadership could change totally.

If the men were the winners, generally the women were the losers. Very few women were recruited—probably no more than 5 per cent throughout the Melanesian labour trade. But women back in the male labourers' home villages often had to take on extra labour to compensate for the temporary loss of some of their menfolk. A dual dependence developed between the village and the colonial state. The rural wage was usually a bachelor wage and there was seldom provision for labourers to be accompanied by wives or families. The village community was responsible for the upbringing of the labourers and for their subsistence after retirement. The village economy subsidised the colonial economy. The colonial state supervised the recruiting process, regulating and monitoring the flow of labour, sometimes closing areas to recruiters. Much of the burden of making the colonial economies function fell on women in the villages. They sustained the gardens, kept the pigs and fulfilled family and community obligations while their sons and husbands went away to work for wages.

Class formation

Kastom (Pidgin for custom) is a term now used to describe the idealisation of the precolonial past. The development of *kastom*, Melanesian nationalism and class formation can be attributed in part to the circular labour migrations. To take the Queensland labour trade as an example, over the last four decades of the nineteenth century three distinct categories of Melanesian immigrants emerged:

1 FIRST-INDENTURE LABOURERS

First-indenture labourers served three-year contracts at six pounds ($12) per year, with food and accommodation. By the 1890s more than one-quarter of them had already served at least one labour contract in Queensland, Fiji, Samoa or New Caledonia.

2 TIME-EXPIRED LABOURERS

Throughout the 1880s and 1890s, 30 per cent of the labourers were time-expired, having served their first three-year contract and now free to re-enlist. They were mobile within districts, quite capable of negotiating with employers.

Table 7.1: Pacific Islander labour migration through regulated labour markets 1860s–1940s

Destination	Numbers	Years
Fiji	27,027	1865–1911
French Polynesia	2,558	1862–92
Hawaii	2,444	1864–85
Nauru	2,000	1880s–1914
New Hebrides (Vanuatu)	54,110	1908–41
New Caledonia	12,000 +	1867–1922
Papua New Guinea		
German New Guinea—Mandated Territory of New Guinea	379,600	1884–1940
British New Guinea—Australian Papua	280,154	1890–1941
Peru	3,634	1862–63
Queensland	62,475	1863–1904
Samoa	12,700 +	1867–1913
Solomon Islands	37,871	1913–40
Total	876,573 +	

Table 7.2: Major areas of Asian migration through regulated labour markets 1852–1942

Destination	Numbers	Years
Fiji	61,270	1879–1916
German New Guinea	6,364	1885–1914
Hawaii	377,251	1852–1929
Micronesia (excluding Kiribati and Nauru)	100,000	1920–42
New Caledonia	47,376	1864–1939
Samoa	6,984	1903–34
Total	599,245	

Tables 7.1 and 7.2 have been compiled from statistics taken from Doug Munro, 'The Origins of Labourers in the South Pacific: commentary and statistics', in C. Moore, J. Leckie and D. Munro (eds), *Labour in the South Pacific*, Department of History and Politics, and the Melanesian Studies Centre, James Cook University of North Queensland, Townsville, 1990, pp. xxxix–li.

3   TICKET-HOLDERS

In 1884 Queensland tightened regulations on Melanesian migration, except for those immigrants who had arrived earlier than 1879. They had complete freedom of occupation and their position in colonial society was closer to Queensland's European migrants than to first-indenture labourers. Between 1885 and 1906, each year between 7 and 11 per cent of the Melanesians were ticket-holders.

Conclusion

Given the high incidence of re-engaging, and the scale of the time-expired market, it could be argued that for many Pacific Islanders the labour trade became a way of life. In Queensland, beginning in the mid-1880s, re-enlisting, time-expired and ticket-holding men and women comprised 40 to 60 per cent of the islanders in Queensland

and were beginning to form the base of a Melanesian segment of the general working class, as distinct from indentured servants. In 1906–08, when the majority of the islanders were deported, almost 2500 (including their families) were able to stay, most from the time-expired and ticket-holding groups. Today their 15 000 descendants are Australian, but maintain their links with the islands.

In Papua New Guinea more than one million people worked for wages between 1884 and Independence in 1975. In the Solomon Islands and Vanuatu virtually every adult male now leaves his village to work on a neighbouring island as a labourer at some time in his life. Meanwhile in rural areas, cash crops such as coffee, cocoa and copra are grown by subsistence farmers, often using local casual labour. In the nineteenth century a working class was slow to develop as governments maintained a dual economic system, with circulating labour moving from the modern capitalist sector to the rural subsistence sector. Since the 1960s in Papua New Guinea and in other Melanesian nations, an urban working class has developed. There is also an urban middle class in the capital cities and the small towns, based on the families of politicians, bureaucrats, businessmen and women, and church leaders. Particularly in Papua New Guinea, the mobility has led to the beginning of a floating group of landless rural and urban workers who are alienated from both their villages and the cities.

Large-scale labour recruiting and indenture was a feature of colonial Melanesia for a century after the 1860s. The labourers, mainly young men, were the human ingredient in Pacific capitalism and were crucial participants in culture contact and change in the South Pacific.

DOCUMENTS

1 Extracts from the Queensland Act (1868)

31 Victoria No. 47 Polynesian Labourers Act

15. All masters of vessels about to proceed to the South Sea Islands in order to obtain labourers therefrom shall enter into a bond in form B with two sufficient sureties for the prevention of kidnapping and for the due observance of these regulations so far as they are concerned.

8(3) [Proper means have to be taken] by the Immigrant Agent or other officer by explanations questions and enquiries amongst the labourers themselves to ascertain whether they have a proper understanding of the conditions of the agreements and did voluntarily enter into same ...

13 No transfer of an immigrant shall be made except with the full consent of the transferor the immigrant and the Government ... and no immigrant shall be allowed to leave his employment under transfer until the same has been recorded in the books of the Immigrant Agent or other appointed office ...

FORM D.

MEMORANDUM OF AGREEMENT made this day between   of   of the first part and   native of   per ship   of the second part The conditions are that the said party of the second part engages to serve to the said party of the first part as a   and otherwise to make   generally useful for the term of   calendar months and also to obey all   or   overseer's or authorised agents lawful and reasonable commands during that period in consideration of which services the said party of the first part doth hereby agree to pay the said party of the second part wages at the rate of not less than six pounds (£6) per annum to provide   with the understated rations daily to provide suitable clothing and proper lodging accommodation and to defray the expense of   conveyance to the place at which to be employed to pay wages in the coin of the realm at the end of each year of the agreement and provide them with a return passage to their native Island at the expiration of three years. No wages shall be deducted for medical attendance.

DAILY RATION.

				lbs.	ozs.
Beef or mutton (or 2 lbs. of fish)...	...	...	...	1	0
Bread or flour	...	...	...	1	0
Molasses (or sugar)	...	...	...	0	5
Vegetables (or rice 4 oz. or maize meal 8 oz.)		...		2	0
Tobacco per week	...	...	...	0	1½
Salt, per week	...	...	...	0	2
Soap (per week)	...	...	...	0	4

CLOTHING.

					Yearly.
Shirts (one of flannel or serge)	...	...	...		2
Trowsers pairs	...	...	...		2
Hat	...	...	...	...	1
Blankets	...	...	...	...	1 pair

In witness whereof they have mutually affixed their signatures to this document.
Witness:

The above contract was explained in my presence to the said immigrants and signed before me by them with their names or marks and by   or his authorised agent at   this   day of   186 .

G.H.

Immigration Agent or Customs House Officer.

Registered at the   office Brisbane Queensland this   day of   186 .

G.H.

Immigration Agent

2   Losing his brother

Faith Bandler from Murwillumbah talks about Wacvie Missington from Biap district, Ambrym Island.

Wacvie swam back to the rock. He was only there for a few moments when he saw something that made his heart thump in his chest like the beating of a drum. It was a boat. As it came from the south, it seemed at first like a white, thick wave, but it was a boat. Although he had seen other boats come into his cove, this one filled him with fear. He stood erect and still, remembering that boats with white wings brought the people with pink skins and yellowish hair, people who gave them knives and axes and beads.

The last time they had come, he had observed that the strangers had long lengths of rope. After they had lured one of his brothers and other men of Biap towards their boat, they had thrown the rope over their heads and pulled them roughly aboard, had taken they away. Some of the older people were saying it would be three moons and then his brother would come back. Now three moons and more had come and gone, but his brother had not returned.

—Faith Bandler, *Wacvie*, Rigby, Adelaide, 1977, pp. 14–15

3   Going home and coming back

Noel Fatnowna from Mackay discusses the case of Kwailiu and Laefira Fatnowna from Fataleka district, Malaita Island

Kwailiu began to think about whether they would go home; whether, if they decided to go, they would be taken to the right island or taken some other place, left to be killed and eaten far from their homeland ... In the end, they had little choice but to go back, when their time was up. And they missed their home, their families ...

Since his return to the islands, he sometimes felt rebellious in his mind. Something kept pulling at his thoughts, even when he was walking round in the bush, going to the gardens, listening to the tribal elders speaking, and discussing the ancient ways of his people. Always in the back of his mind were the canefields of Queensland, the plantations, the other life he knew so well now ...

It was these thoughts, the mixture of memories of good and bad times, that made him think about going back to Queensland. He wanted to try the white man again. He thought he could tackle him now. He wanted to see if he could survive. The white man had axes, guns, and plenty of things he couldn't get in the Solomon Islands.

—Noel Fatnowna, *Fragments of a Lost Heritage*, Angus and Robertson, Sydney, 1989, pp. 101–2, 104

4 Kidnapped?

Ivy Thomas was born in 1914 near Mackay. Her mother, Katie Marller, was born on Aoba Island in what is now Vanuatu (New Hebrides) in the 1860s. Her father, Willie Marlla, was from Fiji. They met at Mackay.

Mother's island name was Natofelinga, she was born in 'Opa' [Aoba island, Vanuatu] a little island in the South Seas, in the Passage of Walariki in the year 1860. She was blackbirded from her little island when she was about fifteen years old.

It was a bright sunny day and my mother and her little girl friend [Jessie Querro] were walking along the island beach, gathering sea shells, to make necklaces for themselves. They saw two dark men coming towards them in a rowing boat, from a sailing ship which was anchored off the island. They were put on board.

The ship was the *Borough Bell*. The Captain of the ship gave them calico clothes to wear and they were all put down into the ship's hold until they left the islands. When Mother arrived at Mackay she worked for the plantation owners; they taught her how to do house-work, and they was taught how to cut cane.

When Mother went home on the *Jabberwock* to the island she took my sister to see her people, but she could not settle down and only stayed nine months, then returned to Mackay and settled down.

—Ivy Thomas, edited extract from 'History of My Mother's Life',
written in the 1960s.

5 Cultural kidnapping?

Henry Stevens Quaytucker's father Kwaitaka (Quaytucker) was born in the 1860s. Kwaitaka recruited to escape retaliation after he killed his sister's boyfriend. He was from the bush in Malaita and enlisted in 1888 on the Myrtle. *He first worked around Ingham, then for the rest of his life at Mackay. He married the daughter of another Malaitan and died in 1919. His son Henry was born in 1911. In 1974, Henry described Malaitan recruiting:*

Some of them said that they saw the full moon when they left their country, and they saw another full moon before they came to Australia. On the way some of them died—over the side.

Time meant nothing to us fellers, time means nothing for a coloured man. Even today, the greatest thing for an Islander is time. We always used to go by the moon. They thought that they would be out there for five or six moons—six full moons—that's nothing. They didn't understand. The first lot came and they seen this, but they never brought nothing with them and then they went back and said 'good country here'. So the next lot would go and bring some foods with them to plant.

6 A massacre on a labour recruiting schooner

In the Kwaio district of Malaita, one of the Solomon Islands in 1886, when attempting to capture a ship, a large number of islanders were killed in the fighting. The surviving crew of the Young Dick *managed to regain control of the ship.*

The following account, told by Talaunga'i of Malaita Island, was recorded in 1966. It is interesting as a piece of labour trade history, but also to illustrate the accuracy of oral testimony over long periods preserved in this case in a stylised narrative. The massacre on the Young Dick *was motivated by a reward (blood money) put up because of the death of the son of one important man. Recruiting from the area increased after the massacre as men left to escape the expected retaliation from a naval ship.*

There was the ship that Arumae and his men attacked down there at Sinalagu; the Tetefou people and their allies. He and his men went. They got to the ship. Only three white men were on the ship then. The rest of them had gone in the ship's boat to Lalobala. They went to pick up recruits at Lalobala.

The three white men were left aboard. The captain was in his cabin. [Actually it was the Government Agent.] Arumae warned his son Fa'auta, 'Not yet; I'll have to take care of the captain in the cabin'. [Literally, 'I haven't hit his body yet.'] But Fa'auta went ahead and struck the first blow against the crewman outside. A second man ran away into the cabin. Arumae grabbed him by the arm, like this [demonstrates]. He pulled and pulled on his arm, to get him from the cabin, but then a timber came back and blocked the cabin door. The captain grabbed a gun in the cabin. He shot Fa'auta. He fell down dead. Then the captain shot Fi'oi. He died. Then he shot Kwainaakwa. He died.

Tafa'au [shortened form of Taafana'au] was killed too. Arumae called for his death and Lamoka killed him. That was because of Tafa'au's son Boosui. Tafa'au had put up blood money to avenge his death; and they killed Tafa'au because [Arumae's son] Fa'auta had fallen. Arumae's thinking went like this: 'You Tafa'au, put up blood money for a ship to be taken to avenge your son Boosui, and now Fa'auta has been killed and his body abandoned because of it.' The captain shot six people. Tafa'au was the seventh who died. And there were the two white men they had killed aboard the ship as well.

—Roger M. Keesing, 'The *Young Dick* Attack: Oral and documentary history on the colonial frontier', *Ethnohistory*, 33:3 (1986), pp. 278–9

7   A labour trade captain defends himself

William T. Wawn, a labour trade captain, defended himself against accusations in the report of an 1885 Royal Commission into Recruiting. This document is from a letter to the editor of The Brisbane Courier *in 1885.*

Sir.—Three weeks ago I addressed a letter to you, which appeared in your columns, commenting on some words of Mr. Griffith's [Premier of Queensland] at the late Maryborough banquet. He accused me and others of obtaining Polynesian recruits from the vicinity of New Guinea—I took none from the mainland—by fraud or force. His accusation was founded on the lying and interested evidence of Kanakas. Mr. Griffith further stated that the Commissioner's Report would be published shortly, he has been in possession of this Report three weeks, but I have heard nothing of any result. Weeks previous to the Report, I was told at the Immigration Office that I was debarred from going to the islands in the labour trade, until, at any rate, the Report was published, but no specific reasons were assigned.

Twice I applied for an interview with the Premier, but was told it was impossible, through press of public business. I have had employment offered me twice, but was debarred from accepting it. Even here this groundless accusation stands in my way.

I have been ten years in the trade, and have always acted in accordance with both the letter and the spirit of the law to the best of my ability; I court inquiry into all my actions; the only unpleasantness with the Immigration Office having been when I could not agree with drunken or otherwise incompetent Government agents.

If I have done wrong, how is it that I am at liberty and not hunted into gaol alongside the *Hopeful* and *Ethel* unfortunates? [Crew from these ships were tried and convicted of kidnapping.] But, if not guilty, why should I be punished by being debarred from engaging in that branch of my profession from which my long experience peculiarly fits me?

It is a Briton's birthright to have a fair trial before punishment, when Mr. Griffith denies me that, he may be acting as a Queensland politician and minister, but not as an impartial judge.

I am, sir, your obedient servant,
W.T. WAWN
Late Master, Polynesian Labour Trade

8   The problem of feedback in oral testimony

Esther Henaway was born at Halifax, near Ingham in 1907. Her father Pargosuggi, was from Epi island and her mother Lemarler Backo from Tongo island, both in the New Hebrides (Vanuatu). Esther Henaway's comments follow:

They used to come to the ships when they see the ships come in. They'd bring their food to trade and the captain would give they knives and beads and things like that, or invite they to come and have a look at the ship. And invite they all up and sometimes they used to get about thirty. Well, they just put them in the hold and that was it. The canoes were left and they didn't dare go back to the same islands again.

... Never told them nothing until they got out here and they can't read or write. They got them to sign this agreement and put a cross on it and each black would make his cross a different way, and that was his signature. He was told, you stop with me three years.

Interviewer:

Have you heard of many cases of the ones that did go back being put down at the wrong place, not their own bay?

Not actually, only what I read. It's a book, by a white chap [Peter Corris] who had travelled all over finding these things about Kanakas. And most of those things that are written in there that I've read exactly happened to my parents. Almost to the letter.

—interview recorded by Clive Moore

9   Girmitiyas: Indian indentured labourers in Fiji

The picture which has emerged suggests that indentured migration was much more complex and varied than has generally been realised. In particular the migrants do not always appear as helpless victims of external forces, as pawns in the hands of unscrupulous recruiters, but also as actors in their own right, responding variously to circumstances affecting them in the late nineteenth and early twentieth centuries.

The important role of deception in inducing migration cannot, however, be denied, because recruitment was carried out on a commercial basis and involved poor and illiterate peasants. The real question is one of perspective and degree. Seen in the context of the nineteenth century and of other types of labour migration from other countries such as China, it has to be admitted that tragic and sensational as the cases of deception in Indian migration were, there was nothing really exceptional about them. This is said not to justify, explain or rationalise those unhappy events that did occur, but to suggest that an awareness of similar experiences elsewhere should put the role of deception in Indian indenture into perspective.

—Brij V. Lal, *Girmitiyas: The origins of the Fiji Indians, The Journal of Pacific History*, Canberra, 1983, p. 129. (Dr Lal is the grandson of Girmitiyas.)

QUESTIONS AND ACTIVITIES

1   What problems was the 1868 Polynesian Labourers Act (Document 1) aiming to clear up?

2   Of the three categories (kidnapping, voluntary indenture and cultural kidnapping) mentioned in this chapter, in which category would Wacvie's recruiting experience (Document 2) belong?

3   What attitudes led to Kwailiu (Document 3) signing on again for Queensland? Into which category would his recruiting experience belong?

4   Compare Wacvie (Document 2), Kwailiu (3), Katie Marller (4) and Henry Kwaitaka's (5) recruiting stories. What are the common elements in their experiences? How important were stories told about Queensland in enticing these recruits to sign on? What was the appeal of Queensland?

5   In what ways was the attempted capture of the *Young Dick* (Document 6) related to complex relationships in Malaitian society?

6   What is your opinion about the evidence provided by W.T. Wawn (Document 7) in his defence against accusations of improper recruiting practices? If the Queensland Premier had written a reply, what might he have written? Draft a response to Wawn's newspaper letter taking the role of either a Queensland sugar planter, the Premier or a fellow labour recruiting master.

7   Explain why there is a difference between the historian Corris's research and book (Document 8) and the stories passed down from one generation to the next.

8   What might be the historian Brij Lal's opinion (Document 9) on the three categories suggested by Clive Moore?

9   Why does Brij Lal suggest there was 'nothing really exceptional' about indenture and the signing on of Indians for Fiji?

REFERENCES

Corris, P., *Passage, Port and Plantation: A history of Solomon Islands labour migration, 1870–1914*, Melbourne University Press, Melbourne, 1973

Moore, C.R., *Kanaka: A history of Melanesian Mackay*, Institute of Papua New Guinea Studies and University of Papua New Guinea Press, Port Moresby, 1985

Moore, C.R., Leckie, J., and Munro, D. (eds), *Labour in the South Pacific*, History Department and Centre for Melanesian Studies, James Cook University of North Queensland, Townsville, 1990

Newbury, Colin, 'The Melanesian Labour Reserve: some reflections on Pacific labour markets in the nineteenth century', *Pacific Studies*, Vol. 4 (1), 1980, pp. 1–25

Chapter 8
Response and Change in Polynesian Societies

Caroline Ralston, Macquarie University

Introduction

Across the Pacific, island societies came into varying degrees of contact with Europeans before Imperial powers imposed formal colonial rule upon them. In many parts of Polynesia, the islanders had experienced more than fifty years of intensive beachcomber, trader, missionary and planter activity by that time. In contrast, there were parts of Melanesia whose people did not see a white person until decades of colonial rule had been established. A Hawaiian living close to the port town of Honolulu in the late 1890s, just before America annexed the archipelago, would probably have been literate, a practising Christian, accustomed to wearing cotton clothing, and using a wide range of European manufactured articles. Her counterpart in the Solomon Islands may have heard of a new religion brought by white strangers, none of whom she had seen, despite the fact that some were very interested in recruiting the menfolk of her clan to go away for long periods of time. Some steel goods may have arrived in her area, including firearms, but traditional settlement patterns, subsistence practices and ways of living were little changed.

Islanders responded in a variety of different ways to the opportunities and challenges which confronted them with the introduction of new goods, economic and political processes and religious ideas. These responses depended on many factors, including the islanders' traditional cultural practices and outlooks, and the number of foreigners and intensity of contact individual island groups experienced. In this chapter we will be looking particularly at the changes that had occurred in Polynesian societies by the end of the nineteenth century.

Even within this fairly unified cultural area, the degree and the rate of change experienced differed greatly. Obviously, for the many Polynesians who were attracted into the recently developed port towns of Honolulu, Papeete, Levuka and Apia, life was very different from that experienced by their counterparts in places distant from these centres of foreign activity. But despite the variety of changes, certain patterns of response can be discerned, which help answer the question: How much had islanders' lives changed by the end of the nineteenth century?

Economic changes in Polynesia

The introduction of a range of foreign goods, from iron axes to fish-hooks to matches and cotton cloth, reduced the number of hours men needed to grind and polish many stone tools, and to make fish-hooks, and that women spent making tapa and weaving mats. The men's stone and shell working skills were rapidly lost, but because tapa and mats remained essential for numerous cultural activities, women retained the requisite techniques as well as acquiring the skills required to sew, wash and iron the newly

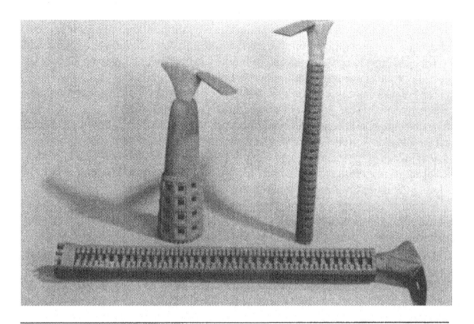

Figure 8.1: Austral Island ceremonial adzes.

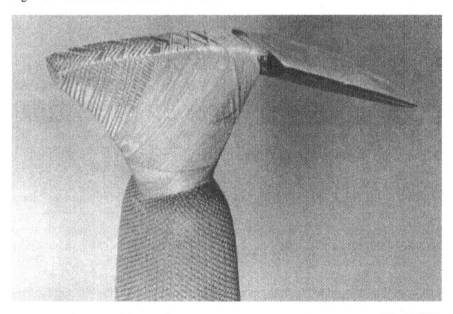

Figure 8.2: Austral Island ceremonial adze.

introduced fabric. In terms of labour-saving devices, the advantage iron had over stone and shell, benefited men more than the introduction of cotton cloth benefited women, who still had to make tapa and mats, and also sew and care for new clothing.

It is not possible to discover precisely how the men filled their spare hours available to them, but some became involved in the new religious learning and leadership roles available to them, while others within trading distance of the new port towns cultivated and sold the newly introduced crops favoured by the foreigners, including white potato, pumpkins and melon. In several societies there was the flowering of intricate wood carving and elaborate feather working stimulated by the new tools available and the greater knowledge of the cultural artefacts from other Polynesian societies. Polynesian women also created new designs and techniques in tapa and mat making, as well as becoming exquisite seamstresses and embroiderers.

The Polynesians' vigorous incorporation of new processes and skills into their lives reveals that they were not overwhelmed or demoralised by the foreign intrusion. Despite the persistent belief amongst Europeans both at the time of contact and later that the islanders suffered a fatal impact to their cultural vitality and integrity, there is clear evidence of the resilience and integrative abilities of Polynesian cultures. This evidence has not convinced all writers on Pacific contact, some of whom were still offering 'fatal impact' interpretations in the 1980s.

Instead of assuming inevitable cultural decline, each Polynesian group must be carefully studied, and the effects of the newly introduced diseases to which the islanders had no immunity, and any other negative impacts of contacts must be weighed against the new directions taken and new patterns that were woven into Polynesian cultures. It is also important to remember that while many nineteenth century Polynesians willingly incorporated new goods and ideas into their current ways of living they could have no knowledge of the possible, long-term consequences of these changes, for example, the impact of the loss of self-sufficiency or the impact of literacy on an oral culture.

The loss of self-sufficiency

In island groups such as Hawaii, Tahiti, the northern shores of New Zealand and Samoa after 1840, which experienced a steady arrival of foreign vessels, the spread of certain basic foreign goods, particularly axes, knives, fish-hooks, cotton cloth, matches, and soap, was widespread, and they rapidly became essentials. The advantages these goods offered the Polynesians in comparison to traditional counterparts were appreciated but once they became necessities, the Polynesians had to supply items valued by the foreigners in exchange for them. The self-sufficiency these communities had enjoyed in pre-contact times was breached and the long process of incorporation into a foreign, world economy had begun.

In the early years the islanders had a variety of natural resources to offer: sandalwood from Hawaii, Fiji and the Marquesas, pork from Tahiti, timber and flax from New Zealand, and provisions from many parts of the Pacific. In time, however, the more lucrative products were depleted and the islanders became increasingly dependent on coconut oil and copra products or the sale of their labour or land, to buy the foreign goods which had become necessities. By the end of the century, many Polynesians also needed cash to pay taxes, church dues and school fees. Marine products and subsistence farming still provided the predominant part of Polynesian diet, but certain foreign goods and cash had also become important items in their lives. Amongst the ordinary Polynesians, men had greater access to cash than women since their labour was in greater demand, so the missionaries offered them more intensive and extended educational advantages, and they had greater marketing opportunities.

The impact of Christianity

The acceptance of Christianity brought changes to many levels of Polynesians' lives. The personal, religious experiences are the most difficult to examine. Few converts left records of the progress or inner meanings of their conversions, but more public changes can be discerned. Church services, choral singing and the new religious personnel, especially pastors and teachers, became integral parts of village life. New concepts of modesty, clothing requirements, notions of time and patterns of work were gradually incorporated into daily life.

At the more personal level, ideas about the nature, roles and responsibilities of men and women were also undergoing change. Both missionaries and certain island rulers valued peace and wanted to see established stable, political regimes in which the new religion and trading opportunities would flourish. The decline of warfare in many societies and the consequent devaluing of the warrior's role deeply affected concepts of masculinity. To counter balance these losses, Polynesian men found new avenues to prestige and value in leadership roles in church affairs and politics, and in trading and labouring activities with foreigners, who all expected men to be exclusively involved in these areas.

The missionaries put great emphasis on the importance of the nuclear family, the husband–wife bond, the adult male role as provider and the domestic responsibilities of women, especially bearing and raising children and sustaining the family unit. In pre-contact times, Polynesian women had played essential roles in large-scale societal and kin activities. But with the advent and acceptance of Christianity, women's lives became more circumscribed, and less valued by society as a whole. Missionaries, some Europeans in the islands and others back in Europe believed that Christianity and nineteenth century, middle class, Western models of appropriate gender relations would improve the lot of Polynesian women, but in fact it can be argued that the combined impacts of new goods, new economic practices and Christian precepts increased the burden of work for women at the same time as it devalued their contribution to society.

Changes in the political sphere

Incoming foreign captains, traders and missionaries sought out male rulers with whom to negotiate; their records give us insights into the activities and varying fortunes of individual male chiefs. The foreigners, not expecting to have to deal with powerful women, ignored the female chiefs, sometimes to their own detriment, as Bingham, leader of the Protestant mission in Hawaii eventually recognised. It was only after three or four years that the missionaries realised their efforts should be focused upon the extremely powerful female chief, Ka'ahumanu, rather than the titular monarch, Kamehameha II, who was relatively powerless. In 1825, after the mission changed strategy, mass conversion occurred under the auspices of Ka'ahumanu. In most Polynesian societies, however, the power of chiefly women was diminished, as their male counterparts enhanced their positions.

In Tahiti, Hawaii and Tonga certain astute, high-ranking, male chiefs variously combined traditional skills and practices, and the opportunities provided by new goods, especially firearms and ammunition, foreign personnel and religious ideas, to establish island-wide monarchies. The debate between historians whether it was the traditional strengths or new opportunities which were the deciding factors in the creation of these new island monarchies remains unresolved, but it is significant that in pre-contact times attempts at island-wide rule had not been sustained.

In Tahiti between 1770 and 1815, a struggle ensued between the highest ranked, chiefly groups to win the right to rule the entire island. The male chiefs Pomare I and II combined traditional attributes of power with the use of foreign firearms and the material backing and concepts of the missionaries who had settled in Tahiti in 1796.

The firearms had become available through the activities of the New South Wales pork traders and were sometimes used for the chiefs by resident beachcombers. In 1815 Pomare II was finally successful in uniting the island under his rule, but the Pomare family's hegemony was challenged after his death by recently defeated chiefs.

Kamehameha I in Hawaii and Taufa'ahau in Tonga also used traditional assets and the new opportunities available to them to create island kingdoms. In these groups daily life became more secure for the ordinary people with the cessation of warfare, but in economic and political spheres the power of the ruling elite was increased. In other parts of Polynesia, ambitious chiefs eagerly traded in firearms, harboured beachcombers in their midst and accepted a missionary in the hope of gaining access to the new learning and the new trade, but no one individual was able to establish himself as paramount ruler.

By the end of the nineteenth century in Hawaii, Samoa and Fiji, foreign planters had appeared in the islands demanding land, security of tenure to that land and access to reliable labour supplies, all of which had serious repercussions on chiefly power and authority. In the political sphere, enormous changes had occurred throughout Polynesia during the nineteenth century. The fortunes of chiefly families had waxed and waned, largely influenced by their access and control over foreign activities. By the end of the century, and much earlier in some Polynesian societies, the threat to island political autonomy was very great indeed.

Major economic developments

Increased foreign trading activities throughout Polynesia led to the rise of the port towns of Honolulu in Hawaii in the 1810s, Papeete in Tahiti in the 1820s, Kororareka, in the Bay of Islands, New Zealand, in the late 1820s, Levuka in Fiji in the 1830s, and Apia in Samoa in the 1840s. These towns appeared in areas that had been of no significance to the islanders in pre-contact times, but such were the opportunities they offered that both political elites and ordinary islanders moved in. At different times the ruling families in the respective archipelagoes recognised the port town area as the

Figure 8.3: Levuka, Ovalau, in 1854.

Figure 8.4: Kororareka, Bay of Islands, New Zealand, 1836.

centre of political power. The towns became the focus of trade, since the incoming foreign vessels concentrated their activities in these harbours. Islanders who wanted access to foreign goods either moved in permanently or had to come in to trade and then return to outlying islands.

The career of the Hawaiian high chief, Boki, illustrates many of the economic and political changes that occurred in Polynesia and the resultant conflicts that individual chiefs experienced. Closely related to the Hawaiian King Kamehameha I, Boki was sent by him to the newly established area of Honolulu in 1818, to control the foreign shipping, increasingly using that harbour. In 1820 Boki was ordered to build houses for the newly arrived Protestant missionaries, who set up their headquarters in Honolulu. In 1823 he travelled to England with Kamehameha II, who died there. On Boki's return to Hawaii in 1825 the missionaries were surprised, but also delighted that he called for calm Christian mourning and orderly funeral ceremonies. In the next four years Boki became closely involved with the sandalwood traders in Honolulu, set up stores and a hotel, but none of his economic ventures was successful. His association with the mission and their schools was half-hearted. He admired certain parts of Western learning but he was also deeply committed to many aspects of traditional culture. Divided between two worlds, Boki was ineffectual in both. In the political sphere, he was the focus of a rival faction within the Kamehameha family, but he was never able to confront successfully the female chief, Ka'ahumanu, who was

Figure 8.5: Chief Boki and his wife, Lilihi, in London, 1824.

acting as regent during the minority of Kamehameha III. Finally, in late 1829, overburdened with debts to foreign traders and politically frustrated, he set sail for the New Hebrides, where there were abundant supplies of sandalwood. He was never heard of again but his life exemplifies the opportunities, challenges and conflicts, chiefly Polynesians faced after the intrusion of the West.

The diminution of islander political and economic power

In an attempt to regulate interactions between foreigners and islanders, the imperial powers from the 1820s onwards, made local appointments or sent junior consuls to the island groups in which port towns

Figure 8.6: George Pritchard, c. 1840.

developed. Their presence did little to protect the power of indigenous authorities, who had no knowledge or understanding of the roles of consuls or the very limited power they could legally exercise. George Pritchard, an ex-missionary and consul from Tahiti, was appointed British consul to Samoa, where he landed at Apia in 1845. Rather than promoting fair transactions between Samoans and British residents, Pritchard turned his consulate building into a public house, thereby flaunting the Samoan chiefs' laws against the importation of liquor, threatened the chiefs with British gunboats when they ignored his advice and in the 1850s set up a foreign residents' protection society in opposition to Samoan authority. His presence and activities in Apia were a continual source of disruption to the chiefs, whose authority was ignored and overridden. Pritchard was a particularly vexatious and partisan consul, but nowhere in Polynesia did consuls enhance or protect indigenous political power.

At the same time that indigenous political power was being eroded, the establishment of large foreign trading companies, dealing particularly in copra, and the arrival of planters, were consolidating the foreigners' economic ascendancy. During the early trading period islanders had control over relatively lucrative trading items, including sandalwood, bêche-de-mer, pork, pearls and pearl shell. But once these assets had been stripped from the islands, they had little to offer except coconut products, their labour and with the arrival of planters, their land. Increasingly, islanders were forced to the economic periphery, unable to compete with the large companies or the encroaching planters.

Conclusion

The formal loss of political control symbolised by the establishment of colonial rule occurred right across Polynesia. It began with the incorporation of New Zealand into the British Empire in 1840 and continued until Hawaii's and Samoa's loss of independence in 1899. Within each individual island society, the opportunities offered by new goods and ideas had been enthusiastically embraced by Polynesians, but the consequences and developments that intrusion from the West involved were only revealed with time.

Individuals had acquired new items of dress, new living patterns, new religious beliefs, and certain new economic activities, but kin, community and land, and respect for chiefly authority remained at the core of their being. Many of the changes had been assimilated into Polynesian values and cultural patterns. On the level of island societies, the male chiefs who had increased their power and status since the arrival of the foreigners found their positions challenged from within by rival, recently dispossessed factions, and from outside by the increasing intervention of foreign consuls, naval officers, company traders and planters.

This chapter has focused on Polynesia, because by the end of the nineteenth century these islanders had experienced between fifty and one hundred years of contact with foreigners. In contrast, foreign intervention into the islands of Melanesia had been much more sporadic and isolated. Missionary forays had been made into the area from the late 1830s onwards, but few conversions had occurred and many missionaries had died in the attempt, or been forced to withdraw. Sandalwood had been exported from the New Hebrides and the Solomons in the 1840s and 1850s and increasing amounts of labour from the 1860s, but few foreigners settled, no port towns developed, no foreign consuls were appointed. For the majority of Melanesians, the changes in political power and economic activity, in religious belief, and patterns of daily living which Polynesians experienced throughout the nineteenth century were to be twentieth century, colonial phenomena.

DOCUMENTS

1 'Everything is changed ... '

Ka'ahumanu:

... But everything is changed with the coming of foreigners. Their wealth, ships, guns, these things change everything. They have made the power of the chiefs weak. I make a law against the sale of rum. A ship comes full of men eager for drink. If the captain does not like the kapu he says 'sell us rum or we'll fire our cannon on your town'. Or perhaps he sends an angry mob to fight and make trouble. What am I to do? Keep the law and have destruction? If we engage him in battle more and more ships with guns will come from his country. Should I relent and give him rum, this makes the chiefs look weak. What will I do? In former days, I did not hesitate to act. My mind did not trouble me. The way was clear. I was not afraid to do away with what I knew to be false or to take up what I wished. But now ...

Hannah:

Everything has changed so much. I know.

Ka'ahumanu:

Ae, the chiefs pass. All the old ones, my counsellors and friends, Keopoulani, gone. My own Kaumuali'i, gone! Liholiho gone! Kalanimoku grows so old. His strength fades. Our people die. I feel as if I am surrounded by darkness ...

—from V.N. Kneubuhl, *The Conversion of Ka'ahumanu*
(unpublished script of a play), 1988, p. 50

2 The God of white men

Ka'ahu:

But my heart still holds itself back from your god. You see, I remember the old days. The gods ruled over us in ways I did not like. So when I saw a chance, I took them down. I did away with them. But this new god, your god; I have seen what happens to those who choose him. He has a strong hold on their hearts. I know if I take this god, the people will follow.

Sybil (wife of a missionary):

As they have always followed you.

Ka'ahu:

But I would never be able to change the beliefs of the people once this god took hold.

Sybil:

He is strength.

Ka'ahu:

He is the god of white men.

Sybil:

Yes.

Ka'ahu:

And it seems that the haole wish to be god over all. I will never be able to stop them here. There are too many ships, too many guns, too many diseases. If I take up this god perhaps there will be some good, some peace. Other nations will see that we believe in the same god and not think us ignorant savages. I know all the names foreigners have for us, but some will want to protect a Christian people from wrong.

—from V.N. Kneubuhl, *The Conversion of Ka'ahumanu*
(unpublished script of a play), 1988, pp. 73–4

3   Civilising the Marquesans

Civilising them [the Marquesans] in its essence was giving them a different sense of time. This new sense of time was not just a concern with regularity, although that was important. Making seven days in a week and one of them a sabbath, making meal-times in a day, making work-time and leisure-time, making sacred time and profane time laid out time in a line, as it were. It removed the irregularity of time in *mau* [memorial feasts] and *koino* [feasts] with their peaks of intensity of preparation and participation and their troughs of inactivity. It removed the cyclical time of rituals in which a legendary past was re-enacted to legitimate and prolong the present. Most important in the new sense of time was a notion of progress and of a break-out from the present. A notion of progress called for a self and a social discipline informed by an image of the future. There was plenty of self and social discipline among Enata [the Marquesans]: their *tapu* [sacred laws] were stringent and their co-ordination in public works, such as making *paepae* [stone platforms] and canoes was remarkable. But their discipline serviced the cyclical renewal of themselves. By it they held themselves always in their present.

—Greg Dening, *Islands and Beaches, Discourse on a Silent Land: Marquesas 1774–1880*, Melbourne University Press, 1980, p. 264

4   The role of women: one view

Although the circumstances of the females [of Rimatara in the Austral Islands] were considerably ameliorated by the abolition of idolatry, yet the cultivation of the ground, and other kinds of labour unsuitable to their sex, were still performed by them. During his [1825] visit, Mr Bourne [a LMS missionary] at a public meeting, proposed an alteration to their established usage in this respect, which was alike derogatory to the female, and mimical to an improvement in morals. Each chief present expressed his sentiments in favour of the proposal, and the result, was an unanimous declaration 'that from that day forward, the men should dig, plant, and prepare the food, and the women make cloth, bonnets, and attend to the householdwork.' The change thus introduced, by instituting a suitable division of labour, has proved favourable to domestic virtue and social happiness, while it has augmented the means of subsistence, and the sources of comfort.

—William Ellis, *Polynesian Researches*, 4 Vols, Fisher & Son, London, 1831, Vol. III, pp. 392–3

5   The role of women: another view

You [the Hawaiians] should act thus. Let the wife remain at home and put the house in order, and the husband go out and cultivate the land, day by day. Be industrious, and fit up your houses and house lots, furnish yourselves with seats, beds, plates, bowls, knives, spoons and glasses; provide separate sleeping rooms for parents and children; and increase the produce of your lands. Rest not until you are comfortably supplied with all good things. Plant all kinds of good trees on your lands ...

Take proper care also of your children, that you be not destitute of heirs. Let the daughters remain at home with their mothers, and learn to sew, wash, iron; to make mats and hats, and to seek after knowledge. The little girls should go to school. The older boys should go out to work with their fathers.

—*The Polynesian* (newspaper), 1850

6   A struggle for power

Among the Hawaiian aristocracy are two rival families, like the houses of York and Lancaster. Governor Boki represents the claims of one, and our good queen the other. Both claim the guardianship of the young king, Kauikeaouli [Kamehameha III], and are equally anxious for paramount influence, but with widely different views. The governor has visited foreign lands. He is ambitious to gain the influence of the resident foreign traders, and the captains of ships to his party. He favours the old order of things, and is very oppressive in his exactions from the common people, but utterly regardless of the public interests in his extravagant expenditures. His levy of sandal-wood has kept the poor people in the mountains for months together, cutting it without food or shelter, other than that afforded by the forests.

Kaahumanu, on the other hand, is anxious to lighten the burdens of the people. She makes frequent tours around the islands, assembling them at each hamlet, exhorting them to forsake every heathen custom, learn to read, and listen to the teachings of God's word and law. She watches the young king with the solicitude of a tender mother, weeping and rejoicing alternately, as he yields to, or resists, temptation to wrong-doing.
—Laura Fish Judd, *Honolulu, Sketches of the Life Social, Political and Religious in the Hawaiian Islands from 1828–1861*, Honolulu Star Bulletin, 1928 (reprint), pp. 17–18. Dated April 28, 1828

QUESTIONS AND ACTIVITIES

Documents

1 In the play *The Conversion of Ka'ahumanu* (Document 1) Ka'ahumanu suggests the 'way was clean' before. Why is she so undecided about what to do?

2 Why does Ka'ahu suggest that the passing of the chiefs is important?

3 Why does Ka'ahu (Document 2) fear the power which the missionaries' God has over people's hearts?

4 What overall message is the playwright trying to communicate to the audience?

5 In what ways does Dening (Document 3) suggest that the introduction of hours, days and months might have affected Marquesan identity?

6 What is the difference between linear and cyclical concepts of time?

7 The historian Dening suggests that Marquesans were very 'disciplined'. Why did nineteenth century European visitors assume that Marquesans lacked social discipline?

8 Upon what model of existing practices was the missionary Bourne (Document 4) basing his new gender role for women on Rimatara?

9 What probably happened to Rimatara Island after the missionary Bourne departed?

10 It is probable that no other Europeans visited Rimatara between Bourne's visit in 1825 and 1831 when Ellis published *Polynesian Researches*. Is Ellis's claim that Bourne's new laws had 'proved favourable' a justified and acceptable claim?

11 Is the fact that Ellis was also a missionary important in judging his account of the impact of changed gender roles on Rimatara?

12 When the advice on gender roles was published in *The Polynesian* in 1850 (Document 5), missionaries had been in Hawaii for thirty years. Why would they now be advocating these gender roles?

13 Why do the missionary writers (Document 6) rely on European examples to describe the Hawaiian political structure? Were European concepts and terms useful for describing Hawaii?

14 What knowledge do you think Laura Judd (Document 6) had of the complex Hawaiian political relationships?

15 Why does Laura Judd favour Queen Ka'ahumanu rather than Governor Boki?

Illustrations

16 Compare the Kororareka and Levuka scenes. Describe the two beach communities in regard to location, layout, size and building construction. Use the timeline in Appendix 2 to place each location in the appropriate context of its growth and decline.

17 What impression would these drawings convey to a reader back in Europe?

18 Although the Levuka scene is set twenty years later than Kororareka, why might it have had fewer European-style buildings?

19 What book might Consul Pritchard be holding in his hand? How has the artist tried to convey the impression that Pritchard is in the 'South Seas'?

20 What impression might readers in Europe adopt from the closeness and relaxed pose of the male and female Hawaiians?

21 Boki was the 'Governor' of Hawaii and an enthusiastic sandalwood entrepreneur who by 1824 had considerable experience dealing with Europeans. From this portrait what can you tell about his attitude towards European culture generally? Why has the artist presented him in Hawaiian clothing?

REFERENCES

Campbell, Ian, *A History of the Pacific Islands*, University of Queensland Press, Brisbane, 1990

Daws, Gavan, 'The High Chief Boki', *Journal of the Polynesian Society*, 75 (March 1966), pp. 65–83

Howe, K.R., *The Loyalty Islands: A history of culture contacts 1840–1900*, Australian National University Press, Canberra, 1977

Quanchi, Max, 'Contact and response: Islanders and Europeans in the Pacific in 1900', *The History Teacher*, QHTA, Brisbane, Vol. 24/7, 1990

Ralston, Caroline, *Grass Huts and Warehouses: Pacific beach communities of the nineteenth century*, Australian National University Press, Canberra, 1977

Scarr, D., *The History of the Pacific Islands*, Macmillan, Sydney, 1990

PART FOUR
FROM COLONIALISM TO
INDEPENDENCE

INTRODUCTION

There was a sudden rush to independence by former colonies between 1962 and 1981, but independence has not come to all Pacific nations. Aspects of colonial rule by the so-called 'great powers' in the late nineteenth century and aspects of the gradual change from colonial rule to self-government in the mid-twentieth century have carried over into the post-colonial period. Today the independent nations of the Pacific face an increasing number of domestic, regional and international issues.

Chapters 9–11 survey a period which runs from the nineteenth to the late twentieth century. What was the relationship between CSR and the Fiji Colonial government? To what extent did government support guarantee the profit margins of German firms in the copra trade? Why did influenza kill more than 9000 Western Samoans? Why were machine guns turned on Mau supporters in the streets of Apia? Why are small nations unable to exploit their EEZ's? Can the writers of a constitution respect both Christianity and ancient ancestral *kastom* and tradition? Why is tourism both desired and criticised as an economic goal? Can a regional organisation of micro-states exert international pressure? Is 'neo-colonial' a term which can be applied to the newly independent nations of the Pacific? How have island people portrayed their relationships with colonial rulers, and with their own indigenous ruling elites after independence?

These chapters suggest that independence has different meanings for people isolated from urban areas and centres of political control and they question whether protest and dissent were widespread in the colonial and post-colonial era. The authors question whether economic autonomy and cultural integrity have accompanied the return of sovereignty.

Chapter 9
Patterns of Colonial Rule

Doug Munro, University of the South Pacific

An early nineteenth century map of the Pacific Ocean would have depicted an expanse of water largely devoid of island groups because at that time the majority of Pacific Islands still had to be 'discovered' for European geography. By 1906 almost every island had been accurately placed on the European charts and coloured to show that every inhabited island group had been annexed by one or other imperial power. Because colonial rule is usually the culmination of earlier European influences, this map was an indication of the extent to which the Pacific Islanders' lives had been changed in little more than a century. Apart from some isolated areas, such as the highlands of Papua New Guinea, the world of the Pacific Islander had been profoundly transformed during the course of the nineteenth century. Whereas Pacific Islanders were their own masters in 1800, by the end of the century they were almost invariably the subject peoples of either Great Britain, France, Germany or the United States.

The first annexations

The spread of colonial rule proceeded unevenly during the nineteenth century. The first major event was Britain's annexation of New Zealand in 1840. Unwillingly, Britain felt forced into the measure because of concern over possible French designs and the internal unrest brought about by the lawlessness of British subjects. As if in retaliation, France extended formal control over Tahiti and neighbouring islands. In this case, however, local commercial rivalries with British traders and the instability of indigenous governments also contributed to the French counter-reaction. France followed this by assuming control over New Caledonia in 1853, to the disgust of the Australian colonies, especially when it became known that the major French motive was to utilise the *Grande Terre* (main island of New Caledonia) as a penal settlement. The first round of European annexations in the Pacific had been accomplished.

It would be a mistake, however, to suppose that Europeans were the first imperialists in the Pacific because centralised governments under Pacific Island monarchies were formed in Hawaii (1810), Tahiti (1815), and Tonga (1830s). In each case, island chiefs augmented their hereditary status and selectively enlisted the aid of Europeans— especially missionaries—to extend their territory and dominions through warfare and diplomacy. But in each case, except that of Tonga, the growing European presence became too demanding. Internal chaos, crises and confrontations with entrenched European interests culminated in Polynesian monarchs losing control over their affairs. The first Pacific Island monarchy to go was Tahiti in 1842. Meanwhile in New Zealand, Fiji and Samoa, attempts at creating centralised indigenous governments were also being frustrated.

The prime example was Samoa. The factionalised nature of the indigenous polity and the disruptive rivalries between British, German and United States citizens and their governments effectively served to put Samoan unity beyond reach. The situation was summed up perfectly in 1880 by a British consular official who observed that:

On looking over the correspondence one cannot help noticing that no representative of a foreign power ever misses the opportunity of telling the natives that there is nothing his government desires to see more than the establishment of a strong and independent [indigenous] government in Samoa, yet some of the stipulations of the treaties which the 3 Powers most interested have concluded with whatever semblance of a government could be found to treat with, are such that even if the Samoans had the highest capacity for government, the formation of a strong and independent [Samoan] Government is rendered impossible.

(Quoted in P.M. Kennedy, *The Samoan Triangle* (1974), p. 20)

Another example of the failure to form a centralised indigenous government was Fiji, although in the late 1860s the chiefs and some European settlers attempted to form a Western-style government. The chiefs had first offered their islands to Britain in 1858. Later, in the face of opposition from the majority of white settlers, and only recently escaped from the wrath of the United States over the debts of one chief to American traders, the chiefs ceded Fiji to Britain in 1874. The reason for annexing Fiji illustrates yet again that imperial expansion was a by-product of both economic activity and the failure of indigenous political systems to accommodate large-scale European intrusion. This in turn raises the basic question: were the underlying causes of European imperialism 'political' or 'economic'? Often the two are seen as being distinct and separable, but it would often be more accurate to say that imperialism was a political act that arose out of the economic activities of Europeans. In the Pacific the economic activities of Europeans on the frontier of European control generally created consequences of a political nature, either by attracting the attention of a rival power and thus creating a focus for international rivalry; or by making an indigenous regime unstable and forcing a metropolitan power to intervene to restore stability, as in the case of Fiji.

Indeed, Britain annexed Fiji under the illusion that this would be an exceptional case. Fiji would serve as the centre of British authority in the Pacific and thus *prevent* the assumption of further territorial responsibility in the region. With that in mind, and in an attempt to regulate the labour trade, the Governor of Fiji was also appointed to the newly created position of High Commissioner for the Western Pacific in 1877, and given extraterritorial jurisdiction over British subjects residing in the western Pacific islands. That is to say, British subjects in any part of this broad area not already under the control of a European power (for example, New Caledonia) could be tried in the High Commissioner's court. In this way, it was hoped, the behaviour of British subjects in the Pacific could be controlled and native independence recognised. Instead, the High Commissioner was hampered by lack of funds, which prevented the appointment of resident officials in places where they were needed. The High Commissioner was also dependent upon the Royal Navy, over whom he had no control, to perform the necessary policing role.

The late-nineteenth century scramble for colonies

Before the 1880s the spread of formal colonial rule was limited to New Zealand, French Oceania, New Caledonia and Fiji. Until that time the various metropolitan powers, such as France, Britain and the United States, had contented themselves with an informal empire in the Pacific. In other words, traders, missionaries and consuls of various nationalities in not yet claimed territories were able to exercise sufficient influence to pursue their interests without the need for formal political annexation. Such a posture was particularly suited to Britain's preference for doing as little as possible, as cheaply as possible, with the least difficulty or trouble. But informal empire has a way of converting itself into formal empire, as the example of Fiji illustrates. In the first place, the development of large-scale plantation systems and trading networks in the Pacific raised the value of European economic assets. This in turn contributed to a rising tide of distrust and antagonism between the various European nationalities in the Pacific. Eventually these pressures made informal empire an unsuitable basis for control. Almost inevitably, the political solution of annexation was imposed in order to provide a satisfactory framework for European enterprise.

These tendencies gained momentum with the emergence of Germany as an imperial power in the mid-1880s. From that point there was a rush of annexations and colonial partitions, commencing with the partition of the New Guinea islands between Britain and Germany in 1884. This was followed by the 1886 Anglo-German Agreement whereby the two imperial powers established a line of demarcation which divided the western Pacific. To the north of a line, Germany was allocated a sphere of influence in which Britain gave up claims to future annexation. The reverse held for the British sphere of influence to the south of the line of demarcation.

The two powers responded to the agreement in quite different ways. Germany regarded the Anglo-German agreement as a means by which she could annex the islands falling into her part, without British objection. Britain, on the other hand, saw it as a device by which she could ignore her side without fear of German intrusion. The Germans quickly took up their territorial options, annexing the northern Solomons, Nauru and the Marshall Islands in quick succession. Germany's motive for annexation was economic, to develop colonies with a view to making a profit. It is no accident that German New Guinea and the Marshall Islands were placed under the control of private chartered companies. Under this arrangement, the private company paid for the cost of colonial government, in return for which the colonial officials involved governed entirely in the interests of the firm. In 1884 Germany also annexed the Caroline Islands and Samoa but withdrew her claims in the face of hostility from Spain and the United States respectively. In the case of Samoa, the local German consul annexed the group without approval from Berlin. The move was disallowed, which illustrates that colonial policy and practice was made at various levels. The consul acted in the interests of the large number of German traders and planters. However, the Imperial Chancellor in Germany thought that no Pacific archipelago was worth a quarrel with another major Power, no matter how preponderant the German community. Wider global policy invariably took precedence over more minor considerations in the distant Pacific.

This increasing complexity of colonial decision making is evident in the case of Britain's eventual assumption of formal responsibility over the Gilbert Islands (Kiribati) in 1892. The Gilberts lay on the British side of the 1886 demarcation line, otherwise Germany would certainly have annexed these islands because of their importance as a source of labourers for plantations in Samoa. When it had been rumoured that the United States was about to annex the group, thereby depriving the German Samoan plantations of a source of labour, Germany took the extraordinary step of actually requesting Britain to annex the group to pre-empt possible American designs. Britain complied with the request, not because they wanted the Gilberts but because they needed German diplomatic support to counter French opposition to the British occupation of the Suez Canal. The alternative for the British was to abandon the 1886 agreement and allow Germany to annex the group. This, moreover, would have had the effect of antagonising the Australasian colonies, which were uniformly opposed to the spread of non-British influence in the Pacific. So for the sake of wider diplomacy and to placate the Australasian colonies, Britain assumed responsibility over a group that was strategically and commercially unimportant, except as a labour source, at a time when her avowed policy was to avoid further colonial entanglements.

Nor did it stop there. The High Commissioner for the Western Pacific then suggested that the French might annex the Ellice Islands (Tuvalu), thereby driving a wedge between the Gilberts in the north and Fiji to the south. To maintain Fiji's position as the British centre of power in the Pacific, the British flag was quickly raised in the Ellice Islands despite their lack of economic potential. Then, fearing that recent events might provoke the French into seizing the southern Solomon Islands, Britain felt impelled to add them to her overseas empire. In other words, Britain could no longer avoid exercising her territorial options within the area defined by the 1886 agreement, despite a disinclination to do so. It was an example of what may be described as *pre-emptive imperialism*, the motivation being to either safeguard existing possessions, as in the case of the Ellice Islands, or to prevent control of unattached areas falling into the hands of a hostile power, as in the case of the southern Solomons.

The final major partition of the Pacific occurred in 1900, when Germany, Britain and the United States resolved their differences over the Samoan islands. Between 1889 and 1898 those three powers had imposed on Samoa a tridominium government in which they had an equal share, though this was so ineffective that it would be misleading to describe it as a system of formal rule. In 1899 at the Treaty of Berlin, however, the partition agreement was thrashed out. It was a foregone conclusion that the United States be apportioned the island of Tutuila (present-day American Samoa) and the harbour that went with it. The British, at first reluctant to surrender Samoa to the Germans and Americans, changed their minds after the British Admiralty gave the opinion that Tonga was the more valuable acquisition because the northern Tongan islands had excellent harbours and these could not be permitted to fall into a rival power's hands given their proximity to Fiji. The British were therefore prepared to concede the western islands of Samoa in return for the German Solomons and concessions in Africa, while Germany for her part wanted Western Samoa, where it had extensive plantation interests. In the North Pacific, Spain 'sold' control of Ponape to Germany in 1899.

The final annexations were the Hawaiian islands to the United States in 1900, and the New Hebrides (Vanuatu) in 1906; the latter were governed jointly by Britain and France under a condominium arrangement. The entire Pacific was now under the formal control of one or other European power with the nominal exception of Tonga, over which Britain had declared a protectorate in 1900 when she lost interest in Samoa. Tonga was the one remaining of the three Polynesian kingdoms established in the nineteenth century, and owed its survival to having established a Western or European style of government that was acceptable to the metropolitan powers. European impact in Tonga also had been relatively light. Strictly speaking, Tonga's status as a protectorate meant that Britain could exercise authority only over her own subjects, but not over Tongans or Europeans of non-British nationality. This gave the Tongan political leaders, comprising a monarch and a cabinet, the right to conduct their country's internal affairs. Britain's formal role was limited to providing advice, which the Tongans were at liberty to accept or reject. Initially the British attempted to exceed their authority and successive consuls gave outright direction instead of formal advice. Only after bitter quarrels were the Tongans able to regain control of their affairs in 1911. (See Appendix 3 for details of all annexation and changes of sovereignty.)

Effects of colonial rule

Colonial rule involved the domination, or at least the attempted domination, of one group of people over another. There was also a pronounced racial dimension because it involved the maintenance of white supremacy. None of the colonial territories in the Pacific—apart from New Zealand and Hawaii—were colonies where Europeans outnumbered the indigenous populations. Yet minority governance of whites over coloured was seen by all but a few as part of a natural order. The idea of colonial peoples eventually attaining their independence would have been dismissed as illusory. Even as late as 1962, a senior Australian official in Papua New Guinea, when asked how long he thought before the territory could become self-governing, replied 'We shall still be there in the year 2000'.

Colonialism was also intrinsically exploitative, and although colonial rule in the Pacific was generally mild by comparison with parts of Africa, it still involved inequalities. If they could not provide prestige, power and profit, colonies were at least expected to be economically self-supporting. To that end, colonies were run by whites, usually for the benefit of whites. Colonial administrations, in the interests of balancing their budgets, facilitated the progress of European commercial enterprise, whether this be trading plantations or mining. In the process, indigenous subjects typically lost a good proportion of their lands, were compelled to provide their labour, and were taxed either in produce or in cash. When their labour power was insufficient, migrant labourers were introduced from other parts of the Pacific or from Asia. In the process, traditional authority was often either subverted or eroded, and rebellions by colonial subjects were normally met with overwhelming counter-force. The subordinate relationship of indigenous subjects extended in other directions; when they attempted to compete in commercial trade with established European interests, their efforts were thwarted by the combined opposition of colonial administrations and European entrepreneurs. Whether harsh or benign, colonial administrations in the Pacific defined their subject peoples' involvement in what was fundamentally a European enterprise. For their part, islanders gave up their lands, gave of their labour, and provided taxes of various sorts. Colonial governments in return provided minimal, if any, social services, preferring instead the cheaper option of leaving the provision of education and health facilities, such as they were, to missionaries.

Despite these commonalities, colonial rule was highly variable in impact. The methods and impact of colonialism varied not only between colonial powers but within the same colonial empire, depending on local circumstances, the guiding philosophies of individual governors, and metropolitan pressures. The German empire in the Pacific provides a case in point. The Germans were economically motivated both in acquiring territory and in governing their colonies. In the Marshall Islands, for example, they prohibited the manufacture of sour toddy (a highly fermented beverage made from the sap of coconut palms). The rationale was not to prevent drunkenness but to protect the copra industry, because toddy manufacture affects the ability of a tree to produce coconuts. In their quest for profits, German administrators were generally more repressive than their British counterparts—if only because faced with fewer constraints. Even so, there were marked differences between different German colonies in the Pacific. In German New Guinea, Governor Albert Hahl was committed to opening up the country to European planters and traders. With that in mind he mounted armed expeditions against recalcitrant New Guineans and adopted other harsh measures, such as the imposition of forced labour programs. Nevertheless, he drew the line at unchecked labour mobilisation, rightly fearing that this would deplete the local labour supply. This provides an ironic twist because in so doing he came into conflict with planters who short-sightedly demanded unlimited recruiting rights.

A quite different approach was adopted in German Samoa by Governor William Solf, who departed from normal German colonial practice by pursuing policies that would protect the indigenous social order. For that reason he discouraged small planters who flocked to the colony from 1902 and resisted their demands that Samoans be conscripted wholesale onto their holdings as labourers. Genuine as Solf was about his native policy, it was only possible because the colony could already justify itself economically through the activities of the German Trading and Plantation Company (DHPG). The DHPG did not need Samoans as plantation labourers because it had an assured and privileged supply from New Guinea. Instead, the Samoans sold thousands of tons of village-produced copra to the DHPG each year, which had the added advantage of enabling them to pay their poll tax to the government. Solf therefore did not need—any more than he wanted—the newly arrived small planters who threatened his protective native policy because the colony was already financially self-sufficient. Whereas Hahl gave planters every encouragement short of unchecked labour recruiting, Solf could restrict further plantation development without endangering his colony's revenues.

British colonial policy presents a further series of contrasts. In general, British colonial administrators faced more restraints than did their German counterparts. Philanthropic pressure groups, such as the Anti-Slavery Society and the Aboriginal Protection Society, exerted a strong influence which resulted in a humanitarian strand in British colonial policy. Even so, there were appreciable differences in the ways that different British colonies were governed. Gilbert and Ellice Islanders, for example, were not exploited because their barren coral islands held so few exploitable resources. Here too an essentially protective native policy was pursued. It was quite a different matter in the Solomon Islands, which had potential for plantation development. Aware that this was the only means to financial self-sufficiency, the British set about establishing the necessary security for commercial development. To this end they followed a vigorous policy of 'pacification', concentrated in the areas most suitable for future plantations, and which involved the occasional use of naval back-up.

Having imposed reasonably durable conditions of security in the places that mattered, the British then set about alienating from indigenous ownership broad acres of prime coastal land, largely through the legal device of successive Waste Lands Regulations. These lands were then put at the disposal of European investors through various freehold and leasehold arrangements. Finally, in 1911, the labour migration of Solomon Islanders to destinations outside the Protectorate was prohibited, forcing Solomon Islanders to work for lower wages on local plantations. As well as lowering the cost of labour by this and other means, the colonial administration also, in 1920, imposed a head tax that took labour mobilisation to its very limits. In areas of the Solomons where the islanders had no other means of earning money, the head tax deprived individuals of a prime means of resisting the plantation regime—namely to decline to offer one's services in the first place. In these ways the humanitarian strand in British colonial policy was compromised in the interest of colonial revenues. Another such example, but far more blatant, is Ocean Island, whose inhabitants were systematically stripped of their lands to make way for phosphate mining.

A further contrast is presented by the French colony of New Caledonia, where a good 90 per cent of the land of the Grande Terre was alienated from the traditional owners for European agricultural and pastoral purposes. From 1871 the demand for native labour for mines, cattle ranches and public works resulted in a program of forced labour, and this was followed by a policy of confinement of New Caledonians onto reserves. To satisfy the growing demands for land by settlers, the administration simply created more reservations, but smaller in extent, more remote in location and in less fertile areas. More thoroughgoing controls were instituted in 1878 with the Code of the Indigenat, which deprived New Caledonians of the protection of French law and placed them instead under the arbitrary authority of administrators. This included restrictions on New Caledonians' freedom of movement. The Code, which remained in force until 1946, also intensified the existing programs of forced labour, and provided severe penal sanctions for non-compliance. Given the severity of these demands, French rule provoked two serious rebellions, in 1878 and again in 1917, which were harshly suppressed.

The need to develop commercial agriculture had different effects in Fiji. In an attempt to reconcile the need for economic development without at the same time drawing on Fijians as plantation labourers, the colonial administration imported nearly 61 000 Indian labourers between 1879 and 1916. As part of a calculated policy to preserve the Fijian way of life—though whether it did is another matter—the colonial administration precluded Fijians from entering into wage labour. Instead, it was decreed that they develop at their own pace and in the context of their traditional lifestyles. The maintenance of the Fijian social structure thus involved keeping Fijians in their villages under the rule of their chiefs and in possession of their lands. This in turn enabled a rigorous system of native taxation from their own produce. A further strand to this native policy was a system of indirect rule through the establishment of a separate Fijian Administration, which used Fijian chiefs as regional, district and local officers. However, these attempts to reaffirm the values of traditional Fijian society had unfortunate and unforeseen consequences. Sheltered from the outside world, the Fijians were ultimately ill-equipped to meet its demands. Another cost of preserving the Fijian way of life was a resident population of Indian migrant labourers and their descendants, whom the colonial government kept separate and unequal, leading to disenchantment and misunderstanding on both sides. This social and political separation contributed to the coups of 1987.

A number of more general comments can be made about colonial rule in the Pacific. In the first place, colonial rule varied from place to place, and over time, and even within a single colony. A prime example is Papua New Guinea, where large numbers of highlanders remained remarkably untouched by colonialism until as late as the 1950s in some cases, simply because they were inaccessible. The contrast with many coastal Papuans and New Guineans is striking. Secondly, annexations entailed the creation of artificial boundaries. In the case of the Gilbert and Ellice Islanders, two culturally quite distinct peoples were joined together in a political union that did not survive the test of time into nationhood. In the Samoan islands, by contrast, a unified culture was divided into two separate political entities and remains so to this day. These were matters over which Pacific Islanders had little or no say.

Finally, and more contentiously, the islanders' response to colonial rule involved collaboration as well as resistance. The motivations for collaboration were various. Many New Caledonians willingly collaborated with the French authorities in suppressing the 1878 rebellion. On the other hand, there was the definitely unwilling cooperation of many New Caledonian chiefs whose unhappy task it was to enforce the labour demands set out in the Code of the Indigenat or else go to gaol. There was in any case an inherent tendency for colonial officials to adopt divide and rule tactics, and indeed colonial rule often depended for its survival on this. The most common experience of many New Guineans during Hahl's governorship was being shot at by other New

Guineans, that is the native police in the colonial administration's employ. The device of indirect rule is another example of collaboration, and it can create tensions. Not infrequently, the autonomy of the Fijian Administration was compromised when chiefs involved had direct pressure applied on them by governors and European magistrates to follow a certain line. Another problem for collaborators was the question of having to answer to their own people as well as to a colonial authority. Governor Solf of German Samoa summed this up perfectly when he accused a chief of being two-faced, and yet colonial rule could not but help create such divisions of loyalty.

From mandates to decolonisation

At the outbreak of the First World War the allied powers seized Germany's Pacific colonies and divided the spoils among themselves at the Treaty of Versailles in 1920. Japan received the Caroline and Marshall Islands, Australia was given New Guinea and Nauru, and New Zealand was left with Western Samoa. These former German colonies were now no longer colonies in the usual sense of the word. Instead, they became League of Nations mandated territories. The acceptance of a mandate by an administering power entailed certain restrictions and obligations. In addition to annual supervision by the League of Nations, the administering authority had a 'sacred duty' to uphold the 'paramount interests' of the subject peoples. The territories involved were being 'held in trust' until they were able to govern themselves. The notion of independence was not taken seriously at the time and the mandated territories were treated much the same as any other colony, apart from the inconvenience of the annual inspection. The lack of effect of League supervision was most graphically portrayed in the case of the Caroline and Marshall Islands. They were systematically settled and exploited by Japan to the extent that a military and civil population from Japan soon outnumbered the Micronesians, who must indeed have felt like strangers in their own houses.

The terms of the mandates were breached time and again with impunity. But at least the notion of eventual independence was being given lip-service, and these sentiments received a boost during the Second World War when colonial administrators beat an ignominious retreat from the advancing Japanese forces. This blow to British and colonial prestige was compounded by United States forces being the rescuers; and in contrast to the aloofness of British colonial officials who operated on shoestring budgets, the Americans were friendly, generous, brought unprecedented wealth to the islands, and voiced anti-colonial sentiments. It was an unsettling experience that created expectations of wealth and opportunity and resentments against colonial domination that left many islanders unwilling to return to pre-war conditions and British rule. The more liberal international ethos following the war was expressed in the United Nations Charter, which espoused such ideals as racial equality and self-determination. This maintained the impetus for change and contributed towards a new climate of opinion less accepting of colonial domination than in the past.

These post-war 'winds of change' set the context for the partial decolonisation of the Pacific and the neo-colonial influences that have since developed.

DOCUMENTS

1 Failure of Samoans to form a centralised government by the 1870s

This failure was ... an almost inevitable consequence of the European impact upon Samoa. Much earlier, in the 1830s, the Tahitian kingdom had become a mockery of sovereign independence when the French had first used threats of force against it. Since the 1850s the Hawaiian government had been forced increasingly to pursue policies that advanced the interests of immigrant planters, often to the detriment of the Hawaiians themselves. When a unified Fijian government had been formed in 1871, under the nominal headship of King Cakobau, settler interests had attempted to use it quite blatantly as an instrument for the establishment of their own supremacy. Only in Tonga, where European interests were minimal, had a modern form of government emerged and remained effective and relatively uncorrupted. In Samoa European interests were too strongly entrenched before a serious attempt was—or, because of the character of Samoan traditional politics, could be—made to form such a government. In the 1870s Apia [Samoa] was, next to Honolulu [Hawaii], the most important port in the Pacific islands. Settlers were engaged in developing, or planning to develop, a large proportion of Samoan lands as commercial plantations. Under these conditions, no Samoan government had any real chance of establishing its authority.

> —J.W. Davidson, *Samoa mo Samoa: The emergence of the Independent State of Western Samoa*, Oxford University Press, Melbourne, 1967, p. 58

2 Variable effects of colonial rule

... in the end no single picture of the German impact on New Guinea emerges. In a country where people's common identity was historically defined by clan or language group, history itself becomes particularised, each community which encountered the Germans having its own history of German rule. Beneficent towards some New Guineans, the Germans were brutal in their dealings with others and their impact must be seen as a mosaic composed of numerous, unique interactions between coloniser and colonised.

> —Stewart Firth, *New Guinea under the Germans*,
> Melbourne University Press, Melbourne, 1982, p. 174

3 The 'blessing' of colonial rule

... never at any time was it thought proper or even advisable to consult the native inhabitants about the form of [colonial] government that they might desire; in the age of 'new imperialism' such a suggestion would have been considered ridiculous. 'Uncivilised' or 'dying' peoples were simply expected to accept what was decided for them in the chancelleries of Europe and, given the temper of the times, the natives might be considered fortunate if a protectorate was established over their lands in one swift, uncomplicated movement. Where great powers quarrelled over the possession of a particular territory, its inhabitants were often ground between rival pressures, and probably suffered the more. In a sense, therefore, the partition treaties of 1899 [relating to Samoa] were an advantage to the Samoans too; neither their economic or political development had been much furthered by the rivalries of the white groups, which had assisted and intensified the Samoan dynastic struggle for the kingship. If actual Samoan independence could not be recovered, was it not better for the islands to be ruled by one responsible government than to be subjected to the pressures of various, often irresponsible, influences? Although we must await a native historian's judgement on this point, to Western eyes this seems certainly to have been the case; and while the cry 'Samoa for the Samoans' never fully disappeared, at least the interests of the islanders were better protected under individual German and American rule than they had been in the days when Samoa was the cockpit of international rivalry in the South Pacific.

—Paul M. Kennedy, 'Germany and the Samoan Tridominium, 1889–98: A study in frustrated imperialism', in John A. Moses and Paul M. Kennedy (eds), *Germany in the Pacific and Far East, 1870–1914* , University of Queensland Press, Brisbane, 1977, p. 110

4 Pressures towards eventual independence

'We admit ... that independence is a stage at which all distant and prosperous colonies are destined ultimately to arrive. If foresight does not voluntarily relax the ties with the metropolis, force will in time assuredly break them.' These words, written to the *Edinburgh Times* in 1808 could well serve as a text for our times. The greater part of the 'colonial world' of twenty years ago has already attained independence or is on the verge of attaining it; and the exodus from colonialism which began mainly with the greater dependencies, such as India and Indonesia, is now beginning to extend to the small territories, such as Western Samoa. Indeed, few political and constitutional processes are at present so greatly affecting human wellbeing as the transition from political dependency to independence.

—J.W. Davidson, 'The transition to independence: the example of Western Samoa', *Australian Journal of Politics and History*, 7:1 (1961), p. 15

QUESTIONS AND ACTIVITIES

1   What change in Pacific Islanders' political status occurred between 1800 and 1900?
2   Describe the events which led Munro to write that in the 1840–53 period the 'first round of European annexations' was accomplished?
3   Why did the British consider Fiji was an 'exceptional case'?
4   Describe briefly the role of the Western Pacific High Commission (WPHC). Why do you think Germany and France did not set up similar organisations to the British WPHC to oversee their colonial presence in the Pacific?
5   Why did Britain and Germany use a demarcation line to divide the Pacific into respective spheres of influence?
6   Form a group of three and prepare a definition of each of these terms:
    • Informal empire
    • Pre-emptive imperialism
    • Divide and rule.
    For each definition select some evidence (an example) which demonstrates the meaning of the term, then present the term, definition and evidence to your partners. After a discussion, if necessary, rewrite your material and present it to the whole class.
7   Appendix 3 lists in table form the details of colonial expansion in the Pacific. Devise a way of presenting this material graphically on a map of the Pacific. Restrict the map to a subregion or group of islands, for example, Melanesia, French territories, atoll colonies or areas under joint control.
8   Compare the colonial administrations of Hahl and Solf in regard to private commercial and company development.
9   Compare colonial rule in the Solomon Islands and the Gilbert Islands in regard to 'native policies'.
10   Why does Davidson (Document 1) claim that it was impossible for a central Samoan-led government to be formed in Samoa in the 1870s?
11   In Davidson's opinion of strong central indigenous government, in what ways was Tonga different from Fiji and Hawaii?
12   Firth (Document 2) uses the phrase 'a mosaic' to describe relations between the German colonial rulers and the peoples of German New Guinea. What does he mean by this phrase?
13   Kennedy (Document 3) claims that 'the interests of the islanders were better protected' when discussing the advantages of colonial rule. What does he mean by this?
14   In the two Davidson extracts (Documents 1 and 4) he uses two similar phrases—'almost inevitable' and 'destined ultimately'—when discussing the presence of colonial rulers. Is he suggesting that events would have occurred naturally? What does he mean by using these terms?
15   Prepare a short argument for or against one of the following statements:
    • 'Samoans were two-faced'
    • Colonial governors could not reconcile native protection and development
    • International rivalry created colonies in the Pacific
    • The only element common to colonial rule in the Marshalls, New Guinea and Samoa was that they flew a German flag
    • Security and strategy were more important than profits in the Pacific colonies.
    Present your opinion to the class as a written or oral presentation, or in a graphic format with maps, illustrations, timelines or photographs.

REFERENCES

See the Select Bibliography on pages 161–3.

Chapter 10
The Path to Independence

Vijay Naidu, University of the South Pacific

Independence in the Pacific denotes the achievement of sovereignty by the people of a former colony. It also involves the renunciation of sovereignty over that colony by the colonising power. In the process leading up to independence, referred to as decolonisation, the attainment of political freedom was linked to the adoption of a number of objects associated with a sovereign state, including a constitution, a national flag and a national anthem. Besides adopting constitutions that provided for political and legal systems mostly modelled along the lines of the British Westminster system, provisions were incorporated to take account of the customs and traditions of the people concerned. The political and legal systems of the departing colonial ruler were usually retained, albeit in a modified way. These, together with budgetary support, foreign aid and technical assistance, resulted in the continuation of influence by the former ruling power.

Independence in the Pacific has also entailed forms of political association which do not lead to a complete severance of relations at the political level. Examples of such arrangements include the self-governing states of Cook Islands and Niue, which are associated with New Zealand, and the various agreements which linked the former Pacific Islands Trust Territories of Micronesia with the United States of America.

The South Pacific region comprises thirteen politically independent or internally self-governing countries: Western Samoa (1962), Cook Islands (1965 internal self-government), Nauru (1968), Fiji (1970), Niue (1974 internal self-government), Papua New Guinea (1975), Vanuatu (1980), Kiribati (1979) and Palau (1981). The United Nations Trust Territory of the Pacific Islands was terminated in the Federated States of Micronesia in 1986. Compared to other regions under colonial rule, Pacific island countries have sought independence fairly recently. Tonga retained nominal sovereignty throughout the colonial era, and has a constitutional monarchy with a partly elected, partly nominated parliament.

Several territories in the South Pacific are still colonial possessions of foreign powers. The French colonies in the Pacific, New Caledonia (Kanaky), French Polynesia, Easter Island and the Indonesian-occupied West Papua (Irian Jaya) fall in this category. In these colonies, movements seeking independence have emerged. There are a number of other metropolitan possessions in the Pacific but these do not have groups seeking self-determination.

As it is not possible to give a full account of the path to independence of each one of the sovereign Pacific states, it is perhaps useful to classify them in terms of some significant features. On this basis, it is possible to designate independent Pacific states into three broad categories:

1 States which have gained full independence as a result of pressure for independence from within
2 States which were impelled towards independence as a result of initiatives by the colonial power
3 Territories which have internal autonomy within the framework of the metropolitan power.

Figure 10.1: Iremia Tabai, former President of Kiribati.

Figure 10.2: Paul Neaoutine, President, FLNKS.

1 Independence as a response to pressure from within

Island states where internal pressures contributed to independence are Western Samoa, Nauru, and Vanuatu. Nationalism as a movement seeking national self-determination was especially strong in these three societies.

By the agreement at the Washington Conference in 1899 Samoa was partitioned into eastern Samoa, which became an American possession, and western Samoa, which became a German colony. The latter was subject to autocratic rule for fourteen years, during which considerable progress was made economically. Samoan institutions, including land tenure arrangements and the *matai* or chiefly system, were allowed to function. In 1909 Lauaki Namulau'ulu Mamoe, an eminent orator from Savai'i, mobilised Samoans against the German colonial authorities in order to gain greater dignity for the orators of *Tumua* and *Pule*, but the Germans deported Lauaki and other leaders to Saipan in the Marianas and sentenced others to periods of hard labour.

The Germans were ousted by New Zealand forces in 1914 at the outbreak of the First World War. Until 1920, Western Samoa was a British Military Administration. For the next forty-two years colonial authority was vested in civilian administration but in the early period this distinction was somewhat superficial as the colonial order was headed by military or ex-military officers. A serious error on the part of the Military Administration led to the death of 8500 people, or 22 per cent of the Samoan population, as a result of the 1918 pneumonia pandemic. The ship *Talune*, which carried afflicted passengers, was allowed to disembark from neighbouring American Samoa spreading the contagion. A Samoan distrust of New Zealand administration was engendered.

Well intentioned reforms by the colonial rulers, such as the repatriation of Chinese and Solomon Island labourers and substituting them with Samoan labour, government marketing of first grade copra to eliminate middleman profiteering, and attempts at land reforms so as to give the ordinary Samoans more say over land matters, were met with strong opposition. The colonial authorities failed to gain the cooperation of either the planter/merchant or powerful factions of the *matai* or chiefly hierarchy. As opposition towards the colonial policies intensified, officials resorted to passing repressive legislation. As a result of repressive measures, including deportation to New Zealand, being deprived of *matai* titles and imprisonment, discontent became even more widespread.

A popular movement, *Ole Mau* or *Mau* emerged and quickly formed an alternative authority structure to the colonial government. The historians Meleisea and Schoeffel point out that:

> The leaders of the *Mau* included many of Samoa's highest ranking chiefs, successful Samoan–European businessmen and other influential local Europeans. The *Mau* had the support of a majority of Samoan villages and took the form of a non-violent protest movement in which Samoans passively resisted New Zealand's attempt to rule them.

During the 1920s and up to 1935, New Zealand colonial rule was made very difficult and scores of Samoans were deprived of their *matai* or chiefly titles. In 1927 three prominent members of the white planter and merchant community, W.A. Gurr, A.G. Smythe and O.F. Nelson were deported to New Zealand. Samoan *matais* were also deported. The refusal to pay taxation, picketing of shops and other forms of non-cooperation paralysed the colonial authorities. New Zealand sent two warships to Samoa to establish control. A petition signed by 8000 male adults out of 9300 (85 per cent) seeking self-government for Western Samoa was sent to the League of Nations.

On 28 December 1929, A.G. Smythe returned after a three year exile in New Zealand and, with police permission, a procession of several hundred *Mau* supporters marched through Apai to greet him. Scuffles broke out when New Zealand policemen

attempted to arrest the Secretary of *Mau*. As police shot at the crowd, a machine gun opened fire from a nearby police station. Eleven Samoans died, including *Mau* leader Tupua Tamasese Lealofi III, who beseeched his supporters not to use violence as he lay dying.

Further repression of the *Mau* followed as marines from a New Zealand warship attempted to round up *Mau* supporters. Most men took to the bush to evade the marines. The marines broke into houses, harassed Samoans and in general displayed 'all the racist sentiments' which were unpopular to express in New Zealand itself.

Although Samoan nationalists continued to be frustrated by New Zealand administrators who received high salaries and maintained a racial hierarchy in the administration, the open hostility of the past two decades subsided. The advent of the Second

Figure 10.3: Tofilau Eti Alesana, Prime Minister, Western Samoa.

Figure 10.4: Paul Neaoutine, Richard Kaloi and Rock Wamytan, FLNKS.

World War and Japan's aggression in the Pacific resulted in an influx of American marines. Samoans enjoyed higher wages and for the first time came across Europeans who treated them as equals. After the war, New Zealand continued as the administering country. On behalf of the United Nations, New Zealand was charged with preparing Western Samoa for self-government. Meanwhile Samoans called a Samoa-wide meeting to seek self-government in place of the trusteeship arrangement confirmed by the UN in 1946.

In 1947 the Council of State was established. This body comprised two *Fautua* members and the New Zealand High Commission. The *Fautua* were members of the new Legislative Assembly which comprised eleven Samoans elected by the *Fono of Faipule*, five 'European' members elected by universal suffrage in European elector-ates, and six official members nominated by the High Commissioner. A Samoan flag, national anthem and national day signified changes at the symbolic level.

According to Meleisea and Schoeffel, there were four issues that needed to be resolved in the process of achieving self-government.

The **first** was the issue of Head of State. It was resolved that the office would be held jointly by two of the *Tama-a'aiga*, Tupua Tamasese Mea'ole and Malietoa Tanumafili II.

The **second** issue was that of the Parliament and parliamentary executive. It was resolved that only holders of registered *matai* titles were empowered to vote or to stand for election in Parliament.

The **third** issue was that of the Lands and Titles Court. This institution developed during the colonial period out of the Lands Commission of the late 1890s. It was empowered to resolve disputes concerning customary land and succession to *matai* titles.

A **fourth** issue arose over the constitutional status of local Europeans who do not consider themselves members of Samoan *'aiga* and who are not represented by *matai*. This problem was resolved by the creation of an individual voter's roll, each of whom could vote independently.

Figure 10.5: Bikenibeu Paeniy, Prime Minister of Tuvalu,1991.

Figure 10.6: Bernard Dowiyogo, President of Nauru, 1991.

An expanded Executive Council was formed in 1953. New Zealand recommended a single legislature to replace the Legislative Assembly and the *Fono of Faipule* and that the New Zealand Reparation Estates, which were plantations seized from the Germans, be handed over to the Samoans. A Working Committee submitted a draft report on matters to be discussed in a Constitutional Convention in 1954.

The Samoan Amendment Act (1957) provided an Executive Council and a single Legislative Assembly. The Executive Council became the most important policy-making body. In late 1959, a Prime Minister was appointed in the place of the leader of government business. The 1960 Constitutional Convention which discussed the draft constitution was dominated by men who were current or previous holders of government positions, church representatives, planters, merchants and storekeepers. Among these men were those who had been 'Europeans' previously but now chose to become Samoans. The conservative *matai* prevailed over issues such as the electoral roll, land reform, religion and selection of a Head of State. In January 1961, the Prime Minister, Fiame Mataafa, took the draft constitution for an Independent Western Samoa to the United Nations.

Under United Nations supervision, a plebiscite based on universal suffrage was held in May 1961. Voters were asked whether they accepted the Constitution and whether they wanted independence on 1 January 1962. Of the 38 000 voters, 83 per cent voted 'Yes' for the Constitution and 78 per cent indicated their support for independence. Samoa became an independent state in January 1962.

Nauru and Vanuatu

The paths of the Republics of Nauru and Vanuatu towards gaining territorial sovereignty were characterised by strong pressure by their respective local leaders in the face

Figure 10.7: Heads of State, South Pacific Forum, 1990.

of metropolitan rulers who were reluctant to relinquish control over their colonies. Of the three countries given the trusteeship of Nauru, New Zealand and the United Kingdom were 'sleeping partners' for much of the period. The responsibility for administering the island fell on Australia. Together with the British Phosphate Commissioners (BPC), the semi-official mining corporation, colonial officials carried out their primary task of delivering at the cheapest cost, phosphate to fertilise the farms and pastures of the three partner countries. A desire to maintain a monopoly over the high quality phosphate explained much of Australia's lack of enthusiasm for Nauru's independence. On the other hand, the unique Anglo-French Condominium (established in 1906) allowed joint administration over the New Hebrides for self-determination, but the French were not prepared to do so for strategic and cultural reasons. The joint administration continued until independence was finally granted to Vanuatu in 1979.

NAURU

Nauru's step towards independence was facilitated by the fact that its trusteeship position ensured that the United Nations Trusteeship Council provided an international forum for the Nauruans to exert pressure on Australia and its partners to win political reforms. The fundamental principle of trusteeship was that paramountcy be given to the wellbeing and development of the Nauruan people so that eventually they would be able to exercise the right of self-determination.

Annual reviews by the UN Trusteeship Council and visits by a UN Trusteeship Commission every three years ensured that Nauruan aspirations received a hearing. In December 1951 the Advisory Council of Chiefs was replaced by the Nauru Local Government Council. Australian-educated Nauruans, particularly Timothy Detudamo and Hammer DeRoburt, began to play a leading role in seeking greater involvement by Nauruans in government and in obtaining more royalties for the phosphate from BPC.

In 1956 DeRoburt was elected Head Chief and Chairman of Nauru Local Government Council. In the late-1950s and early-1960s talks centred around the resettlement of Nauruans as their island was seen as being unable to maintain them after the phosphate ran out.

The Nauruans preferred settlement as a single distinct community and keeping intact their right as a sovereign people. Frazer and Curtis Islands, off Queensland, were suggested as possible sites for Nauruan settlement. The Nauruan wish to retain their 'dignity as a race and community and to control their own affairs' meant accepting nothing short of sovereign independence. In the UN Trusteeship Council Meeting of July 1962, the Chinese delegate suggested independence on Nauru itself and the Soviet Union delegate argued that phosphate resources be handed over to the Nauruan people.

Between 1963 and 1967 DeRoburt intensified demands for sovereignty and a better deal on phosphate royalties. Resettlement was rejected as an option by Nauruans in late August 1964. Australia agreed to establish a legislative and executive council in early 1966 and royalties increased dramatically from 3s 8d (37 cents) to 13s 6d ($1.35) for 1964–65 to 17s 6d ($1.75) for 1965–66. Nauruans utilised the services of Dr J.W. Davidson, a political scientist and constitutional adviser, to assist them in their negotiations with Australian officials. By early 1967, the United Kingdom and New Zealand became directly involved in the negotiations for political change in Nauru. New Zealand opinion favoured the granting of independence to Nauru.

On 15 June 1967 Australia, New Zealand and Great Britain offered self-government to the Nauruan delegation together with a treaty arrangement which would leave Australia in charge of foreign affairs and defence. This offer was rejected. Later, at a Trusteeship Council meeting, DeRoburt agreed to the proposal to establish the Nauru Phosphate Corporation to buy out BPC for $21 million over three years and insisted on complete sovereignty for Nauru. At the special session of the Trusteeship Council in November 1967, it was agreed that Nauru be given independence. On 31 January 1968, on the anniversary of the return of Nauruan people from Truk, where the Nauruans had been resettled during the war, independence was celebrated.

The sudden acceptance of the right of national self-determination after a long period of intense negotiations meant that Nauru went up the path to independence without a constitution and without well conceived, long-term plans for the future.

VANUATU

Under the joint rule of France and Britain there was a dual administrative structure characterised by two education, medical, police and other administration departments—a system described as a pandemonium by Father Walter Lini, Vanuatu's Prime Minister. Grace Molisa, a leader in the anti-colonial struggles in Vanuatu who occupied a number of important posts in the bureaucracy after independence, has described the position of indigenous ni-Vanuatu in the following manner:

> Citizenship—before independence only cattle, coconuts and pigs counted, the people didn't. We didn't have legal status, we were non-existent in our own land. When other people travelled with passports, we could only go as far as identity cards, which hardly anybody recognised. If we ever went out of Vanuatu, you were subject to all kinds of embarrassment and indignity. People would just scratch their heads and ask 'where are you from?' We were legally non-existent. We were stateless, regardless of the fact that we had two colonial powers. These are memories that only people like me will have. The others will just read history but will never know the experience that we lived.
>
> —*Island Business News*, July 1990

Calls for greater access to decision making by New Hebrideans in the Advisory Council (established in 1958) were ignored, and 1971 saw the emergence of political parties, including the pro-independence New Hebrides National Party (NHNP). In August 1973, the National Party took its first major policy step, petitioning the United

Figure 10.8: Michael Somare, Foreign Affairs Minister, Papua New Guinea, 1991.

Figure 10.9: Fred Timakata, President of Vanuatu, 1991.

Nations to intervene in the New Hebrides situation. The following letter was sent along with copies to the French and British governments in Paris and London:

The New Hebrides National Party, concerned for human life and the free development of the indigenous New Hebrideans:
- assert that it is imperative to the future of the territory to have one system of government to enable it to develop self-reliance and stability
- assert that the British and French administrations cease their influence in the territory immediately
- assert that the United Nations send a fact-finding mission to the New Hebrides immediately to ascertain the possibility of establishing one system of government in collaboration with the New Hebrides National Party
- assert that the date of independence will be decided when the new form of government has existed and is functioning under the guidance of the United Nations.

This was the first concrete step that the party had ever taken on the issue of national liberation. After this action the party was increasingly active. Between 1974 and 1975 limited constitutional reforms were made. Municipal councils were established in Vila and Luganville and a Representative Assembly replaced the Advisory Council. While pro-French parties (including Union des Communautés des Nouvelles Hebrides (UCNH) took nearly all the seats in the municipal elections, in the elections for the Representative Assembly which followed in November 1975, it was the pro-independence NHNP that won seventeen of the twenty-nine elected seats, against ten for UCNH and two for Nagriamel and its ally. Thirteen other seats were allocated to the Chamber of Commerce, Cooperative Federations, and customary chiefs. The NHNP, which aimed for early independence, found that although it received 55 per cent of the votes, it did not enjoy a majority in the Assembly. It called for the elimination of the six Chamber of Commerce seats in the Assembly and when this was not accepted by the British and French colonial authorities, the NHNP staged a walkout.

The NHNP put forward a number of conditions to the administration, including the granting of self-government and a referendum to decide if the people of New Hebrides wanted independence. When these conditions were rejected, the NHNP boycotted the Assembly elections of November 1977. Pro-French parties known as 'Moderates' dominated the Representative Assembly and the NHNP proclaimed a 'Peoples' Provisional Government (PPG) and changed its name to the Vanuaku Pati. In 1978 a Government of National Unity was formed with the Vanuaku Pati obtaining 5 seats including the position of Deputy Chief Minister. The pro-French parties were allocated five seats and the position of Chief Minister, who had the casting vote. Father Gerard Leymang held the position of Chief Minister, and the leader of Vanuaku Pati, Father Walter Lini, was the Deputy Chief Minister.

In the general election of 14 November 1978, the Vanuaku Pati won twenty-six out of the thirty-nine seats and Father Lini became Chief Minister. The so called 'Moderates' refused to accept the results of the election. They renamed Santo and Tanna 'Vemarana' and 'Tafea' respectively and declared them independent in February 1980. Encouraged by some French interest as well as the American Phoenix Foundation, Jimmy Stevens of the Nagriamel Movement declared the secession of 'Vemarana' on 28 May 1980. Attempts to delay the granting of independence by fomenting civil disorder failed. British and French paratroopers were deployed in the New Hebrides but did not apprehend the secessionists. Soon after Vanuatu gained its independence in July 1980, the Prime Minister, Father Lini, requested help from Papua New Guinea. A Royal Australian Air Force Hercules carried a contingent of Papua New Guinea troops to Luganville in Santo. Two hundred rebels, including Jimmy Stevens, were captured.

2 Independence fostered by the colonial power

Fiji, the Solomon Islands, Kiribati, Tuvalu and Papua New Guinea received their independence as a result of the initiatives of the British, and in the case of Papua New Guinea, the Australian government.

Universal suffrage was granted in Fiji for the first time in 1963. The Legislative Council consisted of thirty-eight members including the Speaker. There were nineteen official members and twenty-eight unofficial members. The latter were divided equally along ethnic lines so that there were six Ethnic Fijians (two of whom were appointed by the Council of Chiefs, six Indo-Fijians, two nominated by the Governor) and six Europeans (of whom two were nominated by the Governor). This facade of equality masked unequal representation, because proportionately the Indo-Fijian population was much larger than that of ethnic Fijians and Europeans. Meanwhile the United Nations General Assembly demanded that Britain 'take immediate steps to transfer real power to the people of Fiji'.

By the early 1960s, two major political parties emerged, the Federation Party, which represented Indo-Fijian farmers and workers, and the Alliance Party, which represented ethnic Fijian chiefs and civil servants and was supported by ethnic Fijians, Europeans, mixed race people, Chinese and Indo-Fijian businessmen. At a Constitutional Conference in London in 1965, ethnic Fijians were allotted fourteen seats, including two representatives appointed by the Council of Chiefs. Indo-Fijians, who constituted 50 per cent of the population, were given twelve seats. The General

Electors, comprising Europeans, Chinese and mixed race persons, who accounted for 7 per cent of the population, received ten seats or 28 per cent of the thirty-six seats in the Legislative Council. In this pre-independence constitution, communal voting was retained (nine 'Fijian', nine 'Indian' and seven 'General Elector' seats were decided by exclusive ethnic voting) and a category of cross-voting was introduced. This allowed electors to cast votes for 'racial' representatives across ethnic lines.

In the general election of 1966, the Alliance Party won twenty-three seats and received the support of the two Council of Chiefs nominees and two independents. The Federation Party took the nine 'Indian' communal seats but 35 per cent of Indo-Fijians voted against it. Ethnic Fijians and General Electors voted overwhelmingly for the Alliance Party. With a large majority of seats in the Legislature, the Alliance Party introduced the Ministerial system.

Further constitutional discussions began in Suva in August 1969 and concluded in London in April–May 1970. With the death in October 1969 of the Federation Party Leader, A.D. Patel, his successor, S.M. Koya, took a more conciliatory position. The 1970 Independence Constitution had the following provisions: the state's legislature was bicameral with the House of Representatives as the lower house and the Senate as the upper house. The heritage of racial or 'communal' electorates based on three broad categories, 'Fijian, 'Indian' and 'General Electors', were retained. In the lower house, Fijians and Indians had twenty-two seats each (twelve 'communal' and ten 'cross-voting') while the General Electors had eight (three 'communal' and five 'cross-voting'). Indo-Fijians who then comprised 51 per cent of the population had 42.3 per cent of the seats. Ethnic Fijians, then making up 47 per cent of the population, had 42.3 per cent as well, and General Electors, constituting 3 per cent had 15.4 per cent. In this manner, the General Electors were over-represented by more than five times their proportional size.

The Upper House or Senate was formed by appointment. The Fijian Great Council of Chiefs, recognised as the keeper of ethnic Fijian 'traditions', selected eight members, the Prime Minister nominated seven, the Leader of the Opposition appointed six and the Council of Rotuma, one. The Senate was to safeguard the special interests of ethnic Fijians, particularly relating to ethnic Fijian land rights and customs. No significant amendments to the Constitution could be made without the approval of the Council of Chiefs. It was necessary to have the endorsement of three-quarters of the members of both houses to change provisions such as citizenship, the judiciary and the public service commission.

In the opinion of the historian Timothy McNaught, the Constitution therefore gave:
> ... iron clad security, short of revolution to the paramountcy of Fijian interests ... The triumph of Fijian political and European economic interests at national level, matched by the unambiguous commitment of Indian leaders to national peace, allowed the ascendant Fijian leaders to foster multi-racial participation in selected areas of national life such as higher education and civil service, while accepting as historically deter-mined the sharp racial boundaries in community life.

Fiji gained political independence on 10 October 1970, after ninety-six years of British colonial rule.

KIRIBATI AND TUVALU

The process of decolonisation in the Gilbert and Ellice Islands Colony culminated in the formation of two separate states and an unsuccessful attempt by the Banabans to dissociate from an independent Gilberts. The 1967 constitution established in the Gilbert and Ellice Islands a House of Representatives with an elected majority but this forum continued as an advisory body along the lines of the Advisory Council, which had been in existence since the early 1960s. Further political advancement came with the 1974 constitution, which created a full ministerial government with a Legislative Assembly and a Council of Ministers. The Governor continued to hold reserve powers.

Ellice Islanders had become senior civil servants; educated Ellice Island professionals, after doing well at school were succeeding disproportionately to their overall population in the colony. They recognised that if their future was tied to the Gilbertese then they would not be able to maintain their relatively better positions. In a referendum in August–September 1974 organised by the United Nations, Ellice Islanders overwhelmingly (92 per cent of votes cast) accepted secession. Between 1975 and 1976, Ellice Island civil servants and professionals shifted from Tarawa in the Gilberts to Funafuti in Tuvalu.

The name Tuvalu (cluster of eight) was adopted by the Ellice Islands. A Tuvalu House of Assembly was created with the existing eight Ellice Island members and Toaripi Lauti was elected Chief Minister. This tiny state of 25 square kilometres and a population of 7200 acquired its independence on 1 October 1978.

Meanwhile independence for Kiribati (the name adopted by the former Gilbert Islands) was scheduled for mid-1978, but delayed because of unsettled questions over Banaba Island. The isolated but phosphate-rich island of Banaba (Ocean Island) lies to the west of Kiribati. War damage and forty years of mining had allegedly made the island uninhabitable and Banabans had been resettled in Kiribati or on Rabi Island in Fiji. Meanwhile mining continued and royalties poured into the GEIC budget. It was being proposed that after independence these royalties would flow into the budget of the new nation of Kiribati. Finally, special provisions were incorporated into the Kiribati constitution to safeguard the interests of Banabans now in Fiji or Kiribati. (The future sovereignty of Banaba is still being debated.) Led by their first Prime Minister, Ieremia Tabai, the former Gilbert Islands, Phoenix Islands, Line Islands, Christmas Island and Ocean Island (Banaba) gained independence as Kiribati in July 1979.

3 Internally self-governing states in association with metropolitan countries

Cook Islands and Niue are self-governing countries whose external affairs and defence are the responsibility of their former colonial ruler, New Zealand. Their people are also citizens of New Zealand. There are now more Cook Islanders and Niueans resident in New Zealand than in their home islands.

In 1965 after some twenty years of political transition, during which the involvement of Cook Islanders increased in the legislative and executive committee, full internal self-government was granted. Albert Henry, the leader of the Cook Islands Party, became Premier of the Cook Islands.

Niue underwent a similar process of increasing local control over Niuean affairs from 1960. In 1965, the Niue Assembly indicated that they preferred a more gradual approach towards self-government, thereby rejecting New Zealand's timetable for political advancement. Between 1968 and 1974, the powers and the functions of the New Zealand Resident Commissioner were increasingly taken over by the Niuean Legislative Assembly and Executive Committee. A referendum, supervised by a United Nations mission in 1974, saw the acceptance of self-government by Niue. Robert Rex was designated Premier of Niue.

In the North Pacific there are now four political entities variously associated with the United States. These evolved from the former United Nations Trust Territories of the Pacific Islands (TTPI). Until mid-1962, these territories were under the control of the United States Navy and the Americans tested nuclear bombs and missiles in the Marshalls and developed military training facilities in Palau.

American strategic interests have been a dominant factor in the political transition of the TTPI. Political development in this region can be traced back to early 1965, when elections were held for a bicameral Congress of Micronesia made up of a House of Representatives and a Senate. In 1967 the Congress created a Future Political Status Commission which examined the possibilities of future political advancement. During 1968 and 1969, the ten-member Commission visited Puerto Rico and a number of other Pacific Islands to gain first-hand knowledge of their political status, constitutions and political development. In its report to the Congress of Micronesia, the Commission recommended two options: self-government in free association with the United States or complete independence. The USA offered Commonwealth status, akin to Puerto Rico.

Northern Marianas opted for the American offer and became the Commonwealth of the Northern Marianas in political union with the USA in January 1978. During the protracted negotiations for free association, it became apparent that a unified Micronesia was not a desired goal among the remaining districts, and three separate entities emerged: Palau, the Marshall Islands and the Federated States of Micronesia (Kosrae, Pohnpei, Yap and Truk). These political groupings were recognised by the USA following a constitutional referendum on a unified Micronesia, and the former Congress of Micronesia was abolished as a result.

Separate constitutions that were endorsed for the three political entities led to the formation of distinct constitutional governments. Thus Marshall Islands became an autonomous political unit on 1 May 1979; the Federated States of Micronesia (FSM) followed on 10 May 1979; and Palau became self-ruling on 1 January 1981. A Compact of Free Association was signed during 1982 by the US and each of the three emergent states. The UN Trusteeship was terminated in FSM in 1986 but Palau's refusal to change its nuclear-free constitution and the American insistence that this be done, has delayed its change of status. Seven referendums have been held so far to change the nuclear-free clause of the Palauan constitution, which requires a 75 per cent majority for the change.

Under the Compact of Free Association, each of these three states is recognised as sovereign, with the ability to maintain its own foreign affairs, though the USA is responsible for the defence of the Marshalls and FSM for a minimum of fifteen years and for fifty years for Palau. The USA will also operate the Kwajalein Missile Range for a period of thirty years and has the option of using sites on Palau for military activities. The USA has undertaken to provide financial assistance which has been estimated at $2.2 billion for the initial fifteen year period.

Common features in the paths to independence

Three major characteristics may be seen in the process of decolonisation in the Pacific. These are, firstly, the relatively recent and short timetable towards self-government and independence for most island states. National political advancement did not emerge until the late 1960s in nearly all Pacific states. Secondly, there was an absence of nationalistic movements and violent struggles to gain self-determination. For nearly all island states, independence was brought about by negotiations between the colonial rulers and local leaders. Thirdly, the constitutional arrangements for all Pacific states have been based on the British 'Westminster model', with special provisions to take account of local structures, customs and traditions. The latter are sometimes based on concepts that contradict those on which the Westminster system is founded. For most of the colonial period, issues such as the franchise, elections, electoral polities, political parties and legislative bodies were not accountable to local people. These historical factors had considerable impact on the proper functioning of democratic institutions in the post-independence era.

DOCUMENTS

1   Closing address at the Fiji constitutional conference, Marlborough House, London, 5 May 1970

Lord Shepherd, Your Excellency, Honourable Leader of the Opposition, Ladies and Gentlemen:

Today marks the end of a long journey—a journey of close on one hundred years of peace and war, of progress and development, of social and political change. Through it all, we have had the protection, help and guidance of the United Kingdom. Many of her traditions are firmly grafted not only on our political institutions, but on our whole national life. The rule of law, parliamentary democracy, respect for the rights of minorities, a sense of fair play and give and take, are all taken for granted in Fiji, but they are, in a very real sense, a legacy from the British. Should we ever wish to forget the British—which God forbid—it would not be possible. Your ways and your ideals are too much part and parcel of our own way ...

But last year saw a new spirit in Fiji, a new realisation that without harmony among the races there is no hope for Fiji. And this realisation brought a new resolve to seize this moment and to inaugurate the positive actions which see their fulfilment here today. The two parties came together and decided to find where they agreed and where they disagreed and to try to find mutually acceptable solutions. This involved much hard study, a lot of frank talking, and on some occasions sharp definition of position. But throughout, the discussions were carried on in a spirit of mutual trust and goodwill and with the shared objective of the welfare of Fiji as a whole.

—Ratu Kamisese Mara, *Selected Speeches by the Rt Honourable Sir Kamisese Mara, KBE*, Government Printer, Suva, p. 8

2   Radio broadcast on the eve of independence of Suva, Fiji, 9 October 1970

We were admittedly somewhat thrown off course at the 1968 by-elections and we all came close enough to the rocks to have a good look at the dangers. This was salutary for us all.

And the following year we all sat down together and almost to our surprise by going through the 1965 Constitution clause by clause found how much we had in common.

And I would pause here to pay tribute to the late Mr A.D. Patel, who was deeply involved at the outset of these discussions and whose qualities of leadership did so much to pave the way for his party's close association with the new constitutional changes.

It has been said that independence has come very suddenly. But once the 1965 Constitutional Conference in London set us on our way to internal self-government, it was a short step to the Member system. And by the time we moved on to the Ministerial system we were already assuming the responsibilities and actions of Ministers and were firmly set on our course.

We then set ourselves to narrow the differences and after a visit from Lord Shepherd the Minister of State at the Foreign and Commonwealth Office we were able to go to London for a Conference with virtually one major matter unsolved—the procedure for elections and the method of representation. And such was the goodwill and spirit of give and take at that Conference that we came home with a report agreed and signed by all members ...

Meanwhile our representatives at the London Conference in 1965 had affirmed the unquestioned ownership of Fijian land as well as title to other lands and this was reaffirmed in the 1970 Constitutional Conference. And very firm safeguards are clearly written in the new Constitution on Ordinances particularly dealing with Fijian interests. The strong representation of members nominated by the Council of Chiefs in the Senate is another bulwark for Fijian interests.

But I remind Fijians that the best and strongest safeguard we can have in our own land is a happy and harmonious society. Given this, I am confident that all will work together and that it will be from the goodwill of the other races that the Fijian people will derive their most lasting guarantees.

—Ratu Kamisese Mara, *Selected Speeches by the Rt Honourable Sir Kamisese Mara KBE*, Government Printer, Suva, pp. 13–14

3   Western Samoan–New Zealand relations

The Constitutional Convention, in this, its final meeting—

1. Reaffirms the profound desire of the People of Western Samoa that Western Samoa should become an Independent State and expresses the hope the General Assembly of the United Nations will, in its current Session, agree to institute the procedure necessary for the termination of the Trusteeship Agreement.
2. Affirms its belief that, in view of its adoption of a Constitution for the Independent State of Western Samoa and of the transfer in October 1959 of the functions of the High Commissioner and Executive Council to the Council of State and Cabinet, no reasonable doubts can be held as to the readiness of Western Samoa for independence.
3. Welcomes the clear and friendly understanding between the Governments of Western Samoa and New Zealand, whereby both Governments agree that the sovereignty of Western Samoa should be complete and unqualified and that the two countries should continue to work together, on terms agreeable to both Governments.
4. Welcomes the offer of the Government of New Zealand to provide assistance to the Independent State of Western Samoa.
5. Recommends:
   (*a*) That the framework of future co-operation between New Zealand and the Independent State of Western Samoa should be laid down in a Treaty of Friendship between the two sovereign states to be signed after Independence Day.
   (*b*) That, in particular, the Government of the Independent State of Western Samoa should request the Government of New Zealand to afford—
   (i) administrative and technical assistance;
   (ii) assistance in carrying out its external affairs in such a manner as will not detract from the responsibility of the Government of the Independent State of Western Samoa to formulate its own international policy.

   —from 'Resolutions Adopted by the Constitutional Convention of Western Samoa 1960' in J.W. Davidson, *Samoa mo Samoa: The emergence of the modern state of Western Samoa*, Oxford University Press, Melbourne, 1967, pp. 400–1

4   From the Constitution of Western Samoa

IN THE HOLY NAME OF GOD, THE ALMIGHTY, THE EVER LOVING

WHEREAS sovereignty over the Universe belongs to the Omnipresent God alone, and the authority to be exercised by the people of Western Samoa within the limits prescribed by His commandments is a sacred heritage;

WHEREAS the Leaders of Western Samoa have declared that Western Samoa should be an Independent State based on Christian principles and Samoan custom and traditions;

AND WHEREAS the Constitutional Convention, representing the people of Western Samoa, has resolved to frame a constitution for the Independent State of Western Samoa;

WHEREIN should be secured to all the people their fundamental rights;

WHEREIN the impartial administration of justice should be fully maintained.

AND WHEREIN the integrity of Western Samoa, its independence, and all its rights should be safeguarded;

NOW THEREFORE, we the people of Western Samoa in our Constitutional Convention, this twenty-eighth day of October 1960, do hereby adopt, enact, and give to ourselves this Constitution.

—Preamble, The Constitution of the Independent State of Western Samoa, from
Pacific Constitutions, Vol. 1: Polynesia, p. 455

5   The Western Samoa Act 1961

1961, No. 68

An Act to make provision in connection with the attainment of independence by the people of Western Samoa

[24 November 1961]

WHEREAS at the date of the passing of this Act the Government of New Zealand is the administering authority for the Territory of Western Samoa under the Trusteeship Agreement for that Territory approved by the General Assembly of the United Nations on the 13th day of December 1946: And whereas the Trusteeship Agreement will terminate on the 1st day of January 1962 and Western Samoa will thereupon become a fully independent sovereign State under the name of the Independent State of Western Samoa having a constitution which has been adopted by the people of Western Samoa: And whereas it is expedient that provision be made declaring that Her Majesty shall have no jurisdiction over the Independent State of Western Samoa on and after the date on which the termination of the Trusteeship Agreement takes effect and for the repeal or amendment of such of the laws of New Zealand as would be incompatible with the status of Western Samoa as a fully independent sovereign State:

1. Short Title—This Act may be cited as the Western Samoa Act 1961.

2. Commencement—(1) Except where this Act otherwise provides, this Act shall come into force at the hour of 11 o'clock in the evening on the 1st day of January 1962, being the time in New Zealand corresponding to the commencement of the 1st day of January 1962 in Western Samoa (that date being the date appointed by the General Assembly of the United Nations for the termination of the Trusteeship Agreement for the Territory of Western Samoa).

(2) The period of 24 hours following the commencement of this Act is hereinafter referred to as Independence Day.

3. Independence of Western Samoa—It is hereby declared that on and after Independence Day Her Majesty in right of New Zealand shall have no jurisdiction over the Independent State of Western Samoa.

4. Future New Zealand Acts not to be in force in Western Samoa—No Act of the Parliament of New Zealand passed on or after Independence Day or passed before Independence Day and coming into force on or after Independence Day shall be in force in Western Samoa.

—*The Western Samoa Act*, 1961

6 From the Constitution of Tuvalu

PREAMBLE

WHEREAS the Islands in the Pacific Ocean then known as the Ellice Islands came under the protection of Her Most Gracious Majesty Queen Victoria in September 1892 and on 12th January 1916 in conjunction with the Gilbert Islands became known as the Gilbert and Ellice Islands Colony;

AND WHEREAS on 1st October 1975 Her Most Excellent Majesty Queen Elizabeth II was graciously pleased to establish the Ellice Islands as a separate colony under their ancient name of Tuvalu;

AND WHEREAS the people of Tuvalu, acknowledging God as the Almighty and Everlasting Lord and giver of all good things, humbly place themselves under His good providence and seek His blessing upon themselves and their lives;

AND WHEREAS the people of Tuvalu desire to constitute themselves as an Independent State based on Christian principles, the Rule of Law, and Tuvaluan custom and tradition;

NOW THEREFORE the people of Tuvalu hereby affirm their allegiance to Her Most Excellent Majesty Queen Elizabeth II, Her Heirs and Successors, and do hereby proclaim the establishment of a free and democratic sovereign nation, of which the following provisions shall form the Constitution.

—Preamble, The Constitution of Tuvalu, from *Pacific Constitutions Vol. 1: Polynesia*, University of the South Pacific, Suva, p. 289

7 Tuvalu Act 1978

1978 CHAPTER 20

An Act to make provision for, and in connection with the attainment by Tuvalu of independence within the Commonwealth.   [30th June 1978]

Be it enacted by the Queen's most Excellent Majesty, by and with the advice and consent of the Lords Spiritual and Temporal, and Commons, in this present Parliament assembled, and by the authority of the same, as follows:

1.—(1) On and after 1st October 1978 (in this Act referred to as 'Independence Day') Her Majesty's Government in the United Kingdom shall have no responsibility for the government of Tuvalu.

(2) No Act of the Parliament of the United Kingdom passed on or after Independence Day shall extend, or be deemed to extend, to Tuvalu as part of its law; and on and after that day the provisions of Schedule 1 to this Act shall have effect with respect to the legislative powers of Tuvalu.

—*Tuvalu Act* 1978, Parliament of the United Kingdom

8 The Niue Constitution Act 1974

1974, No. 42
An Act to make provision for self-government by the people of Niue, and to provide a constitution for Niue

[29 August 1974]

1. Short Title and commencement—(1) This Act may be cited as the Niue Constitution Act 1974.

(2) This Act shall come into force on a date to be appointed for the commencement thereof by the Governor-General, by Proclamation.

This Act came into force on 19 October 1974. See the Niue Constitution Act Commencement Order 1974 (S.R. 1974/286).

2. Application to Niue—This Act shall extend to Niue as part of the law of Niue.

3. Niue to be self-governing—Niue shall be self-governing.

4. Constitution of Niue—(1) The Constitution set out in its Niuean language version in the First Schedule to this Act and in its English language version in the Second Schedule to this Act shall be the Constitution of Niue (in this Act called the Constitution), and shall be the supreme law of Niue.

(2)Where the Constitution provides that any New Zealand Court or Department of Government or statutory authority shall perform any function or exercise any power in relation to Niue, that Court, or, as the case may be, the officers of that Department or the members and staff of that authority are by this Act authorised and required to perform that function or exercise that power in accordance with the Constitution.

5. British nationality and New Zealand citizenship—Nothing in this Act or in the Constitution shall affect the status of any person as a British subject or New Zealand citizen by virtue of the British Nationality and New Zealand Citizenship Act 1948.

6. External affairs and defence—Nothing in this Act or in the Constitution shall affect the responsibilities of Her Majesty the Queen in right of New Zealand for the external affairs and defence of Niue.

7. Economic and administrative assistance—It shall be a continuing responsibility of the Government of New Zealand to provide necessary economic and administrative assistance to Niue.

8. Co-operation between New Zealand and Niue—Effect shall be given to the provisions of sections 6 and 7 of this Act, and to any other aspect of the relationship between New Zealand and Niue which may from time to time call for positive co-operation between New Zealand and Niue, after consultation between the Prime Minister of New Zealand and the Premier of Niue, and in accordance with the policies of their respective Government; and, if it appears desirable that any provision be made in the law of Niue to carry out these policies, that provision may be made in the manner prescribed in the Constitution, but not otherwise.

—The *Niue Constitution Act* 1974, from *Pacific Constitutions, Vol. 1: Polynesia*, University of the South Pacific, Suva, pp. 283–4

QUESTIONS AND ACTIVITIES

1   Why did Ratu Kamisese Mara (Document 1) place so much emphasis on British links in his address at the Constitutional Convention?

2   In stressing the British connection, is Mara's speech (Document 2) a denial of Fijian identity and Fijian contribution to Fiji's government and political organisation?

3   What link does Mara suggest exists between 'races and parties' in Fiji?

4   In his independence eve speech, who is Mara referring to when he says 'we'?

5   What phases does Mara identify in Fiji's progress towards independence?

6   Why would the Western Samoan Constitutional Convention (Document 3) bother to say 'no reasonable doubts can be held' regarding readiness to proclaim independence?

7   Section 5 (ii) of the Western Samoan Constitutional Convention Resolutions suggests that New Zealand and Western Samoa would still be linked after independence. What type of relationship was being suggested?

8   In the Western Samoa Act of 1961 (Document 5), how was the relationship to New Zealand worded?

9   Compare the provisions regarding Western Samoa–New Zealand relations to sections (6)–(8) in the Niue Constitution Act (Document 8). How was Niue's proposed relationship with New Zealand different to that of Western Samoa's?

10 Compare the Niue and Western Samoa relationship with New Zealand to Tuvalu's relationship to the United Kingdom (Document 7).

11 Compare the preambles to the Tuvalu and Western Samoan Constitutions (Documents 6 and 4). To what degree are western introduced religion, Kastom, and forms of introduced and traditional political organisation integrated into the constitutions?

12 Why do you think one Preamble refers to, and one does not refer to, the former colonial ruler?

13 For further research, you might investigate how many Pacific Island constitutions are published in vernacular language, how many have been revised since independence and how often political, social or cultural problems have been solved finally by reference to the wording of a constitution.

REFERENCES

See the Select Bibliography on pages 161–3.

Chapter 11
Neo-colonial Influences and Issues

John Anglim, Australian National University

Figure 11.1: The flag of independent Papua New Guinea

By 1980 most of the island peoples of the Pacific had achieved independence or had chosen a status somewhat short of full independence:
- The Cook Islands and Niue chose 'free association' with New Zealand
- The Marshall Islands and the Federated States of Micronesia chose free association with the United States
- The Northern Marianas elected to become a Commonwealth of the United States
- Others were fully independent—but when we say that a state is 'independent', what do we actually mean?

The meaning of independence

In formal terms, independent countries have charge of their internal and external affairs. They have certain rights: for example, they can enter into treaties, defend (and exploit) their territories and resources, and make laws. They also assume responsibility for their people's welfare and their nation's obligations to the international community. But for rights to be exercised, responsibilities to be met or aspirations to be realised, a nation needs resources, and formal independence does not guarantee those.

The small island nations of the Pacific have particular problems, commonly referred to as 'constraints to development'. These constraints make it difficult for them to exercise real control over their affairs. For example, in 1984, nearly all of Kiribati's export earnings of $A8.8 million were derived from the export of seafoods and copra, but Kiribati paid out nearly two-and-one-half times as much on imports, including $A3.1 million on fuel. Its major source of income was the $A13.5 million aid it received from outside donors. Clearly, a significant fall in the price of seafoods or copra or a rise in the price of oil would have made Kiribati even more dependent on external sources of funds, or forced it to accept a lower standard of living.

Kiribati's problems are common to most small island nations. Their economies are said to be very 'open', in that they rely on the export of a few primary products, the prices of which can fluctuate markedly but are mostly falling over the long term. Because each country is only one producer among many, it has little ability to influence prices. They generally lack the biological diversity to change over to other products. Producers are spread over many islands and even their major ports are far from the major trading routes, so transport costs are high. Volumes are too low to justify investment in expensive processing plants, so there is considerable spoilage and the exporters miss out on the increased profits to be made from selling processed products. The local economies are too small to justify such investment for domestic consumption.

There are other problems associated with smallness. A jetty which serves 300 people may be no cheaper to build than one to service 3000 people: but the cost per head would be ten times greater. Similarly, it may require nearly as many people to staff a small medical clinic as it does to staff a larger one, so the cost per patient is greater. Indeed, the costs of providing many services in small island nations are proportionately much greater than in, say, Australia or New Zealand. Tiny nations may be unable to afford to be represented at negotiations where decisions will be made which will directly affect their wellbeing, for example, on Law of the Sea, sea level rise, the General Agreement on Tariffs and Trade, nuclear-free zones or international loan meetings. And they are vulnerable through their absence to the influence and depredations of powerful countries and lobby groups.

Economic threats to independence

In 1984, the Solomon Islands impounded the *Jeanette Diana*, an American purse seiner (tuna fishing boat) for fishing illegally within the Solomons' 200 mile (320 km) exclusive economic zone (EEZ). The United States government, pressed by the powerful American Tuna Association, placed a ban on all fish imports from the Solomons. As fish have provided up to one-third of the Solomons' export revenue, with America a major market, the impact on the Solomons was naturally severe. Ultimately, the two countries negotiated a settlement. However, the point remains that the Solomon Islands was an independent country asserting its internationally recognised rights, yet it was unable to exercise those rights effectively because its open economy made it highly vulnerable to actions in a single major market.

Tuna fishing returned to prominence in 1985. The United States once again supported its tuna fishermen by declining to pay adequate royalties for the right of its tuna fleet to fish within Kiribati's EEZ. Kiribati, with only two export commodities, was even more vulnerable than the Solomons to the power of the American Tuna Association. Besides, it could not afford to patrol, let alone defend its enormous EEZ. In short, it could do nothing. Fortunately, the USSR was looking to fish for tuna in the South Pacific, and was prepared to pay its way. Kiribati and the Soviet Union signed a one-year agreement for $A1 million. Vanuatu followed suit in 1986. The United

States, Australia and New Zealand (the ANZUS countries) were concerned at Soviet 'encroachment' into the region and tried to convince Kiribati and Vanuatu to reject the Soviet offers. The US attempted to buy-off Kiribati with increased aid, but Kiribati President Tabai declined, preferring a commercial deal with the Soviets to a handout from America.

The Pacific Island countries were clearly and vocally upset at what they saw as economic exploitation by US fishermen, supported by the American government, and resented the ANZUS countries' unsolicited and unwarranted interference in the exercise of their sovereign rights. The United States was stunned into action to close what it saw as a 'window of opportunity' for Soviet influence in the region. US negotiators sat down with the nations of the South Pacific Forum and, in 1987, signed the South Pacific Regional Fisheries Treaty which would, in effect, pay the royalties of the American Tuna Association and provide technical assistance to the South Pacific countries to help them develop their own fishing industries. Most importantly for the US, the Treaty went some way towards restoring the goodwill lost through their hamfisted and (to the islands) bullying behaviour.

The politics of aid

While it is clear that Kiribati's and Vanuatu's deals with the Soviet Union were commercial in nature, the non-communist Western-alliance ANZUS nations' responses related to their own political and strategic concerns. However, Pacific Island governments had already shown themselves to be quite adept at taking advantage of such concerns.

In 1976, the King of Tonga had approached Australia, New Zealand, the USA and other donors for funding to build an airport. When his appeals were rejected, he approached the Soviet Union for assistance. Australia, New Zealand and the USA were shocked to find an independent Pacific nation acting independently, developing its own foreign policy and not simply 'toeing the ANZUS line'.

After warning the island leaders about Soviet intentions in the region, Australia's reaction was to quadruple its aid to the islands from $A15 million in 1974–76 to $A60 million in 1977–79 and to increase its diplomatic representation in the region. This activity was so clearly designed to deny Soviet access to the region that, when Australia disingenuously claimed humanitarian concern, the island leaders rightly felt insulted.

'Playing the Soviet card' (and later the 'Libyan card'), as it came to be known, is one means by which the small island states have been able to secure for themselves funds or other assistance which would otherwise have been denied to them. But whether such exploitation of superpower rivalry will continue to be effective in the post-cold war era of Soviet–US detente is another question.

The use of strategic importance as a bargaining chip is clearest in the case of the former USTT of the Pacific Islands, where the Marshall Islands, the Federated States of Micronesia and the Commonwealth of the Northern Mariana Islands openly bartered the granting of US access, and the denial of Soviet access, to their territory for very high levels of US aid. Indeed, US aid is the major source of funds for all of these new political entities. But what do these pacts mean for the people's long-term independence?

The Marshallese have access to a level of material goods which they cannot possibly afford to acquire through their own efforts. However, because their economy is propped up by US aid funds, they have been able to avoid or put off 'hard' decisions about the allocation of resources. Bureaucracy can grow unchecked and projects can be commenced whose recurrent costs (maintenance, fuel, parts, etc.) will require a high level of funding for years to come. In such circumstances, when things come so easily, it would be a brave or foolhardy politician who recommended tightening belts or making the sacrifices necessary to restructure the economy so as to make it more self-sufficient in the long term or to diversify the sources of income.

The problems associated with reliance on external funding sources apply just as much to foreign investment as they do to foreign aid. A single company can establish or destroy an industry with the stroke of a director's pen. A decision seen simply as 'good business' to the Paris, Tokyo or Sydney based investor may devastate a small country's development plans. When the Van Camp Sea Food Company began operations in Palau in 1964, Palau envisaged a viable fishing and canning industry. However, when it closed down its operations there in 1983, Palau was left with a fleet of mostly idle fishing vessels and an inactive freezing plant.

In striking their deals with the US, the Micronesian peoples understood that they were sacrificing foreign affairs and defence powers, but many also saw that in relying on incomes generated elsewhere, they were passing control over their material wellbeing to others, indeed to a single other—the United States. Unless they invest wisely, the Marshallese will be even more dependent on the US at the end of their Compact of Free Association and, in what may be a different strategic environment, there is no guarantee of continued US generosity.

Tourism

One industry claimed to have particular potential for the economic independence of small island nations is tourism. Indeed, tourism is rapidly increasing throughout the Pacific, where it is seen as:
- a way of obtaining 'hard' currencies which can be used to promote local development
- a source of employment and skill development for the local people
- a chance for people of different cultures to mix and learn about each other.

But tourism is a mixed blessing. Consider a typical package tour. An Australian airline flies tourists to an Australian-owned hotel, where they eat food imported from Australia, participate in activities run by the Australian operator or its local subsidiary, and perhaps conduct their duty-free shopping in Australian-owned stores (usually purchasing goods made in Europe or Asia). If they do shop locally, they tend to push up prices. In some cases, not only the accommodation, but even the food and recreational activities are prepaid in Australia, greatly reducing the money flowing into the local economy. Profits will remain in-country only if taxes are low, forcing tourist destinations to compete with each other in offering the lowest tax rates. The operator will also wish to minimise costs, so wages will be kept low. Senior staff will probably be Australian, leaving only menial tasks for the locals.

The cultural impact can be harmful. The Pacific is already replete with examples of 'cultural shows' which demean the performers and misrepresent the local culture. The 'Polynesian' dance shows at one resort in Guam are a particularly reprehensible example. Guam is part of Micronesia, not Polynesia, but the resort operators presumably found Micronesian customs too dull for their customers—mostly Japanese or young American servicemen. Meanwhile, the local people are exhorted to smile at the tourists so as not to spoil the impression that they are visiting a tropical paradise.

Not even the 'tourist attractions' are safe. A walk along Waikiki in Hawaii or Garapan in Saipan, where vegetation (and once-productive farmland) has given way to beachfront hotels, shows that the tourists are rapidly destroying the very things they came to see—and one wonders what this might mean for the long-term viability of the tourist industry itself. Which brings us to the fickle nature of tourism. It is subject to changes in taste and wealth, to rising fuel costs, to changing air routes, even to changing technology; when long-range aeroplanes no longer have to island-hop to refuel, only the 'best' destinations survive.

Consequences of migration

The economies of island budgets are also affected by remittances from family members who have migrated to New Zealand, Australia or the United States of America. The flow of money from remittances combined with reliance on aid donors, and the dominance of paid employment opportunities in government or public-sector jobs, has created a new Pacific acronym: MIRAB societies (Migration, Remittances, Aid and Bureaucracy). However, temporary or permanent migration to take jobs, for example in New Zealand, is becoming less an option as rim countries tighten their entry permit rules. Island people also travel to urban centres, to other islands and beyond the region for study and training. Migration and mobility are characteristics of island life, but the impact of population loss, separation of families and the loosening of community responsibilities is only now being highlighted.

Several regional organisations have been created in the post-independence era with the expressed aims of forging solidarity among the micro-states of the Pacific. It has been argued that this solidarity will enable small states to exercise an influence on international forums and relationships with super-powers, which their solitary voices might not achieve. Since 1945 a number of regional links have been established—a regional shipping line, a regional university (based in Suva), organisations such as the Pacific Island Producers Association, South Pacific Commission, South Pacific Forum, South Pacific Bureau of Economic Cooperation, South Pacific Board of Evaluation and Assessment (which administers regional Year 12 subjects), and CCOP/SPOAC (joint prospecting for off-shore mineral resources). More recently, subregional political groupings have appeared, including a 'Melanesian Spearhead' group formed by Vanuatu, the Solomons and Papua New Guinea.

The enthusiasm for this regional identity came from within the new nations of the Pacific, but also from former colonial rulers. Australia has been one of the 'rim' and metropolitan nations to promote regionalisation. In 1979 the Harries Report (on Australia's relations with the Third World) noted that Australia's main interest in the island states of the Southwest Pacific involved security considerations. 'One motivation for Australia's active support for the South Pacific Forum and other forms of subregional collaboration is to encourage a sense of collective identity among these small nations which may serve to lessen their vulnerability to inimical external influence.' It was clear to Pacific island leaders that 'inimical' referred not to the islands' security but to Australia's.

In many ways religion has also been regionalised. At the same time churches have become more indigenous and less influenced or directed by metropolitan authority. The legacy of the missionaries can be found throughout the Pacific. While traditional belief is important, in formal ways such as the wording of the constitutions written by each new Pacific nation, the influence of the introduced religions is still strong. This must be contrasted to the taking over of churches by indigenous leaders and the founding of, for example, distinctly Melanesian churches. Although Christianity has maintained its prominence as a major plank of island society and culture, the introduction of indigenous churches and the adoption of new forms of spiritual life have been a feature of the late-twentieth century.

International pressures

Independent nations may own their island world, but they are also drawn into membership of the wider international community. Rainforest milling, sea-bed mining, the marketing of passports, off-shore tax havens, drift netting, chemical waste dumping, and nuclear testing are local issues with international profiles. Papua New Guinea and the Solomons want to open their rainforests to timber milling, but there is considerable international pressure being exerted to protect rainforests. In regard to huge mining developments, can Papua New Guinea, for example, maintain control over multinational operations while maintaining profits for the company, their own government and land-holders? Relationships between regional neighbours, multinational corporations, central governments, provincial governments and local land-holders often create complex difficulties.

Independence carries with it the right to make decisions on the basis of sovereign and local considerations. However, international pressure can be exercised against individual nations which have been seen to be breaking international law. For example, military action by the French in New Caledonia and Ouvea, the Santo rebellion in Vanuatu, the coups and military takeover in Fiji, and Papua New Guinea's actions in Bougainville have raised international and regional questions about the use of military solutions to solve domestic political issues. Each of these military actions was criticised internationally but they were in essence local issues, needing local solutions. Island nations have regained their sovereignty and independence. Now they are striving to establish ways to protect that independence in a complex economic world system and global environment.

The examples used in the chapter show that formal independence does not guarantee de facto independence. The power of the large and rich countries and the economic constraints and other vulnerabilities of the small Pacific Island nations, illustrate that there are varying degrees of independence. However, the larger nations are also constrained in many ways and the island nations have shown themselves willing and able to take advantage of those constraints.

DOCUMENTS

1 Bad effects of migration for Tonga

While the total population has remained static, the work force has dramatically declined, i.e. those from 18 to 40 years of age. These are the important people in an agricultural economy and these are the people who are largely migrating. More and more of those who remain are taking up white collar jobs, which are now relatively easy to obtain. Most of the land lies idle. There are fewer and fewer people to work it. Many of the older generation are living off remittances from their sons and daughters overseas, so they no longer have to push themselves to do anything more than grow food for themselves.

Some of the land is still held by people living overseas, and provision has been made for them to sublease their land, thus giving rise to 'absentee landlords'.

There is also some wooing of overseas capital to Tonga and this usually is associated with some land being leased to overseas interests.

Family life has suffered enormously by the separation of spouses. Most host countries demand that only individuals be accepted, and only after long years of separation when that person has obtained some qualifying status is it possible to bring over a spouse and children. Many couples cannot survive this long separation and it has been the cause of divorce, one parent families and de facto relationships. A whole generation of people are growing up who have never had an experience of normal family life. For them the very concept of marriage involves the long separation which other countries only experienced in wartime. Every village has its quota of those 'migration widows', very often young women in their 20's and 30's struggling alone to look after 3 or 4 children. At the other end of the scale there are the matriarchs in their 50's with a tribe of adolescent children whom they alone are trying to guide into adulthood.

Another problem occurs when young couples marry overseas. To meet the demands on them both in the host country and home country they must both work, some even having two or three jobs. As the babies come along they are sent back to the grandparents to care for while they continue to work.

Private remittances of money are a part of life in Tonga. Whenever something occurs which demands money in any quantity the first thought is to get it from those members of the family who are overseas …

Among those at home a hand out mentality has developed. To some extent they are being caught up in consumerism, desiring more and asking for more. It is very often 'easy come—easy go' so that the money obtained is not always used wisely. Enormous amounts can go into funeral expenses, big feasts, building bigger and better buildings not commensurate with the country, excessive consumption of alcohol and cigarettes, etc.

Now that a decline in population has begun it is not imprudent to expect that it will continue. There is no reason to believe that migration as such will slow down or cease, but even more marked will be the drop in replacement births. When one sees the enormous number of school children in Tonga one may question that. But primary school rolls are dropping annually in many of the village schools, some to the extent of a class a year. Church statistics show a marked decline in both marriages and baptisms, and this will surely escalate as present parents get past the child bearing years and their young people continue to migrate before marriage.

How long remittances will continue to come to Tonga is difficult to estimate. It is difficult to see that they will extend into second generation migrants for whom the ties of home will be much weaker and who will be much more a part of the culture of the host countries. So at the moment we may be riding the crest of the wave, but it will require a very good balancing act to stay there.

—from a speech by Patelisio P. Finau, SM, at the Pacific Islander Migration and Settlement Conference, Sydney, September 1990

2   Indigenous history

No non-western educated Tongan can claim to present a pure authentic view of Tongan history. Neither does his European counterpart. However, a European scholar is restricted in many areas in what he wants to know or find out about local history due to his being culturally different. A Tongan history from a purely local perspective, if there is such a thing, is only a different version of mythology. On the other hand, a scholarly history of Tonga without consideration of local values and applying Christian value judgements is a sterile academic exercise. If we are to accept the view held by many sympathetic historians, either of European or indigenous descent, we are committing ourselves to treating mythology as real history. By doing so, the objects of historical investigation are either given a false image and reflection of realities (which in practice does not do them any good), or we are too overly patronising. Both are unacceptable. Let me illustrate this point by making reference to a Tongan myth—the myth of dynastic origins. 'Aho'eitu was said to have had an earthly mother Va'epopua and a heavenly father Tangaloa. If we are prepared to accept, unquestioningly, this assertion because it is an indigenous perspective, we are creating the worst history of all times. Without an analytical and critical approach which is the tool of Western education, we are committing ourselves to treating mythology as reality ...

It should be put straight that the European intellectual tradition does not have a similar or equivalent tradition in Tonga. Here I specifically refer to the traditional period which, for our purposes, covers the beginning of the original settlement up to the establishment of the first formal schools in 1866. The process of learning in Tonga in this period can be correctly called a socialisation process. Margaret Mead and Raymond Firth have documented this socialisation process quite thoroughly in two different areas of the Pacific, Manu'a and Tikopia respectively. The socialisation process in Tonga was similar, although it was extremely authoritative due to the rigidly stratified nature of the society. Consequently, the critical faculty of Tongan minds was undeveloped and enclosed. If it did exist, it did so quietly. The nature of Tongan society greatly contributed to this uncritical mindset of its members. Life without criticism is the life of a servant or slave. In Tonga a critical stance was suppressed and treated as unacceptable, if not rude ...

As previously mentioned, there are a growing number of scholars who would like to see the emergence of indigenous history. If a real 'indigenous history' is to emerge, I expect to see a development within Tongan society of an intellectual tradition similar to that of Europe. I think this is unrealistic since no authentic indigenous culture exists on its own and in total isolation. The Tongan culture is not authentic, nor any other culture. George Marcus refers to it as a 'compromise culture' (that is, Tongan culture dynamically affected and changed by contact with Europeans). The best we could hope for is a compromise history which is sensitive to indigenous values and cultural practices. Albert Wendt, as quoted in Howe, a well known Pacific scholar, has repeatedly called for an indigenous history. He proposes that real history of the Pacific can only be written by Pacific Islanders. I do not believe that this is the case. Statements and assertions of this kind should be treated cautiously. A non-Western trained historian cannot write genuine history. Only a person with academic training, like Wendt, who has learned his trade from Western institutions of education, is capable of such a task. There have been recent publications in which the authors are indigenous persons, such as *Tuvalu: A History*, edited by Hugh Laracy. These works claim to be history written from the perspective of the indigenous people. They contain a somewhat straightforward transcription of legends and myths of the past and about their society. I do not believe they should be called indigenous history; rather they should be treated as a source of history. Any direct recording and publication of oral tradition is not history itself.

> —F.O. Kolo, 'Historiography the myth of indigenous authenticity', in P. Herda et al. (eds), *Tongan Culture and History*, Australian National University, Department of Pacific and Southeast Asian History, 1990, p. 1

3 Protest and dissent

Colonial rule in the Pacific did not impinge evenly on Islanders, even in the same places or at the same time. In areas like Papua New Guinea, it spread through corridors of influence, piecemeal and spasmodic. Groups entered the system at different points from the late nineteenth century through to the 1950s, so that knowledge of the system's demands—and of its advantages—was erratically spread, at times even contradictory in nature. But in the time of New Zealand rule, Samoan chiefs and orators knew what colonialism was all about and began to formulate a program for liberation. But it is questionable whether at that point villagers in outer districts took much notice of European matters in their daily lives ...

We must beware—Europeans and Islanders alike—of fighting anti-colonial battles which the ancestors of present-day independent Pacific peoples did not fight, or of celebrating the protest that did occur as always heroic, altruistic and effective. There are many historical instances of villages ignoring colonial demands, of evading them, or of rejecting them. And there are examples of elites who worked through the colonial system to better their communities—guardians of traditions and proto-nationalists upon whom the generation of today can call as standard bearers of modern protest. But it would be unhistorical to deny that protest in the colonial Pacific also involved being cowed by foreign collaboration for personal gain. The reasons for resistance to or cooperation with foreign rulers were in many instances complicated, as proven by the varied responses of Samoan elites to New Zealand during the mau period. In the end the adoption of simple categories like 'resistance', 'collaboration', 'patriotism' or 'revolution' becomes dangerously emotive when dealing with the history of new states in the Pacific. What we must look to uncovering is the range of subtle encounters going on between Europeans and Pacific islanders, the series of exchanges—social, economic, legal, religious, educational—that proceeded with both conflict and cooperation, and which in the process were changing all parties.

> —P. Hempenstall and N. Rutherford, *Protest and Dissent in the Colonial Pacific*, University of the South Pacific, Suva, 1989, pp. 147, 152

4 Anaibolafafawa: Big Man of Suremada Village

'You have sinned in the eyes of the Christian religion. You will be taken to court to be questioned for what you have done. You're answerable to that. You understand?' asked the officers.

'I do not understand what you are trying to convey to me,' replied Anaibolafafawa. 'What you say is just an excuse,' replied the government officers. 'But the tribes of Tarafikwai did something wrong too. So I wanted to kill Kirima to settle the problem,' answered Anaibolafafawa. 'You're a stupid man. You must be hanged according to the law. The other friends of yours too. They must be tried in the court as well. Your stupid accomplices, where are they?'

'It's your duty to bring them here,' answered Anaibolafafawa. The people of Suremada wanted to go and burn the jail which the men were kept in but Anaibolafafawa sent word not to do it. 'You must not do that,' said the Big Man. 'They will shoot you. They are people from another world.'

The government in its anger even sent men to Suremada to confiscate the wealth of the Big Man. They took the hoard of red shell money the Big Man had stored in his treasury. The people of Suremada said, 'We are raped. The red shell money is our strength. We'll do nothing but live in hopelessness. We are nothing. We are now slaves of the Whitemen.' The government of the Whitemen took Anaibolafafawa and his other friends to court. Anaibolafafawa and his men did not know what to say. In those days they did not have a public solicitor to defend them in court. Around the court house Whitemen stood with guns. Silence hovered over the court house. The people of Suremada did not want to come to the court house. They did not want to see their Big Man entangled with the power of the Whitemen. After hearing the case for many weeks the Whitemen finally found Anaibolafafawa and his men guilty of the crime. They took the Big Man of Suremada north of the court house area. There was a tree for hanging people. They handcuffed the men of Suremada and marched them to the tree. They were all hanged. The Whitemen saw the tongues of the men of Suremada coming out of their mouths while they were hanging on the tree. Their tongues were the dogs' panting for water in the dry season.

The people of Suremada heard of the death of the men. Did they mourn over the death of their men? Some men of Suremada said, 'Our Anaibolafafawa has done a great wrong. Our ancestors were not right in establishing that ritual.' And some said, 'But why did the Whitemen come and live on our land without our consent?' And others said, 'Let us follow the laws of the Whitemen. Let us stop fighting each other. Let us heal ourselves with the medicines of the Whitemen. Let us worship the gods of the Whitemen.'

And not many days after the hanging of the men of Suremada, a missionary went to the village with a Bible. The missionary said, 'My brothers and sisters, you know Adam and Eve? I am from their genealogy. You too belong to the same genealogy. I come to visit you to ask you to dismantle your religious houses. I want you to throw away your incantations. I want you to allow me to say that Almighty God was not here before I came. You worshipped stupid gods.'

'Come tomorrow and build a church house here', replied the people of Suremada. 'Come here tomorrow and tell us the story of a man who loved this world and saved us from all its evils. Come and put our true god in the church house'. My mother said, 'That's why you see that church house there. And the book the missionary brought here is the Bible you're holding in your hand now. And every day of the week the people of Suremada sing songs in their new church. They have forgotten the story of Anaibolafafawa, the Big Man of Suremada.'

—Rexford Orotaloa, *Suremada: Faces from a Solomon Island village*, Mana Publications, Suva, 1989, pp. 5–6

5 Poems

COUNTRY ROAD

The road down the country
was once earth-trodden
Ten years ago, strange men came
Ploughed down the trees and
Dug the earth with rough machines.
Today that same road lies
Breathless, beneath the hard tar-mac
In the name of development for
Exclusive politicians and
Executive businessmen.

Who'd wave to the natives
As they whiz down the lane
In their luxurious limousines.

Country Road! Were you not betrayed!

REWRITING HISTORY

Archeologists dig the ruins for prehistory,
discover that even our history
does not begin with sailors and settlers
(Let's pardon the educationists).

Colonial days: Our history discontinued.

Now, our historians must rewrite that:
    Place Irian Barat on the chart
    Maubere, Niugini, Solomoni,
    Vanuatu, Viti, Kanaky—

ALL, as one chain of archipelago.

OUR COMMON WEAKNESSES

Absolute power in corrupt hands,
Over-paid and under-worked,
In-house fightings, privilege-abuse.

Globe trotting on public funds,
Perennial borrowings, big spendings
Riotous living.

Widespread malpractice,
Nepotism, mass corruption
And graceful ignorance of

'what really goes on'.

RUSTIC NO MORE

My people!
I scream
The rustic life:
carving, hunting, gardening—

are now yours alone.

I will only be a part-timer
Or, perhaps more so an observer.

For I am a rustic no more:
money madness, bureaucratic pretences
and exclusive
invitations to some bourgeois soirees

are now eating deep into my bones.

My people!
I scream
No-one cares.

My people!
I scream
No-one cares.

WORKERS: TWO PROFILES

The well-educated public servant
draws up self-reliance policies, signs
official letters and answers the phone
in his air-conditioned office.

The un-educated subsistence grower
slashes and burns the bushes,
plants his crops,
sweats under the sun.

Before sun-set both men retire:

The public servant goes to the
Supermarket,
buys imported food.

The subsistence grower,
he reaps his harvest.

—All poems from S. Ngwele, *Bamboo Leaves: A collection of poems*, South
Pacific Creative Arts Society, Suva, 1989, pp. 5, 15, 24, 28, 42

6 French occupied Polynesia

Mr Chairman, I would like to thank you for your very kind welcome to the regional conference that you have organised for us, the indigenous people of the Pacific. It is a pleasure to meet some of my colleagues of the Pacific countries for the first time. I hope we will have an occasion to understand each other's problems before we leave for home.

I have a statement to make to the National Aboriginal Conference from *Ia Mana Te Nunaa*. The attack of one civilisation against another can take on various forms—genocide, economic or cultural assault. After having lived through a period of military colonisation, the Polynesian Ma'ohi have undergone an economic and cultural colonisation for a century.

That economic and cultural colonisation specifically grew with the settling of the Pacific Nuclear Tests Centre in our country. While the external trade balance of Polynesia was in equilibrium around the 1960s, it is today in a 98 per cent deficit. This means that Polynesians largely count upon foreign transfers without being able to cover more than 2 per cent of their debt …

The economic dependence on the outside world also resulted in a cultural dependence with regard to habits, mental outlook and the way of life, leaving the Polynesian people deeply estranged from their identity and traditional socio-economic balance.

Now, in the colonial society which increasingly extends its influence to all the fields of life, the Polynesian has turned into the throw-away individual of a consumer civilisation. In our eyes the Ma'ohi people's cultural estrangement is one of the most harmful aspects of colonisation. Our Party—Ia Mana Te Nunaa—firmly committed itself since 1975 to fighting against that cultural process in order to give back to the Ma'ohi people the cultural tools of an autonomous reflection and the economic means for a true political emancipation. Ia Mana Te Nunaa means Let the People Decide the Power.

—Jacqui van Bastolaer, 'French Occupied Polynesia', *Indigenous Struggle in the Pacific*, World Council of Indigenous People/National Aboriginal Conference, 1984, pp. 33–4

7 Common origin

Unlike nation states which come into existence through divergent processes, a Melanesian community usually comes into existence by a common origin, natural or metaphysical. The origin was natural in the case of Wautogig when the first ancestor, Suonu, slew his brother, following jealousy over Suonu's wife and fled to another ridge and started Wautogig Village. Origin may come about when someone establishes a new village even on an inhabited island through intermarriage and prowess. In yet other communities, the people accept that they are descended from the stars or from pigs, fish, birds, plants, or other phenomena. Even when begotten in mystery, it becomes their common heritage, giving them social solidarity, a network of common bonds, the basis of unity and oneness.

In modern Melanesia common origin is not essential to create new social units. For example, in many squatter settlements in Melanesia, people come from different backgrounds as in the case of Bumbu settlement in Lae of Morobe Province. Nevertheless, they function as a new or modern village. Melanesian suburbs are as diverse in ethnicity as many modern countries are diverse in nationality and linguistic communities.

In the wake of new demands for cash cropping and education many independent villages relocated on new sites. For example, the villages of Waganara and Magopin among the Arapesh are modern conglomerates of ancient, autonomous villages. Whilst they function together under this common modern history, each has a unique historical identity and origin. These are real social forces which give rise to varying social relations on a day-to-day basis. These notions of affinity continue to play a part in national affairs in Melanesian states.

—B. Narokobi, *Lo bilong yumi yet: Law and custom in Melanesia*, University of the South Pacific, Suva, 1989, p. 23

QUESTIONS AND ACTIVITIES

1 What policies might the Tongan government adopt to counter the problems identified in Bishop Finau's description of migration (Document 1)?

2 Are these problems unique to Pacific Island external migration situations? Could the origin of these problems also be found in local conditions not related to migration?

3 What is Bishop Finau's main fear over migration? In your opinion what is the main issue?

4 Why does F.O. Kolo (Document 2) criticise the acceptance of local history based on mythology?

5 What is F.O. Kolo's opinion on the difference between indigenous history, genuine history and compromise history?

6 In writing colonial history, what dangers do Hempenstall and Rutherford identify (Document 3)?

7 Hempenstall and Rutherford use the term 'unhistorical'. What do they mean by this term?

8 Does Rexford Orotaloa's story (Document 4) from Suremada village fall into Hempenstall and Rutherford's unhistorical category? How would F.O. Kolo respond to the Suremada story?

9 How would Hempenstall and Rutherford and F.O. Kolo respond to Ngwele's poem 'Rewriting History' (Document 5)?

10 How might Ngwele and Rexford Orotaloa respond to Kolo's criticism of oral local history?

11 What does Ngwele mean by the phrase 'all as one chain of archipelago'?

12 What message is the author of the Suremada story conveying to readers? How would ni-Vanuatu villagers react to this story? How would former British colonial officials react? How would urban, western educated ni-Vanuatu react?

13 Jacqui van Bastolaer (Document 6) identifies economic dependence as a major issue in French Polynesia. What link does he suggest between economic dependence and Ma'ohi cultural identity?

14 In describing his own coastal village of Wautogig, urban squatter settlements and other 'new' settlements, what message is Bernard Narokobi (Document 7) conveying to readers?

15 Is there a theme which links the five Ngwele poems (Document 5)? Describe this theme in your own words.

16 Compare the images of the Tahitian or Ma'ohi (Document 6) with the ni-Vanuatu (7) and the Solomon Islanders in the Suremada story (4). Which of Ngwele's poems best captures the messages these authors are trying to convey?

REFERENCES

Australia's Relations with the South Pacific: AIDAB Submission to the Joint Committee on Foreign Affairs and Defence, AGPS, Canberra, 1987

Connell, John, *Sovereignty and Survival: Island Microstates in the Third World*, Research Monograph No. 3, Department of Geography, University of Sydney, 1988

Commonwealth Consultative Group, *Vulnerability: Small states in the global society*, Commonwealth Secretariat, London, 1985

Douglas, Norman and Ngaire (eds), *Pacific Islands Yearbook*, 16th Edition, Angus and Robertson, North Ryde, 1989

Firth, S., 'Sovereignty and independence in the contemporary Pacific', *The Contemporary Pacific*, Vol. 1 1/2 (1989), pp. 75–96

Islands '88 Proceedings, Papers of Islands '88, 2nd Conference of Islands of the World, Hobart, 1988

Karolle, Bruce G., and Ballendorf, Dirk A., *Prospects for Self-Sufficiency in the New Micronesian States*, Centre for South East Asian Studies, Occasional Paper No. 25, James Cook University, Townsville, 1986, p. 15

Munro, D., 'Migration and the Shift to Dependency in Tuvalu', in Connell, J. (ed.), *Migration and Development in the South Pacific*, Australian National University Press, Pacific Research Monograph No. 4, Canberra, 1990

Select Bibliography
on Colonialism and Independence

General

Brookfield, H. (ed.), *Colonialism, Development and Independence: The case of the Melanesian Islands of the South Pacific*, Cambridge University Press, Cambridge, 1972

(*) Brooks, M., and Codrington, S., *Australia's Pacific Neighbours*, Geography Teachers Association of NSW, Sydney (*a school level text)

Campbell, I.C., *A History of the Pacific Islands*, University of Queensland Press, Brisbane, 1989

Crocombe, R., and Ali, A. (eds), *Foreign Forces in Pacific Politics*, Institute of Pacific Studies, Suva, 1983

Crocombe, R., and Ali, A. (eds), *Politics in Polynesia*, Institute of Pacific Studies, Suva, 1983

Crocombe, R., and Ali, A. (eds), *Politics in Melanesia*, Institute of Pacific Studies, Suva, 1983

Crocombe, R. (ed.), *Micronesian Politics*, Institute of Pacific Studies, Suva, 1988

Davidson, J., 'The decolonization of Oceania', in *Journal of Pacific History*, Vol. 6, 1971

Douglas, N., and Douglas N. (eds), *Pacific Islands Yearbook* (16th Edition), Angus and Robertson, North Ryde, 1989

Ghai, Y. (ed.), *Law, Government and Politics in the Pacific Island States*, Institute of Pacific Studies, Suva, 1988

Hempenstall, P., and Rutherford, N., *Protest and Dissent in the Colonial Pacific*, Institute of Pacific Studies, Suva, 1984

Hooper, A., et al. (eds), *Class and Culture in the South Pacific*, Institute of Pacific Studies, Suva, 1987

Howe, K., *Where the Waves Fall: A new South Sea Island history from first settlement to colonial rule*, Allen and Unwin, Sydney, 1984

Mamak, A., and Ali, A., *Race, Class and Rebellion in the South Pacific*, Allen and Unwin, Sydney, 1979

Maude, H., 'South Pacific; Independence and regionalism in the South Pacific Islands', in *Round Table*, Vol. 234, 1971

Oliver, D., *The Pacific Islands*, University of Hawaii Press, Honolulu, 1961

(*) Quanchi, M., *People and Place: The Pacific in the twentieth century*, Cambridge University Press, Melbourne, 1991 (*a school level text)

(*) Ridgell, R., *Pacific Nations and Territories*, Bess Press, Honolulu, 1988 (*a school level text)

Robie, D., *Blood on Their Banner: Nationalist struggles in the South Pacific*, Pluto Press, Sydney, 1989

Scarr, D., *The History of the Pacific Islands*, Macmillan, Melbourne, 1990

Cook Islands

Gilson, R.P., *The Cook Islands 1820–1950*, Victoria University Press, Wellington, 1980

Fiji

Scarr, D., *Fiji: A short history*, Allen and Unwin, Sydney, 1984

French Polynesia

Aldrich, R., *The French Presence in the South Pacific 1842–1940*, Macmillan, London, 1989

Newbury, C., *Tahiti Nui: Change and survival in French Polynesia*, University of Hawaii Press, Honolulu, 1980

Hawaii

Daws, G., *The Shoal of Time: A history of the Hawaiian islands*, University of Hawaii Press, Honolulu, 1968
Fuchs, L., *Hawaii Pono: A social history*, Harcourt Brace Jovanovich, New York, 1983
Joesting, E., *Hawaii: An uncommon history*, Norton, New York, 1972
(*) Menton, L., and Tamua, E., *A History of Hawaii*, University of Hawaii Press, Honolulu, 1989 (*a school level text)

Kiribati

Koch, G., *The Material Culture of Kiribati*, Institute of Pacific Studies, Suva, 1986
Macdonald, B., *Cinderellas of Empire: Towards a history of Kiribati and Tuvalu*, ANU Press, Canberra, 1982
Mason, L. (ed.), *Kiribati: A changing atoll culture*, Institute of Pacific Studies, Suva, 1985
Talu, A., et al. (eds), *Kiribati: Aspects of history*, Institute of Pacific Studies, Suva, 1979

Loyalty Islands

Howe, K., *The Loyalty Islands: A history of culture contacts*, ANU Press, Canberra, 1977

Federated State of Micronesia

Heine, C., *Micronesia at the Crossroads*, University of Hawaii Press, Honolulu, 1977
Hezel, F., *The First Taint of Civilization: A history of the Caroline and Marshall islands in pre-colonial days 1521–1885*, University of Hawaii Press, Honolulu, 1983

Nauru

Viviani, N., *Nauru: Phosphate and political progress*, ANU Press, Canberra, 1990

New Caledonia

Connell, J., *New Caledonia or Kanaky? The political history of a French colony*, ANU Press, Canberra, 1987
Fraser, H., *Your Flag's Blocking Our Sun*, ABC Books, Sydney, 1990
Spencer, M., Ward, A., and Connell, J. (eds), *New Caledonia: Essays in nationalism and dependency*, University of Queensland Press, Brisbane

Papua New Guinea

Dorney, S., *Papua New Guinea: People, politics and history since 1975*, Random Century, New York, 1990
Griffin, J., et al. (eds), *Papua New Guinea: A political history*, Heinemann, Melbourne, 1979
Turner, M., *Papua New Guinea: The challenge of independence*, Penguin, Ringwood, 1990

Solomon Islands

Bennett, J., *The Wealth of the Solomons: A history of a Pacific archipelago 1800–1978*, University of Hawaii Press, Honolulu, 1987
Lamour, P. (ed.), *Solomon Island Politics*, Institute of Pacific Studies, Suva, 1983
Laracy, H., (ed.), *Ples bilong yumi: Solomon islands, the past four thousand years*, Institute of Pacific Studies, Suva, 1989

Tonga

Herda, P., et al. (eds), *Tongan Culture and History*, Department of Pacific and Southeast Asian History, ANU, Canberra, 1990

Rutherford, N. (ed.), *Friendly Islands: A history of Tonga*, Oxford University Press, Melbourne, 1977

Tuvalu

Koch, G., *The Material Culture of Tuvalu*, Institute of Pacific Studies, Suva, 1981

Laracy, H. (ed.), *Tuvalu: A history*, Institute of Pacific Studies, Suva, 1983

Macdonald, B., *Cinderellas of Empire: Towards a history of Kiribati and Tuvalu*, ANU Press, Canberra, 1982

Munro, D., 'Migration and the shift to dependency in Tuvalu', in Connell, J. (ed.), *Migration and Development in the South Pacific*, ANU Monograph series, Canberra, 1990

Vanuatu

Sharma, D., 'Vanuatu: The first ten years', in *Island Business News*, July 1990

Van Trease, H. (ed.), *The Politics of Land in Vanuatu: From colony to independence*, Institute of Pacific Studies, Suva, 1987

Western Samoa

Boyd, M., 'Independent Western Samoa', in *Pacific Viewpoint*, Vol. 9, No. 2, 1968

Davidson, J., *Samoa mo Samoa: The emergence of the independent state of Western Samoa*, Oxford University Press, Melbourne, 1967

Gilson, R., *Samoa 1830–1900: The politics of a multi-cultural community*, Oxford University Press, Melbourne, 1967

Meleisea, M., *The Making of Modern Samoa*, Institute of Pacific Studies, Suva, 1987

Meleisea, M., *Lagaga: A short history of Western Samoa*, Institute of Pacific Studies, Suva, 1987

PART FIVE
THE CHANGING IMAGE
OF THE PACIFIC

INTRODUCTION

Many themes have been introduced by the authors of the preceding chapters. Some of these themes are applicable for a study of people in Asia, Africa and elsewhere, and some are themes distinctly 'Pacific' in origin and expression. This concluding chapter seeks to draw these themes together by applying them to one, virtually unrecorded incident in the narrative of contact, encounter and response between Pacific Island people and Europeans.

The incident involves a small Australian gold prospecting expedition which travelled through the headwaters of the Fly River in Western Papua in 1914, which found little gold and would have passed by without notice except that a motion picture camera was carried along on the voyage. The film of this expedition was prepared for commercial screening. Although not uncovered for another sixty years, it provides blurred and poignant images of the Fly River region just as it was being mapped and 'discovered' by Europeans, and at the same time as the Upper Fly River people and Ok mountain people 'discovered' white men.

Chapter 12
The Changing Image of the Pacific

Max Quanchi, Queensland University of Technology

'Long ago a man dreamed about a white man. In that dream a man said to him, sometime you will be watching on the beach and a man will come to you. He will bring good tools to use for the garden and to change your minds with. His skin will be different from yours ...'

—Koete Lorou of the Iokea people, Gulf of Papua

' ... From close to D'Albertis' furthest, every shovelful of sand and shingle gives "colors" of gold; and many stones contain interesting organic remains in silica or lime. It will not be necessary to do anything administrative more than 200 miles up the Fly. Above that the people are wanderers; the country does not look as if it were of much account ...'

—Sir William McGregor, Administrator of British New Guinea, after sailing 1000 kilometres up the Fly River (1890)

'I have just returned from observing the beastly devices of the heathen on the Fly river. We went 530 miles but only found a scanty population ... We went to look for a site for a government station but I do not think that there are enough people. Sir Rupert Clarke, one of my chief enemies in Australia, is going up with a party looking for gold next month.'

—Sir Hubert Murray, Lieutenant-Governor of Papua (1914)

Acknowledging the presence of strangers

There is a tradition among many language-speaking groups in Papua New Guinea, that some men journey away from their own lands and then return home bringing with them new ideas, new knowledge and a desire to change the existing order. These men are known as wanderers because they have travelled beyond their own culture and beyond the horizons of their known world with its laws, morality and value systems. Wanderers often return unexpectedly with a vision of a transformed world and set out to create change.

These wanderers are soon absorbed and restored to an accepted, defined place in the community. The first missionaries, miners, adventurers, anthropologists and government officials to cross the beach in Papua New Guinea, and elsewhere in the Pacific, were often absorbed in the same way. The Iokea people living in the Gulf of Papua were able to explain in this way the arrival in 1883 of 'Tamate'—the enigmatic and peripatetic missionary, James Chalmers. For many generations a wise Iokea man, an elder and 'dreamer' had foretold the arrival of a wanderer who would cross their beach and bring good tools, and good news to change their minds with. So in 1883 when Chalmers appeared with the east coast Motu people during one of their *hiri* trading voyages west into the Gulf, he was immediately identified and accepted. There was no need to ask whether he was a spirit, why he had come, or what he wanted—his presence was already explained and included in the Iokea's world.

For his part, as a European establishing settlements along an unknown coastline, Chalmers saw the Fly River as a pathway—a pathway into the darkest heathen world.

He was determined, like missionaries before and after, to conquer a dark void and make Christians out of what he saw as 'naked, beastial tribes'. Chalmers moved west establishing stations at Toaripi, then at Saguane on Kiwai island and finally at Daru, near the Fly River estuary. His aim was to progressively move further and further into unknown territory. (Seventeen years later Chalmers was killed by the Goaribari people when he wandered into their lands at a time when they wanted a body for a ritual ceremony. When asked, they replied that they always killed strangers who entered their lands.)

Along the Fly River in 1914, it was that fascinating point in time when two worlds were coming into contact. The map of Papua marked out an official boundary—the Western Division—but the Australians who governed from Port Moresby had made only one or two forays into the interior using the rivers which flow from the central mountains south into the Gulf of Papua. It was a mysterious, daunting territory—a blank space on most European maps—stretching from the Puarari River delta in the east to the maze of estuaries, banks and islands at the mouth of the Fly River and then north through swamps and foothills to the towering peaks and ridges of the central range.

Luigi Maria D'Albertis, an Italian explorer, adventurer and amateur anthropologist, had been the first European outsider to enter this world. He travelled more than 800 kilometres up the Fly River in 1876. William McGregor, from 1888 to 1898 the Administrator of British New Guinea (as it was then called), later travelled up the Fly and its many tributaries claiming he was extending the districts under government control, but admitting privately that he was following an irresistible urge just to see what was there! McGregor had found good 'colour', and the prospect of gold was noted in official reports and in both Papuan and Australian newspapers. Several diggers, anxious to find 'colours' in the fast south-flowing rivers, made tentative expeditions into the 'wild country' between the Gulf of Papua and the mountain ranges to the north, and gold continued to draw a constant trickle of keen and desperate men to the newly proclaimed Australian Territory of Papua. (The name change occurred when British New Guinea passed to Australian control in 1906.)

In April 1914, John Hubert Murray, the Lieutenant-Governor of Papua, also visited the Fly and reported that he had found good 'colour'. But Murray was worried about exploring parties or teams of diggers rushing into a territory where there was no government control or presence. He feared the consequences of gun-toting diggers confronting the allegedly fierce warriors of the West. As Lieutenant-Governor, it was his job to protect 'natives', but also to foster development, defined as opening up economic opportunities for white investors, agriculturalists, commercial and business interests. While determined to balance the little colony's budget by promoting sensible, responsible Australian investment, Murray made it clear he had little time for the gold-seeking, filibustering plans of wealthy, opportunist investors from down south.

The Fly River expedition

It was into this part of the Pacific that the Rupert Clarke expedition was heading in June 1914, hopefully to uncover a mother lode, or at least a 'jeweller's shop' where nuggets would lie thick in the sand and gravel of a tumbling mountain stream. Elements of the 1914 Clarke expedition may sound familiar, for they are indeed themes repeated many times over in the centuries before, and in the century which was to follow.

The Fly River expedition was financed by Sir Rupert Clarke, a wealthy Australian pastoralist, businessman and investor who had already developed plantations in the more settled areas along the Papuan coast. His primary aim was to discover a new gold field. In Europe, alliances and diplomatic relations were crumbling and international conflict was imminent. A payable field in Papua with long-term potential, and easy access for large vessels up the Fly River, was judged from Melbourne and Sydney to be a very promising enterprise in an economy and world market about to be disrupted by war far away in Europe. Melbourne, which had recovered from the depression of the 1890s, was full of post-Federation confidence in its own destiny and in the pioneering entrepreneurship of its leading citizens. Sir Rupert Clarke and his sons were pictured as adventurous, confident and successful. In his youth Rupert Clarke had been Commander of a Battery of three nordenfeldt machine-guns in the local militia and, although it was his father's wealth that supported the troop and provided him with his officer's braid, none was surprised twenty years later to see him heading off into largely unknown territory in search of fame and fortune.

This was a grand adventure, but in the plain talk of the day, Clarke was out to make money. He belonged to what Hubert Murray, the Lieutenant-Governor in Port Moresby, suspiciously but probably justifiably, called 'a pack of capitalists' interested in Papua only for what they could get out of it.

A journey of 1000 kilometres upstream to Kiunga, where much later a government station was established, was only half way to the source of the Fly, one of the world's great river systems. The Italian, D'Albertis, had not found it picturesque, being a journey hemmed in by forest, interminable twists and turns and with only occasional glimpses of the lands beyond. But to gold seekers glancing at a map in far-off Australian cities, the Fly River was a pathway to the interior, where tumbling mountain streams hid nuggets and panning was easy.

The lower coastal parts of the Fly River were a flat maze of banks, sand bars, shifting islands and mangroves. But the coast and off-shore islands were already popular as labour recruiting grounds for the bêche-de-mer, pearl shell and gold mining industries. In Port Moresby and other plantation centres, men recruited from the Western Districts and Gulf had a fearsome reputation. The busy little port and township at Daru was the main European settlement. When a crew was needed in 1914 to head up river with Rupert Clarke's expedition in the *Kismet*, there were plenty of experienced 'Gulf men' in Daru ready to sign on.

On the lower reaches of the Fly, the people had memories of the river expeditions of D'Albertis and McGregor. Indeed some fifty years after D'Albertis had bulldozed his way up and down the river, the details of his encounters were well remembered by villagers along the banks of the Fly. Both D'Albertis and McGregor had sailed by many villages without stopping but at others they had traded for curios, firewood and water. There had been confrontations and both real and threatened violence as local people disputed the right of the strangers to pass through their lands. D'Albertis, who was later officially questioned about his violent tactics, had gone prepared with special dynamite charges attached to fireworks so he could throw a charge into a distant crowd or village.

In the mountain ranges, limestone gorges and fog shrouded valleys beyond the headwaters of the Fly River, there was a sizeable population. As the Clarke expedition steamed up the Fly on the *Kismet*, the party looked with anticipation north to the rain-shrouded central ranges. They were being led by Frank Pryke, an experienced miner with fifteen years fossicking in Papua. On Clarke's behalf, Pryke had recruited nineteen 'boys' from Daru Island, and they formed the expedition party along with Clarke, McAlpine (Clarke's plantation manager from Kanosia on the Gulf coast), Pryke's brother Jim, and Mackay, an engineer.

The expedition spent June testing for colours in the upper Fly, Black and Palmer tributaries, and then, after Rupert Clarke returned to Daru Island (heading for England to sign on in the Great War), the Pryke brothers and Mackay stayed on for two months, using a launch, canoes and cross-country treks to test the Tully and Alice (now called the Ok Tedi) tributaries. They traversed country where no European had been before, but failed to find enough gold to justify opening up a major field. As he trudged for two months over ridges and up creeks, stopping to break rocks and swirl gravel in search of colour, Frank Pryke's journal recorded his impressions of the local people.

On the Alice (Ok Tedi) River, Frank Pryke made the members of the expedition adopt a casual indifference, but wary attitude, towards the threats of local people who gathered with posture and gesture to insult and mock the strangers. As a result conflict was avoided. The only violent encounter occurred when the exploring party was heading down stream near where D'Albertis had been attacked in 1876. After the Prykes declined the sexual overtures of women sent to lure them ashore, a large party of warriors fired a barrage of arrows. As the warriors defended their territory and the Pryke party defended their right of passage, five of Pryke's crew were wounded, and both Pryke brothers suffered arrow hits. When the Prykes landed after the melee they found one native dead. The local people marshalled to continue the attack but with a final menacing and insulting display the warriors made a tactical withdrawal. The Pryke party sailed downstream after burning canoes and houses and destroying crops in retribution and as a warning of the white-man's power (sic). The memory of this encounter remained in the minds and language of the warriors and their community, and in the few terse sentences scribbled in Pryke's journal.

The people on the tributaries and upper reaches of the Fly, Alice, Black and Palmer rivers remained isolated for many more years as the Great War intervened and exploring expeditions, either private or government funded were curtailed. In 1922 Hubert Murray went up the Fly as far as one of Clarke's camps, and on the basis of a cursory look around, reported that the people were friendly but few in number.

Today, the upper reaches of the Alice and Fly rivers are recorded prominently on the balance sheets, geological maps and stockbroking boards of multinational companies as home for the giant Ok Tedi mine.

In the 1930s the people on the lower and middle Fly River witnessed another wave of strangers. The river became a busy thoroughfare with oil and gold exploration teams swarming over the Western and Gulf districts. Aeroplanes were 'as thick as mosquitoes' and Daru became a busy port, with new buildings and a bustling anchorage. However, high up on the Fly River in the tributaries and foothills, it was not until the mid-1960s that the area north from Kiunga to the ranges and the border (by then the Indonesian border) was declared pacified and under government control. The opening of the vast Ok Tedi mine was the next phase in the history of encounters, contact and mapping of this area.

A fast helicopter ride across the ridges and valleys now allows villagers to soar above and over their traditional territorial enemies and to live in two or more distinct worlds. Villagers speak the languages of their ancestors, wear the grass covering of their ancestors and also drive four-wheel-drive utilities, operate power sluices and utilise a range of Japanese and German electronic gadgetry.

Others as strangers—in a customary manner

The journals of D'Albertis and McGregor, fourteen years apart, record many instances where the European 'strangers' were welcomed with hospitality and friendship. In other places and in other situations they were treated as 'strangers' and threatened, abused, attacked, derided or mocked. The designation of others as strangers, with a corresponding form of behaviour, is a complex issue and depends on many factors.

Village communities in the upper reaches of the Fly and its tributaries and deeper in the ridges and valley of the central cordilla, had knowledge of the outside world, but they did not or could not go out to reach it. Nor did their knowledge and language extend as far as the European settlements at Daru or Port Moresby. This was so firstly, because it would have meant crossing the lands of neighbours and enemies and secondly, because long journeys were not commonplace. For example, when the anthropologist Roy Rappaport visited the Simbai people in the central highlands in 1962, although there had been a government station in their valley since 1959, only a couple of young men out of group of 300 people had ventured the 40 kilometres from their village to see what happened at the patrol post. Local people probably knew about strangers or white-skins before they arrived, but when Frank and Jim Pryke strode into their village, it still demanded a response. What was the appropriate behaviour? Rumours and stories may have travelled inland from the coast and reached small scattered communities along trade or warring paths, but face-to-face contact was a new and possibly challenging situation.

Whereas the Iokea people had not been troubled by the Chalmers appearance among them, on the upper Fly the people suddenly confronted by the Clarke and Pryke party would have been asking such questions as:

- Why had these men come?
- Were they men?
- What did they want?
- What valuable goods did they carry?
- Where did they belong?
- Were they spirits?

In 1914 one of the founders of anthropology was nearby, having just arrived in Papua to begin his research. Due to his 'enemy alien' nationality, at the outbreak of war he was confined (with Australian government support) on the Trobriand Islands. Based on these experiences, Bronislaw Malinowski, later a distinguished professor of anthropology at London University, set off on a long career which gave anthropology a new set of definitions.

One of these was that culture contact was not a one-way imposition by the dominant white culture. Malinowski argued that mechanisms existed in indigenous cultures for the handling of incursions from an outside world. That is, when they saw film of the Clarke expedition, what seemed to theatre-goers in Sydney to be a momentous, world-shaking event for primitive, simple natives, was for the people of the Fly River area, merely another dream come true, another legend brought to life, or a routine reaction to another perhaps unexpected but not unusual event in their lives. The encounter did not shatter their existence, cause their value system to crumble or cause their life to have new meaning. They were able to handle and absorb it, using their own mechanisms.

However, we don't know for sure. Clarke's cameraman could not capture the meaning of the encounter on film. We are left with a set of images, frozen, divorced from their own context of action and meaning. Outsiders must rely on the terse paragraphs in Pryke's diary, a few photographs or the few feet of motion picture film which remains from the Clarke expedition. In contrast, the descendants of Fly River people who were there when the *Kismet* tied up to the bank near their village, carry with them a memory (a story) passed down through several generations of meanings and purposes. When European researchers or tourists visit the places where these encounters occurred, they might share these memories and stories. More than likely, the stories will now be embellished so that the tourist, anthropologist or aid worker hears what they want to hear.

During these first encounters, the stranger's habit of taking away artefacts such as weapons, skeletons, totems and carvings, may have reinforced in the local people's minds that Clarke, Pryke and their companions were powerful spirit figures. They took away symbols with spiritual meaning for the carver and owner. They also took utilitarian things like utensils and weapons, to store in their own far-off land. The strangers were perhaps their very own ancestors returning to gather things they had left behind in an earlier life.

It has often been pointed out that for pre-contact Papuan and New Guinea people, there was a thin line, hardly recognisable, between their real world and their spirit world. Perhaps the encounter with the Prykes was part-way between dream and reality, part-way between the spirit world and actual behaviour—a contact with spirits in the grey vagueness that lies between the dreaming half-awake world and the reality of daylight.

Encounters, contact and response—the themes

The possibility that strangers could enter your world and your territory was accepted reluctantly by the small communities of the upper Fly River. As many as 800 men confronted G.M. Massy Baker when he was 'discovering' the lower Fly in 1913. Well to the north, 50 kilometres up from the junction of the Fly and Alice Rivers, 200 men disputed the advance of the Clarke expedition in 1914. In the southwest Pacific, Niueans had taunted and thrown stones at Captain Cook's landing party on Niue in 1774 and 200 years later, in 1990, a regional organisation, the South Pacific Forum, angrily attacked the USA's chemical waste dumping plans for Johnston Island.

A friendly welcome was as common as a rebuttal. Sonrosol Islanders had welcomed the first Spanish to their island in 1710. The missionary Samuel Macfarlane, after visiting the lower Fly River area in 1876, reported rather ambitiously that he had established 'what appeared to be a genuine and firm friendship between the natives and ourselves'. Higher up, on the Tully River, Jim Pryke, who was leading the Clarke prospecting expedition, found that communities which had certainly never made contact with Europeans before, came most days to trade, leaving their bows and arrows behind in the bush. Pryke's journal noted regularly that, 'Natives appeared friendly'. The Pryke party were certainly strangers in other people's lands, but a willingness to trade, friendship and curiosity with an element of caution, were a normal enough and routine response for the owners of those lands.

The story of the Clarke expedition also raises another theme—of the three-way relationship between colonial governments, economic development and 'native protection' policies. Another theme in the preceding essays has been the relationship that exists between events in the islands and events in Europe and to a lesser degree events in the USA, Australia and New Zealand. A further theme that emerges from the Clarke expedition of 1914, and that runs through the study of contacts and encounters in the Pacific, is the degree to which island peoples and Europeans were changed by the contact. The 1914 Fly River expedition also raises questions about the ways that island peoples interpreted and recorded these cross-cultural experiences, and the ways in which Europeans interpreted and recorded the same events.

A story—a history

What happened on Sonrosol Atoll in 1710 may be compared and contrasted to what happened on the Fly River in 1914 or to what happened at the South Pacific Forum meeting in Pohnpei in August 1991. They each constitute a different form of culture contact. They may be studied and recorded as cross-cultural interactions or encounters—Spanish meeting Micronesians, gold prospectors meeting isolated inland communities, independent island nations meeting each other with their former colonial rulers sitting alongside as equals. Each encounter may be told as a story, important and interesting because of its own unique context. It also may be linked in a grand story running through several generations or centuries.

Contact, encounter and response in the Pacific in the distant past, recent past and as you read this today, is a story, which each of us has to tell in our own way. One historian has finished a book on the Pacific—his history of the Pacific to 1900—by stating that history has no separate existence; it is what we make it. The authors who compiled the collection of essays you are now reading take the story of encounter, contact and response in the Pacific Islands, past 1900 for another ninety years, and have also told a story—or made history.

The story of the Clarke and Pryke expedition on the Fly River is just that—a story. It is a story told in one culture as grand adventure, as capitalism, as entrepreneurship or as a civilising mission opening up the dark interior. In another culture it is a story told as a dream, a vision come to life or perhaps as a routine event of no long-term political, economic or social significance. Each participant tells his or her own story.

Each of us—the authors who have written these essays and you, the student reading these lines—also create and tell our own story from the shreds of evidence we uncover. This is history—the creation and the telling of a story anew, each time we contemplate the 'past'. In this sense the history of culture contact in the Pacific is an ongoing process of which we are all a part.

QUESTIONS AND ACTIVITIES

1. What are the 'great themes' which appear in the essays in this book?
2. Why was Chalmers' presence accepted by the Iokea people?
3. Why did the discovery of payable gold in Papua have such good prospects?
4. What did missionaries such as Chalmers in Port Moresby and entrepreneurs such as Clarke in Melbourne think of the Fly River?
5. Why did the Prykes burn the village where the attack took place?
6. What did communities in the upper Fly River know of the outside world beyond their normal walking and visiting range?
7. What was Malinowski's contribution to the study of anthropology?
8. Why are we are all part of the history of culture contact in the Pacific?
9. Choose one of the following statements.
   - Everything that happened to Pacific Islanders was a reaction to European presence.
   - Europeans provided a new opportunity to achieve old goals.
   - Relationships between Europeans and islanders were based on mutual dependence.
   - In the contact between islanders and Europeans, it was the chiefs who benefited most.
   - The frontier where contact took place was a moving frontier.
   - The conclusion to be drawn from three hundred years of European contact was that it was a fatal impact.
   - Europeans were changed by their meeting with Pacific Islanders.
   - There is no history of the Pacific—there is only what we think of the past, at the moment we write.
   - The telling of a story (oral history) is a reliable method for recording the past.

   Present a response to one of these statements, using both evidence from events and incidents described in this book (or elsewhere), and conclude with one or more of the general themes related to contact, encounter and response.

REFERENCES

Connolly, R., and Anderson, R., *First Contact*, Viking, New York, 1983 (See also a 50-minute documentary film by the same name)

Hezel, F., *The First Taint of Civilization*, University of Hawaii Press, Honolulu, 1983

Keddie, R., *Fly River* (a documentary film), RK Films, Melbourne, forthcoming

Linekin, J., and Poyer, L. (eds), *Cultural Identity and Ethnicity in the Pacific*, University of Hawaii Press, Honolulu, 1990

Lacey, R., 'Journeys and transformations ... ' in Chapman, M. (ed.), *Mobility and Identity in the Island Pacific*, Pacific Viewpoint (special edition), Vol. 26, No 1, 1985

Lacey, R., 'To Limlimbur, the wanderers ... ' in *Pacific Studies*, Vol. 9, No. 1, 1985

Schieffelin, E., and Crittenden, R. (eds), *Like People You See in a Dream: First contact in six Papuan societies*, Stanford University Press, 1991

Appendix 1

Chronology: The Arrival of Missionaries in the Pacific

	LMS	Meth.	RC	Ang.	Pres.	SDA	Other
Tahiti	1797–1863		1839			1891	Paris Evangelical Missionary Society 1863
Marquesas	1797–98		1838				
Cook Islands	1823		1894			1895	
Samoa	1830	1835–39 1857	1845			1895	
Tonga	1797–1800	1822	1842	1902		1895	
Gilbert Islands (Kiribati)	1870		1889			1947	American Board of Commissioners for Foreign Missions (Cong.) 1857
Ellice Islands (Tuvalu)	1865		1878–99 1940			1947	
Fiji		1835	1844	1870		1895	
New Hebrides (Vanuatu)	1839–48		1848–50 1887	1849	1848	1912	Churches of Christ 1908
New Caledonia	1840–1920		1843	1850–59		1954	Paris Evangelical Missionary Society 1897
Solomon Islands		1902	1845–47 1898	1850		1914	South Sea Evangelical Mission 1904
New Britain		1875	1882	1925		1929	
Papua	1874	1891	1847–55	1891		1908	Numerous new missions since World War II
New Guinea (Mandated Territory)			1896	1929		1929	Lutheran 1886. Many since World War II
New Zealand (Maoris)		1822	1838	1814	1843	1885	Lutheran 1844
Hawaii							1820

—Prepared by David Hilliard, Flinders University

Appendix 2

Chronology: Beach Communities and Port Towns

Date	Honolulu	Papeete	Kororareka	Levuka	Apia
1642			Tasman first sighted New Zealand	Tasman sailed among the Fiji Islands	
1722					Roggeveen first sighted Samoa
1767		Tahiti discovered by Captain Wallis			
1778	Cook discovered Hawaii				
1779	Cook died at Kealakekua Bay				
1787	First beachcomber landed in Hawaii				Massacre of La Perouse's crew. First major European contact with Samoans
1797		First missionaries arrived			
1801		Beginning of the salt pork trade to NSW			
1804	Kamehameha returned to Waikiki: John Young left as governor of Hawaii Island. Honolulu rapidly became centre of European population			Beginning of sandalwood trade in Fiji	
1809	Kamehameha moved into Honolulu from Waikiki. Foreign population about 60				
1814			First CMS missionaries settled at the Bay of Islands. Kendall appointed J.P.	End of sandalwood trade	
1815	Whites in Honolulu threatened with exile	Peace—spread of Christianity. Name 'Papeete' becoming established	Timber trade flourishing	Decline in beachcomber population	
1820	Arrival of first American missionaries. J.C. Jones appointed first US consular agent. Chiefs decided that Honolulu should be king's principal residence. Exile of whites to Fanning Island. Foreign population in Honolulu growing rapidly.	S.P. Henry employed by Pomare II, Ebrill and Bicknell in the islands. English church services given at Papeete for whalers	Flax trade established		Number of convict beachcombers settled in Samoa
1824		Twenty foreigners on Tahiti—very little economic development	First settlers at Kororareka—large number of whalers anchored off shore		
1825	Kamehameha III confirmed as King (Kamehameha II died in England). Charlton arrived as British consular agent. Missionaries gaining ascendency—first 'blue laws' promulgated. Missionary/Merchant split intensified	Pritchard re-established mission at Papeete		David Whippy arrived	

Date	Honolulu	Papeete	Kororareka	Levuka	Apia
1827	First RC priests arrived	Papeete established as royal seat. First Chilian ventures for pearls. Foreign population rapidly increasing		Beginning of first intensive period of bêche-de-mer fishing	
1830	Foreign population about 260	Expansion of Papeete–Valparaiso trade. Decline in missionary influence.	Kororareka fired		Williams and Barff arrived. First missionary voyage to Samoa. Island teachers left
1834	Theatre Club established	Liquor prohibition	For Res built church	First vessel built at Levuka	
1836	First publication of *Sandwich Island Gazette.* Dancing becoming fashionable. Fourteen women living in Honolulu. Lord Russell incident	Moerenhout installed as US consul. First attempt by RC priests to land on Tahiti	Temperance society established and survived one meeting. Foreign population growing. Crime rate higher		Missionaries established at Apia. First whaler reported in the harbour
1840	*Polynesian* established. *Sandwich Island Mirror* collapsed. Kekuanaoa governor of Oahu	Foreign population about 70	Annexation. Auckland named as site of future capital	Whippy's leadership firstly established. Self-governing body set up	
1858				Levuka fired. W.T. Pritchard arrived as British Consul. Left November for England with request for secession. J.B. Williams moved to Levuka from Laucala. Whippy and his followers left Levuka for Wakaya Island	
1874				Annexation by Great Britain	
1875					Steinberger returned and established a new government
1876					Steinberger deposed and deported

—Prepared by Caroline Ralston, Macquarie University

Legend: Appendices 1 and 2

CMS   Church Mission Society (Anglican)
RC   Roman Catholic
LMS   London Missionary Society
Meth.   Methodist
Ang.   Anglican
SDA   Seventh Day Adventist

Appendix 3

Short Chronology of Colonial Rule

First Claimed	Island or Island Group	Colonial Power	Comments
1838	Pitcairn Island	Great Britain	Absorbed into British Empire.
1840	New Zealand	Great Britain	Became a colony. Responsible Government in 1856 and progressively the constitutional links with Britain were severed.
1842	French Oceania	France	Protectorate declared over Marquesas Islands and the domains of Pomare, including Tahiti. At that time called French Oceania. Protectorate gradually extended to other islands in present-day French Polynesia, including Rapa in 1867.
1850	French Polynesia	France	Renamed French Polynesia. Reconstituted as an overseas territory of France in 1957.
1853	New Caledonia (and dependencies) [e.g. Loyalty Islands and and Isle of Pines]	France	Initially administered as part of French Polynesia. Became a separate French colony with its own naval governor in 1860. Penal settlement, 1854–1890s. First civilian government appointed in 1882. Reconstituted as an overseas territory of France in 1946.
1874	Fiji	Great Britain	Ceded by the chiefs and became a British Crown Colony. Governor also became High Commissioner for the Western Pacific from 1877. System of indirect rule through a separate Fijian Administration established. Rotuma incorporated into Fiji in 1881.
1884–1906	British New Guinea	Great Britain	British Protectorate declared. Colony created in 1888. *See 'Australian Papua'.*
1884–1914	German New Guinea	Germany	Between 1884 and 1899 German New Guinea was run by a private business firm and was called the Protectorate of the New Guinea Company; from 1899 until 1914 German New Guinea was an Imperial Colony administered by government officials. *See entry for 'New Guinea'.*

FFirst Claimed	Island or Island Group	Colonial Power	Comments
1885	Caroline Islands	Spain	In August 1885 Germany took possession of the Carolines but the Spanish reaction was so hostile that Germany submitted the quarrel to Papal arbitration. The Pope found in favour of Spain, which annexed the group in December. In 1899 Germany purchased the group from Spain. Japan took over the Carolines after 1934, when Japan left the League of Nations. United States forces took over the Carolines in 1945. *See entries on the 'Trust Territory of the Pacific Islands' and the 'Federated States of Micronesia'.*
1885	Guam	Germany	Initially included in the German Caroline Islands, which were then handed over to Spain 1885–99. Seized from Spain by the United States in 1898. Seized by Japanese 1941–44. Since then a United States military base. Has always had a separate political status from other US territories in Micronesia. Although people of Guam are US citizens, they have no representation in the US Congress, nor do they vote in US Presidential elections.
1886–1914	North Solomons	Germany	Initially comprised Shortland Islands, Buka, Bougainville, Choisel and Santa Isabel. In 1900 reduced to Buka and Bougainville; the remainder were incorporated into the British Solomon Islands Protectorate. Buka and Bougainville seized from Germany in 1914. Became part of the Mandated Territory of New Guinea in 1920.
1887	Wallis and Futuna	France	Protectorate declared in 1887. Annexed in 1913. Reconstituted as an overseas territory of France in 1961.
1888–1914	Marshall Islands	Germany	Chartered company government until 1906 when incorporated into German New Guinea as its 'Island Territory'. Seized by Japan in 1914. *See entry on 'Marshall and Caroline Islands'.*

First Claimed	Island or Island Group	Colonial Power	Comments
1888–1970	Nauru	Germany	Incorporated into the Marshall Islands Protectorate in 1888. Taken by Great Britain 1914–20 (military rule administered by Australia). Australia granted League of Nations Mandate, 1920–42. UN Trust Territory with a civil administration, 1945–70.
1888	Easter Island	Chile	Possession proclaimed.
1888–1900	Cook Islands	Great Britain	Protectorate initially extended over the southern Cook Islands; administered by New Zealand.
1900	Cook Islands	New Zealand	Sovereignty transferred to New Zealand, which formally annexed the entire group in 1901. Self-government in free association* with New Zealand since 1965.
1889	Tokelau	Great Britain	Protectorate declared in 1889. Incorporated into the Gilbert and Ellice Islands Protectorates in 1908. Incorporated into the Gilbert and Ellice Islands Colony in 1914 along with Ocean Island, Fanning, Washington and most of the Phoenix Islands, as was Christmas Island in 1919.
		New Zealand	Tokelau a territory of New Zealand in 1926.
1892–1916	Gilbert Islands	Great Britain	Protectorate proclaimed. Although the Gilbert and Ellice Islands were technically separate protectorates they were, for administrative convenience, treated as a single entity, and they shared the same Resident Commissioner.
1892–1916	Ellice Islands	Great Britain	The Gilbert and Ellice Islands Protectorates were consolidated into a single Colony in 1916. *See entry under 'Gilbert Isands'.*
1893–1978	Solomon Islands	Great Britain	British Protectorate declared in 1893 but administration not established until 1896. Internal self-government between 1976 and 1978.
1895	Kermadec Islands	New Zealand	Possession proclaimed.
1900–59	Hawaii	United States	In 1959 the territory of Hawaii became the fiftieth state of the United States of America.

First Claimed	Island or Island Group	Colonial Power	Comments
1900–79	Ocean Island (Banaba)	Great Britain	Incorporated into the Gilbert and Ellice Islands Protectorates.
1900–70	Tonga	Great Britain	Friendship treaty with Britain gave Tonga Protectorate status in 1900.
1900–01	Niue	Great Britain	Protectorate declared in 1900.
1901		New Zealand	Sovereignty transferred in 1901 to New Zealand. Niue initially incorporated within the Cook Islands administration; Niueans objected and in 1903 a separate Niue administration established. Self-government in free association* with New Zealand since 1974.
1900–62	Western Samoa	Germany New Zealand	1900–14: Imperial Colony. 1914–19: military rule. 1920–45: Mandate (League of Nations). 1945–62: civil administration.
1900	American Samoa	United States	Unincorporated territory of the United States. Administered by the US Navy, 1900–50; then by the US Department of the Interior.
1906	Australian Papua	Australia	Sovereignty over British Papua transferred to Australia.
1906–80	New Hebrides (Vanuatu)	British–French Condominium	Possession (joint) proclaimed.
1914–42	Australian New Guinea	Australia	1914–20: military rule. 1920–42: Mandate (League of Nations). *See entry on 'Papua New Guinea'.*
1914–45	Marshall and Caroline Islands	Japan	Mandated territory until Japanese withdrawal from the League of Nations in 1934. *See entries on 'Trust Territory of the Pacific Islands' and the 'Federated States of Micronesia'.*
1916–75	Gilbert and Ellice Islands	Great Britain	In 1975 the Ellice Islands separated from the rest of the Colony to become a separate British dependency. As Tuvalu it attained independence in 1978. As Kiribati the Gilbert Islands achieved independence in 1979.

First Claimed	Island or Island Group	Colonial Power	Comments
1942–75	Papua New Guinea (Formerly British NG, Australian Papua and Australian New Guinea)		The northern (New Guinea) and southern (Papua) territories were first combined under the Australian New Guinea Administrative Unit (1942–49), followed by the civil administration of the Territory of Papua New Guinea (1949–75).
1945-77	Trust Territory of the Pacific Islands	United States	United Nations territory under US administration.
1975	Northern Marianas	United States	Opted to become a Commonwealth of the US.
1977	Federated States of Micronesia	United States	Comprise the districts of Yap, Chuuk, Pohnpei and Kosrae. Free association* with the US.
1979	Republic of the Marshall Islands	United States	Free association* with the US.
1979	Belau (Palau)	United States	Last remaining trusteeship territory in the world.

* 'Free association' means different things. The territories freely associated with New Zealand (the Cook Islands and Niue) 'may terminate the relationship unilaterally by simply amending their constitutions'. This is not the case with the various Micronesian territories in 'free association' with the United States. 'Free association for the Republic of the Marshall Islands and the Federated States of Micronesia ... specially prevents a full and final decolonisation by binding those states to the former administering authority in perpetuity.' See Stewart Firth, 'Sovereignty and Independence in the Contemporary Pacific', *The Contemporary Pacific*, 1:1–2 (1989), pp. 75–96.

—Prepared by Doug Munro, University of the South Pacific

Index

Lightning Source UK Ltd.
Milton Keynes UK
UKOW07f0602190317

296925UK00002B/91/P

9 780521 422840